IMAGES
of America

NEW LONDON

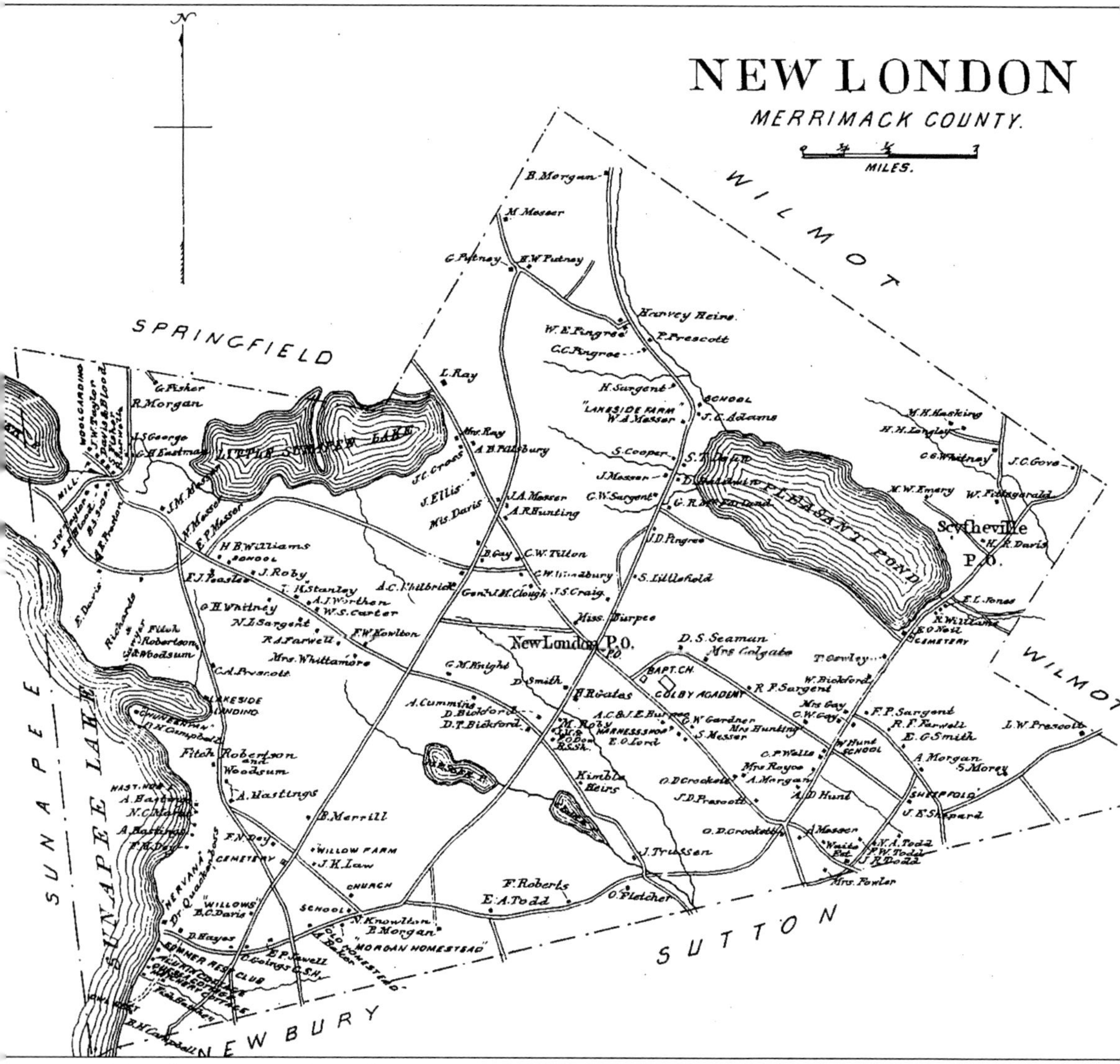

New London, 1892. This map was taken from *Atlas of New Hampshire*, compiled by D.H. Hurd and Company in Boston, Massachusetts. This source is popular with genealogists because each house is identified with the name of its owner.

IMAGES
of America

NEW LONDON

Lianne E.H. Keary

ARCADIA
PUBLISHING

ISBN 978-0-7385-1322-5

Published by Arcadia Publishing
Charleston, South Carolina

Printed in the United States of America

Library of Congress Catalog Card Number: 2003107811

For all general information, contact Arcadia Publishing:
Telephone 843-853-2070
Fax 843-853-0044
E-mail sales@arcadiapublishing.com
For customer service and orders:
Toll-free 1-888-313-2665

Visit us on the Internet at www.arcadiapublishing.com

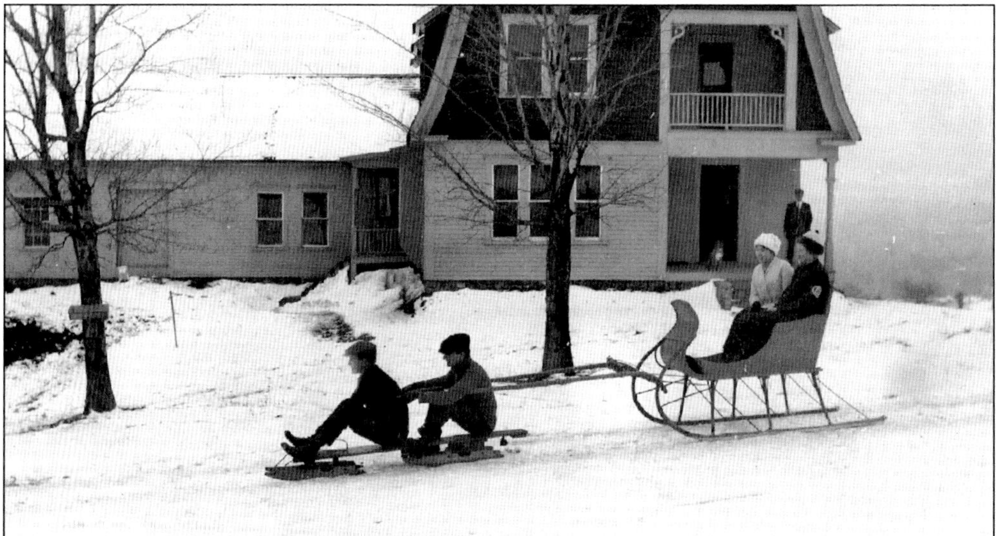

WINTER FUN. Colby Academy students survive the long, snowy winters of New London the best that they can.

Contents

ACKNOWLEDGMENTS

This book would not have been possible without the cooperation and generosity of many people, especially Peg Moreland at the New London Town Archives and everyone at the Cleveland Library at Colby-Sawyer College.

Special thanks are due to my family and friends, especially my parents and husband, for their unrelenting love and encouragement.

Introduction

In his 1855 book *New Hampshire As It Is*, Edwin Charlton wrote of New London, "Its location is healthy and its scenery delightful." Although many things have changed during almost 150 years, it can be argued that Charlton's statement is just as true today.

New London is situated about 30 miles northwest of New Hampshire's capital city of Concord. On its western border is Lake Sunapee, and on its northern border is Little Lake Sunapee. To the east are Pleasant Lake and the village of Elkins. The scenery in New London is dominated by views of Mount Sunapee and Mount Kearsarge to the south.

The town was incorporated under the name of Heidleburg on June 25, 1779. Like most of New England, New London was primarily agricultural. Industry in the town consisted of a scythe factory in Elkins (established in 1837), as well as a few sawmills, blacksmiths, and shops. Tourism has always been an important industry. Resorts, hotels, fishing, skiing, and golf have always drawn visitors to the area. By the early 1800s, the population had grown enough that the town was divided into six districts (Colby Hill, Elkins, Low Plain, West Part, Burpee Hill, and Pleasant Street) for the school system. In 1837, a Baptist academy was founded. This school would develop over time into a women's junior college and then into Colby-Sawyer College, a coeducational liberal arts college.

Like most small towns, New London has a very strong sense of community. Many present-day residents are descendants of original town settlers. Many summer residents return to New London year after year, which may explain the cohesiveness of the community and a surprising lack of friction between full-time and part-time residents.

Selecting photographs for this book was a very difficult task since there were so many wonderful images from which to choose. Many people at the New London Town Archives have helped with the research for this book, but the author assumes responsibility for any mistakes contained herein.

Photographs in this book appear through the courtesy of the New London Town Archives unless otherwise indicated.

One

NATURE

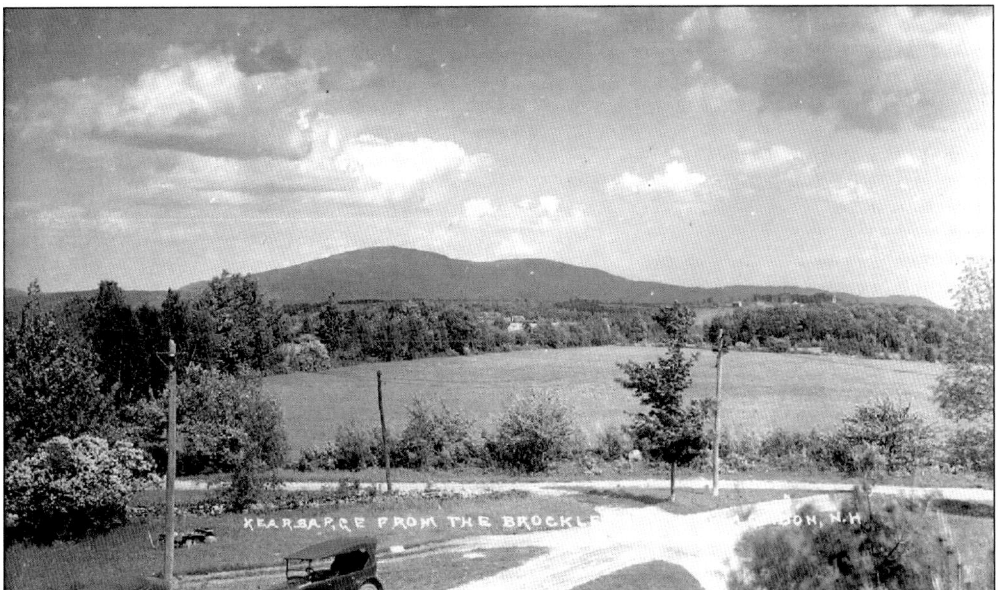

MOUNT KEARSARGE FROM THE BROCKLEBANK HOTEL. There are few places in New London where a view of Mount Kearsarge does not dominate. The Brocklebank was located on County Road.

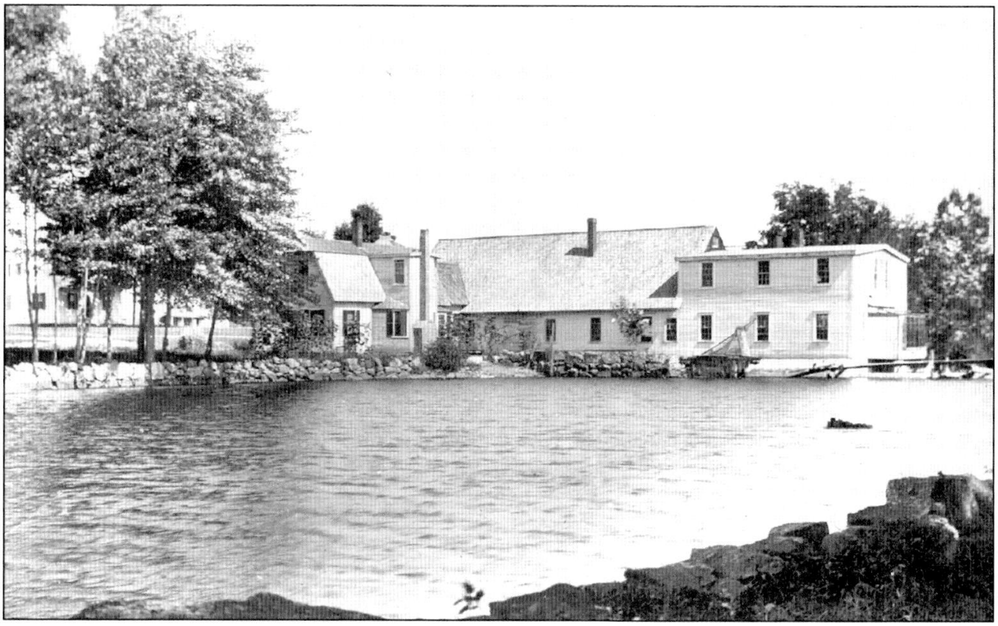

Mill Pond, c. 1900. Elkins Village became the industrial section of New London in the late 1830s, when a scythe factory—Phillips, Messer and Colby—was established there.

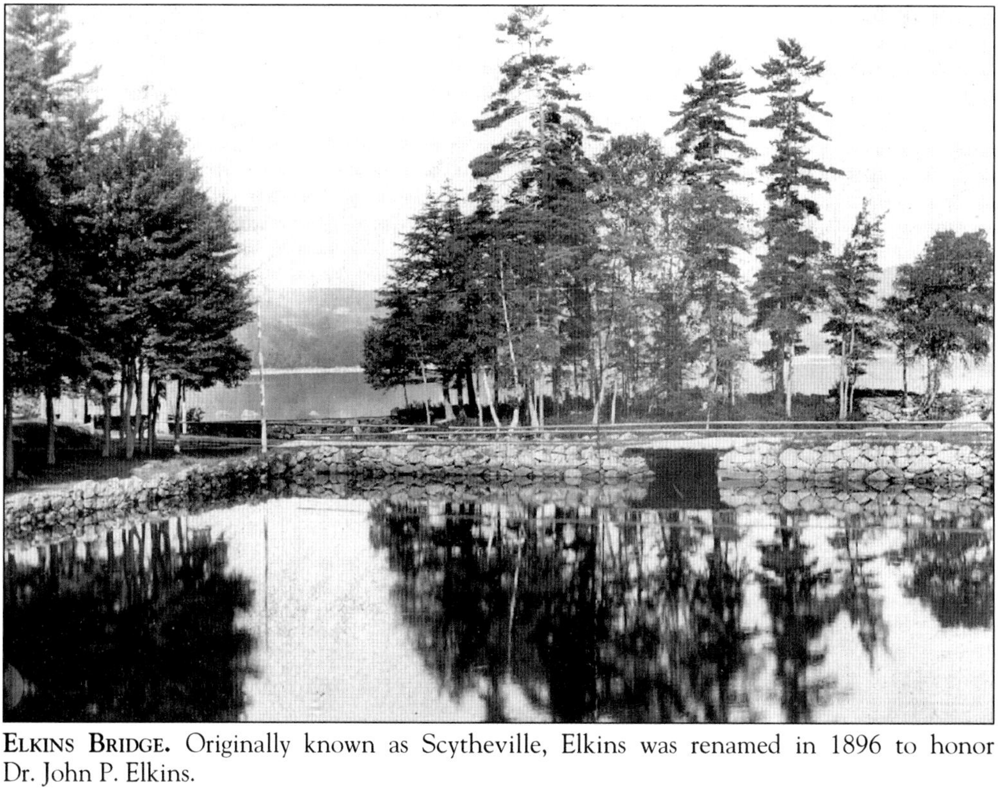

Elkins Bridge. Originally known as Scytheville, Elkins was renamed in 1896 to honor Dr. John P. Elkins.

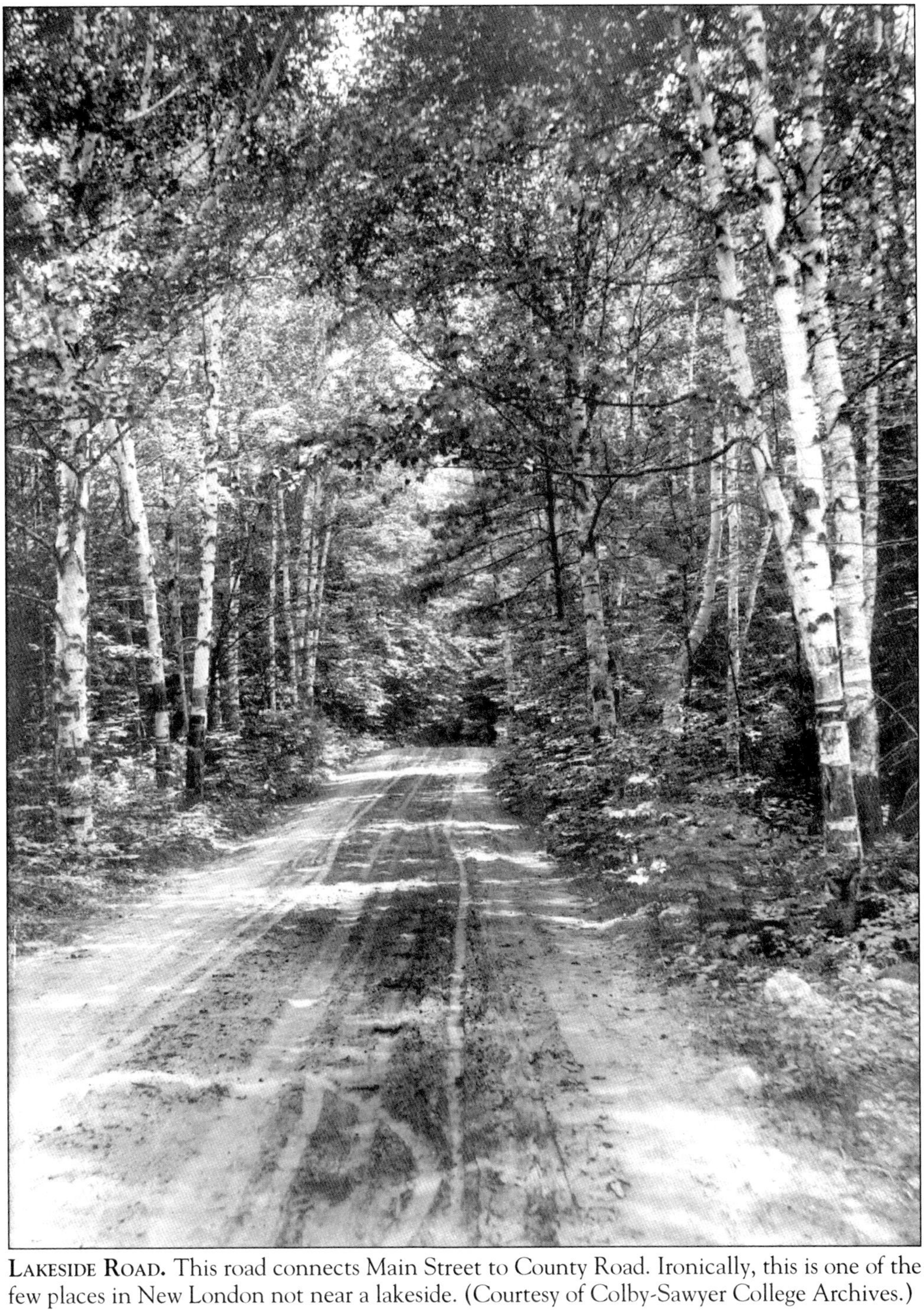

Lakeside Road. This road connects Main Street to County Road. Ironically, this is one of the few places in New London not near a lakeside. (Courtesy of Colby-Sawyer College Archives.)

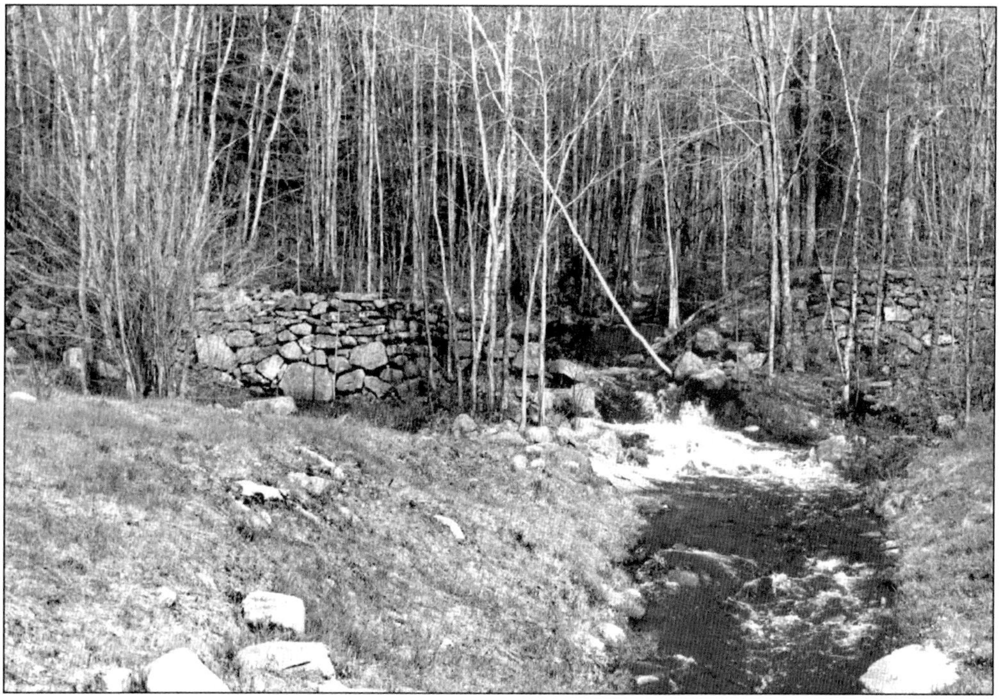

A Hominy Pot Dam. Located just south of Clark Pond, Hominy Pot is the area where New London's first homes and schoolhouse were built. Eventually, a sawmill, gristmill, and hat factory were built along the brook.

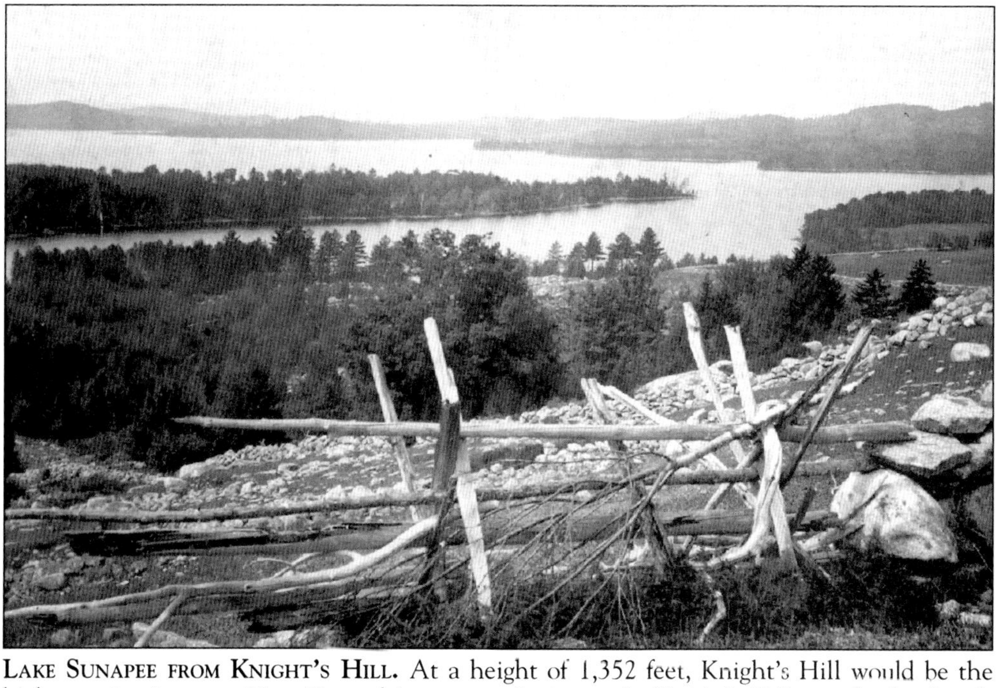

Lake Sunapee from Knight's Hill. At a height of 1,352 feet, Knight's Hill would be the highest point in many New Hampshire towns. As it stands, Knight's Hill is only the fourth highest point in town.

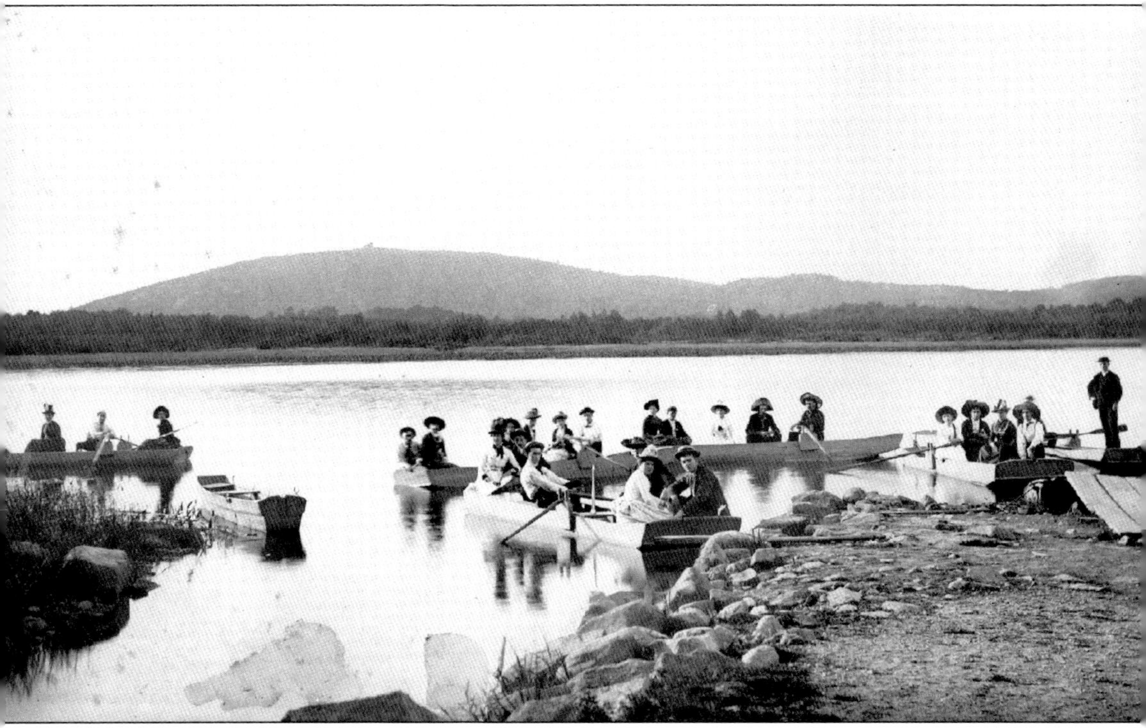

PLEASANT LAKE. This photograph was taken at the Red Gables hotel *c.* 1910. New London continues to be a popular tourist spot because of its lakes and mountain views.

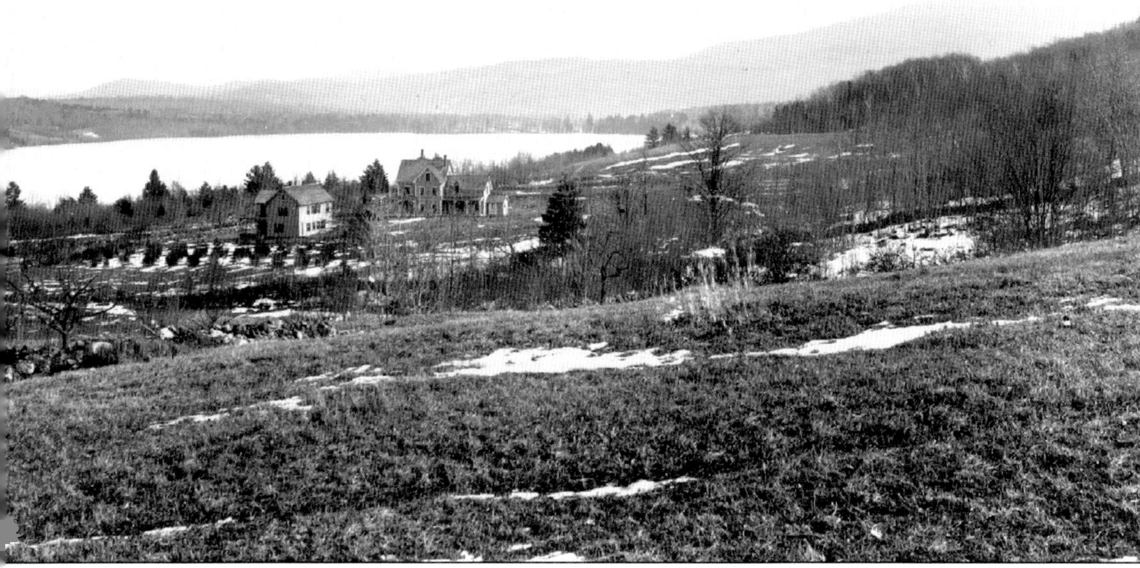

A View of Pleasant Lake from Pleasant Street. Pleasant Lake is another of New London's many bodies of water. Elkins Village is located at the southern end of this lake. This photograph was taken *c.* 1900.

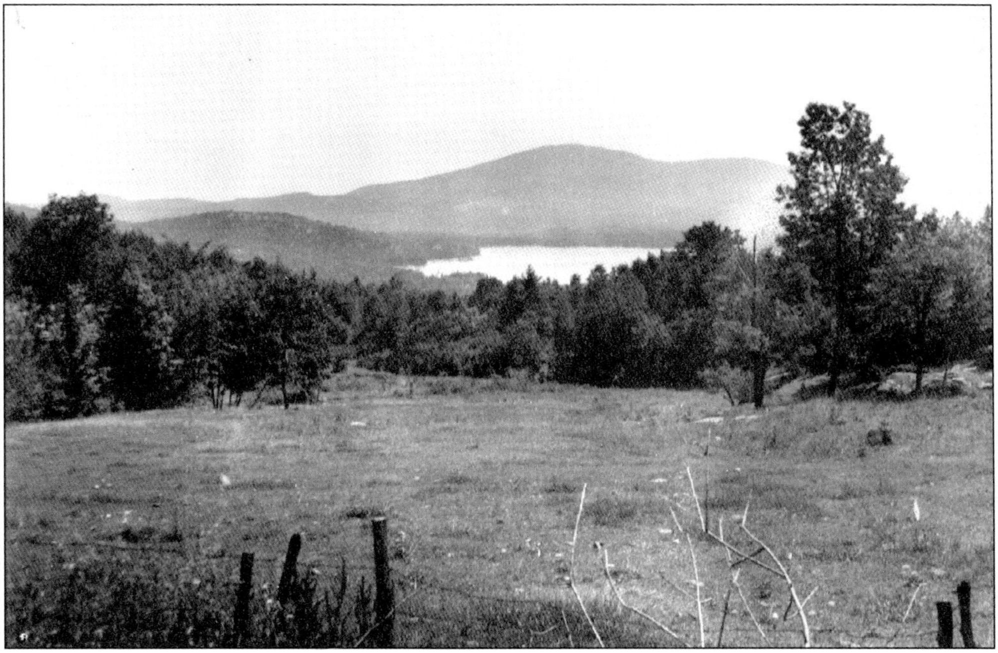

Pleasant Lake and Mount Kearsarge from Morgan Hill. At a height of 1,760 feet, Morgan Hill is New London's highest point.

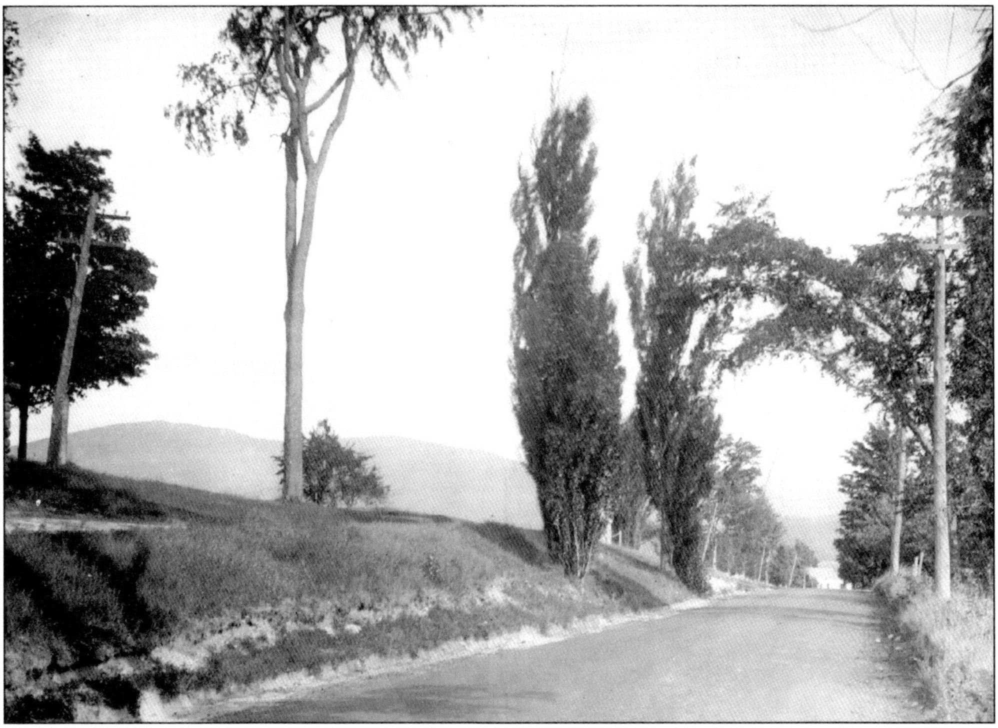

Main Street, Looking toward Crockett's Corner, c. 1924. Crockett's Corner is at the intersection of modern-day Routes 11 and 114.

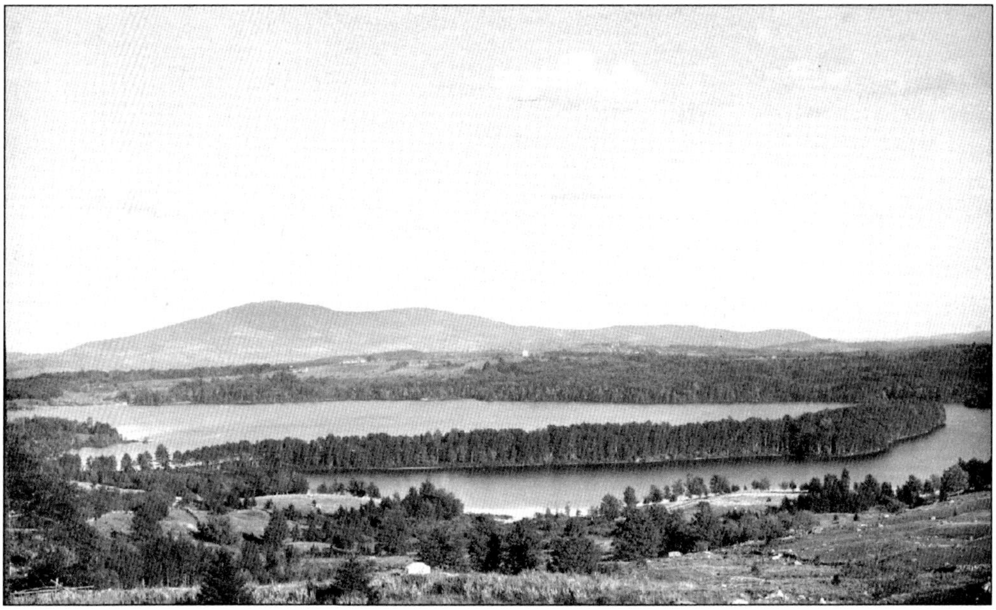

LITTLE LAKE SUNAPEE. Little Lake Sunapee is located in the northern part of New London. It is nearly cut in half by the long, narrow peninsula of Colby Point.

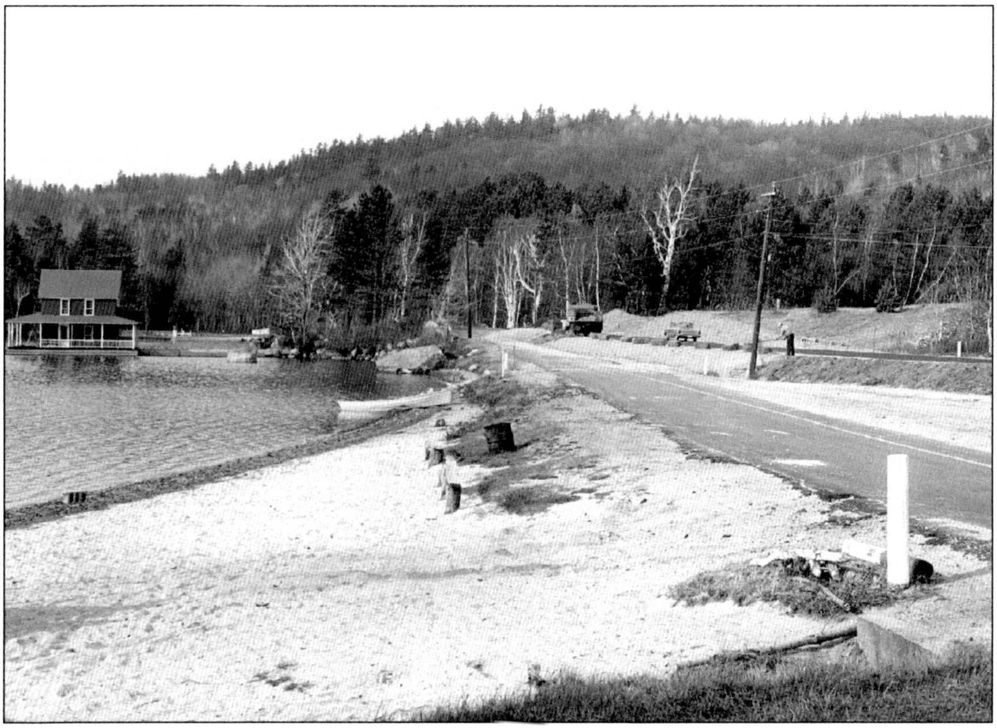

BUCKLIN BEACH. Taken in October 1963, this photograph shows the new highway of Route 114, which runs north to south on the eastern edge of Little Lake Sunapee. (Photograph by Don Eggleston.)

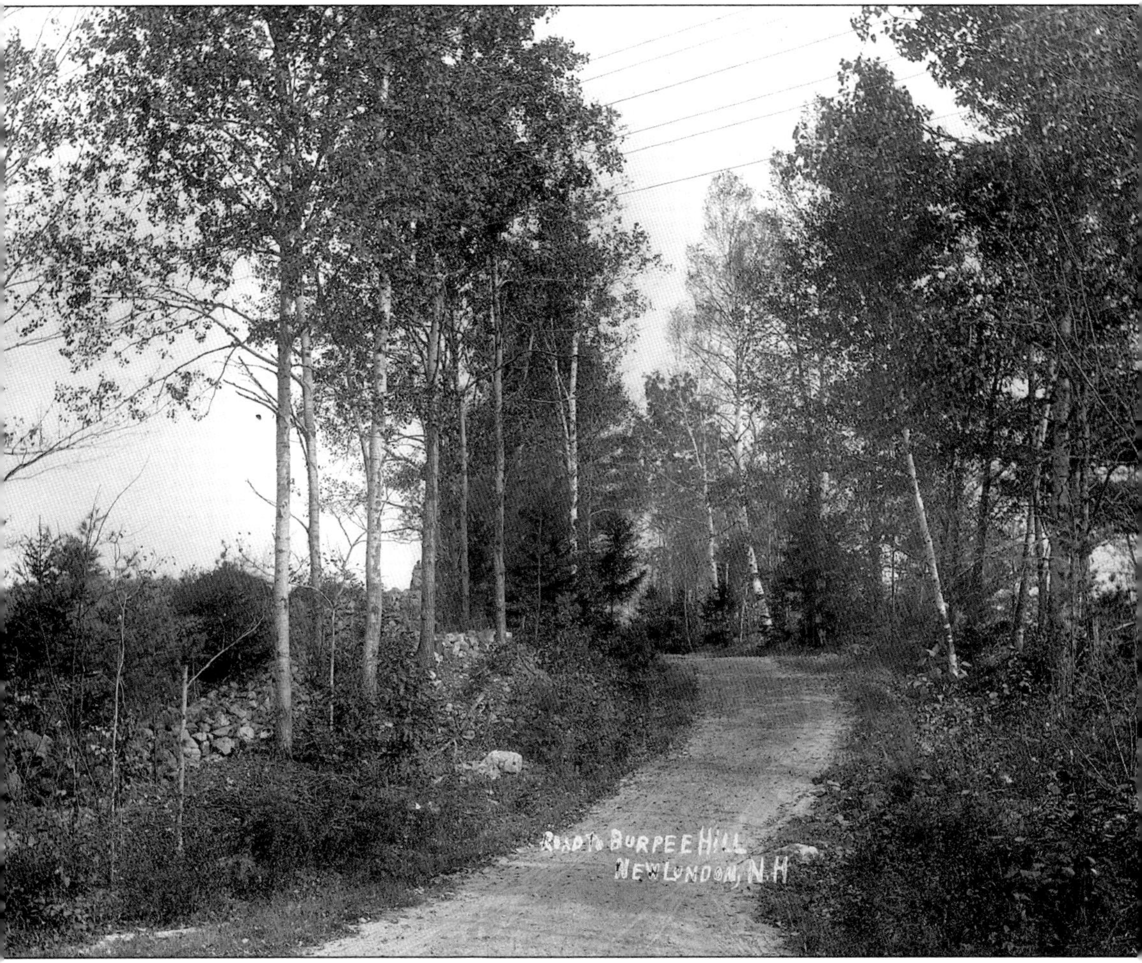

The Road to Burpee Hill, c. 1902. Located just south of Little Lake Sunapee and east of Lake Sunapee, Burpee Hill is a little higher than 1,400 feet. (Courtesy of Colby-Sawyer College Archives.)

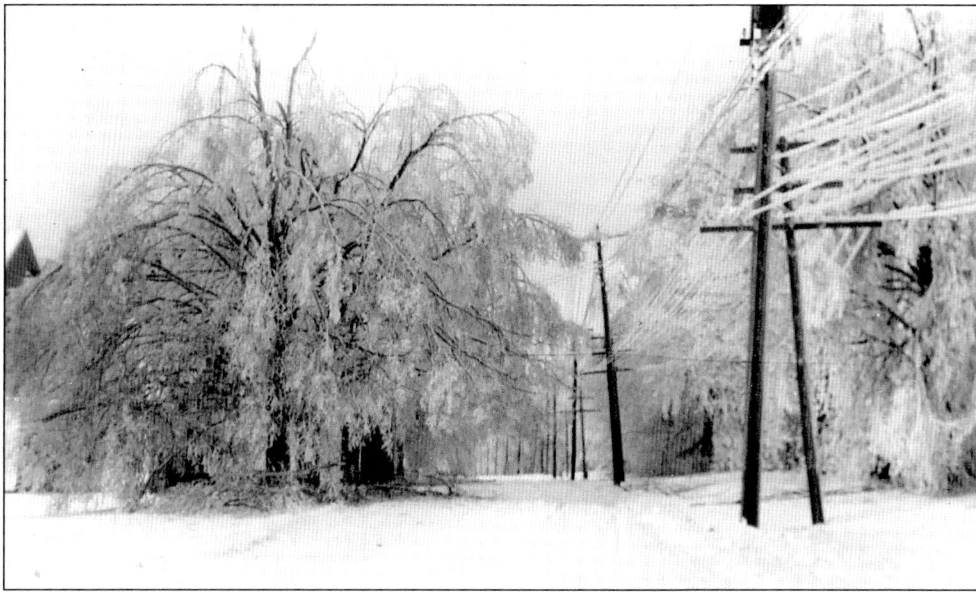

AN ICE STORM IN THE WINTER OF 1929–1930. In January 1998, New London was gripped by an ice storm that crippled a large part of New England. Roads were impassable; power and water were unavailable for 10 days. This photograph documents a similar storm that hit New London in the winter of 1929–1930. (Courtesy of Colby-Sawyer College Archives.)

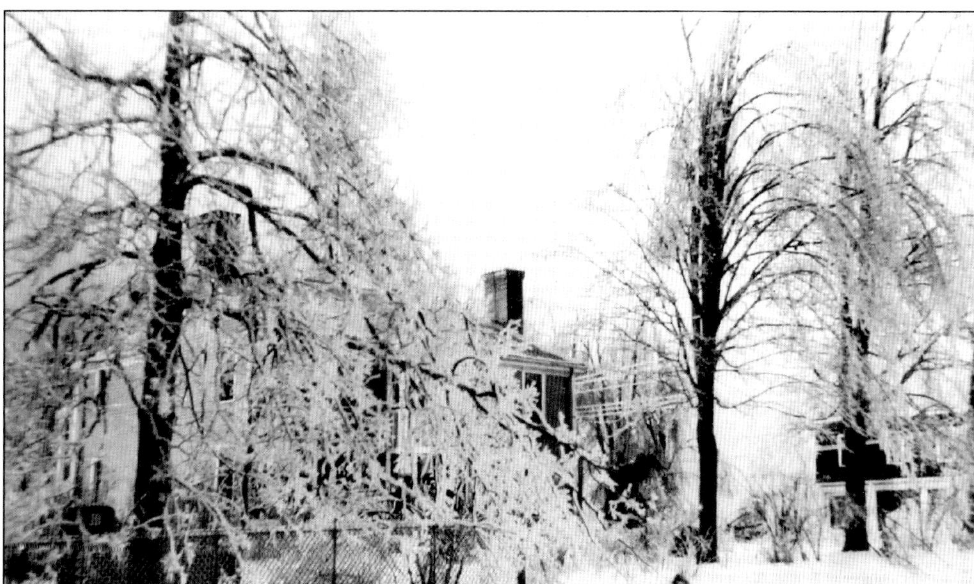

THE LIBRARY AFTER THE ICE STORM. The building obscured by ice-covered trees is the Tracy Memorial Library, on Main Street. (Courtesy of Colby-Sawyer College Archives.)

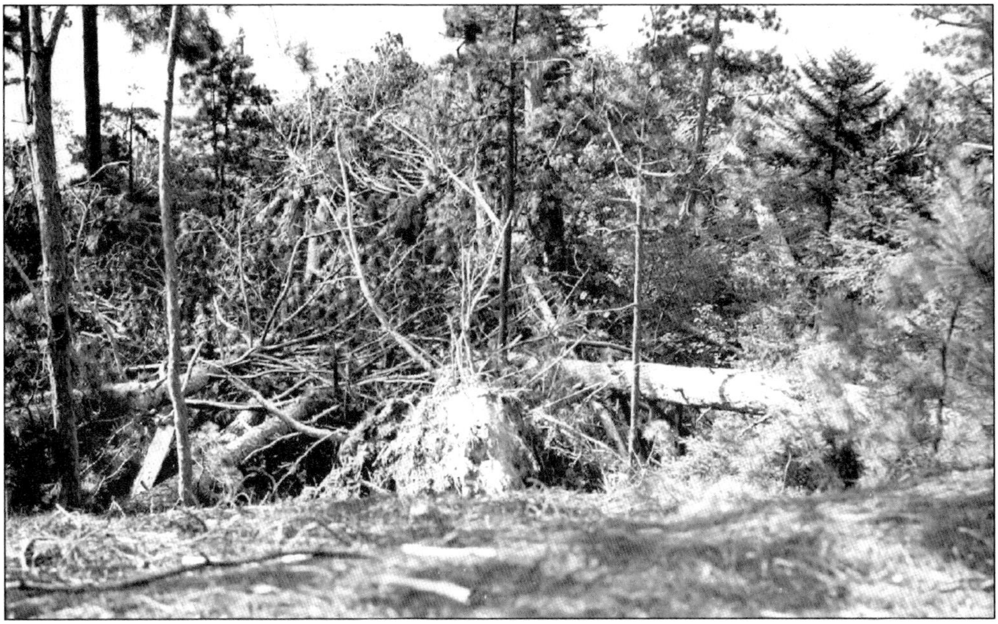

The Hurricane of 1938. In September 1938, a hurricane ripped through New England, tearing up trees and destroying homes. New London was not immune to the devastation. (Photograph by Joseph Hague.)

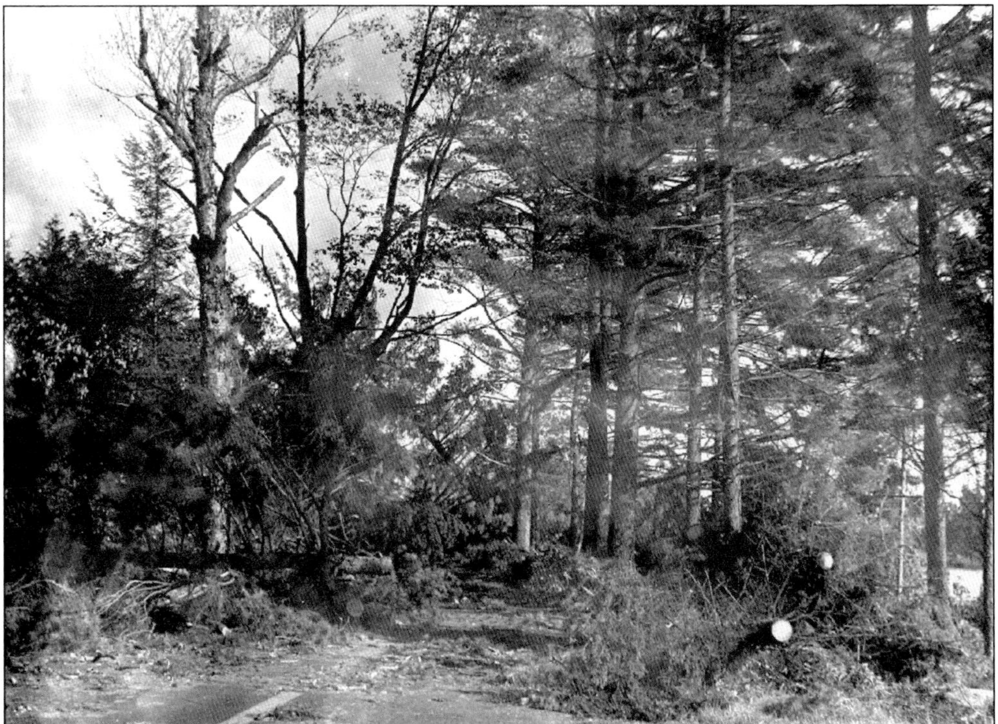

The Road around Twin Lake after the Hurricane of 1938. Twin Lake Villa, a summer lakeside resort, is located on Little Lake Sunapee. (Photograph by Joseph Hague.)

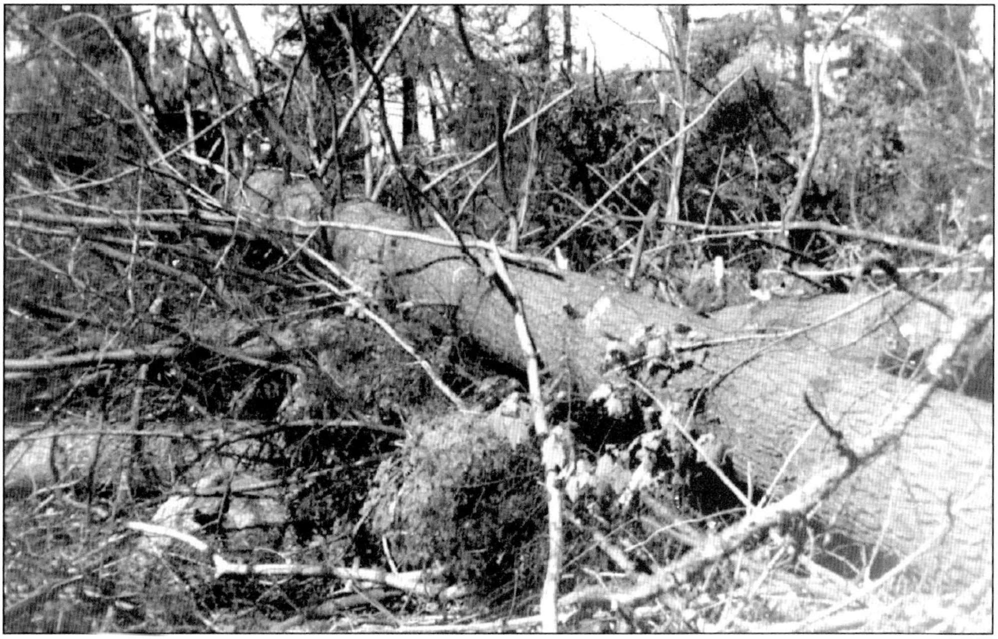

HURRICANE DAMAGE, 1938. This view shows the damage at the back of the barn of the Messer farm.

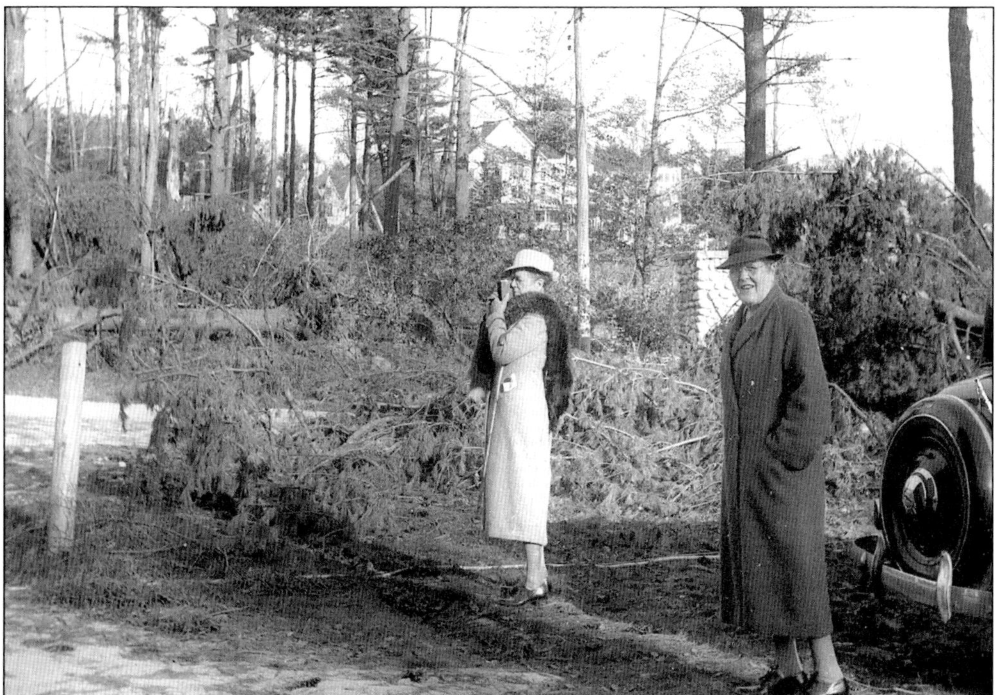

MORE HURRICANE DAMAGE. Eliza Burpee Robbins (right) and an unidentified person document the hurricane damage at Soo-Nipi Park, located on the shores of Lake Sunapee. Note the Soo-Nipi Lodge in the background. (Courtesy of Colby-Sawyer College Archives.)

Two

PEOPLE AND HOMES

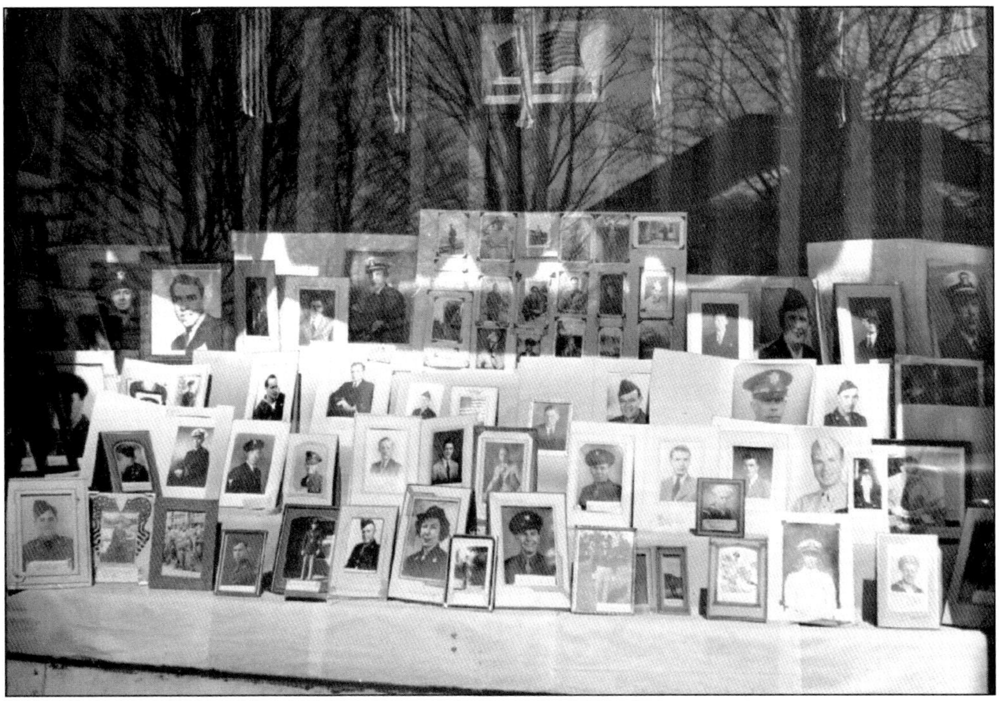

WORLD WAR II PHOTOGRAPHS ON DISPLAY AT NEW LONDON PHARMACY. During the course of the war, more than 100 New London residents served in the armed forces.

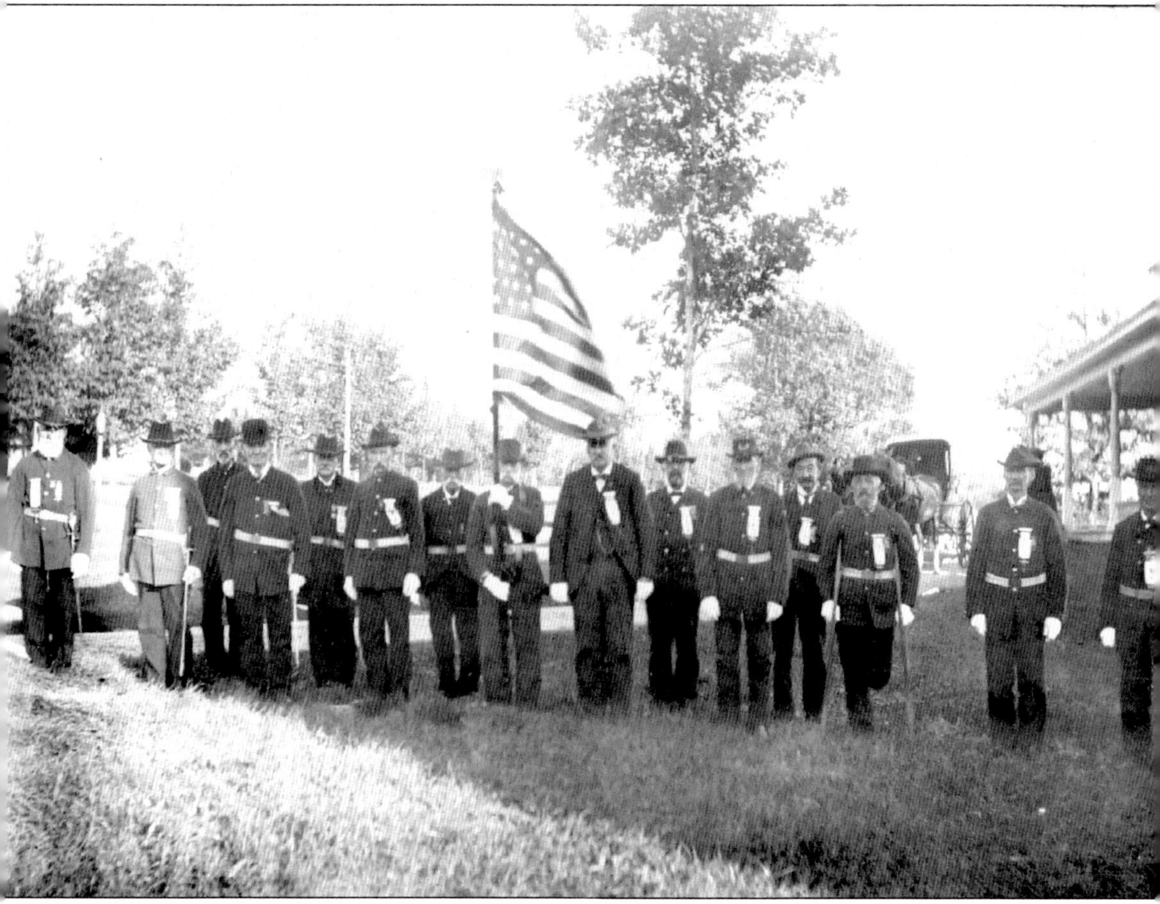

The Grand Army of the Republic, c. 1880–1900. Pictured, from left to right, are A.J. Sargent, Robert McConnell, C.W. Woodbury, Frank Messer, Joseph Clough, Charles Woodward, Ransom Sargent, Walter Pingree, William Messer, John K. Law, Page Colby, Alston Brown, Solon Cooper, George Sholes, and ? Palmer.

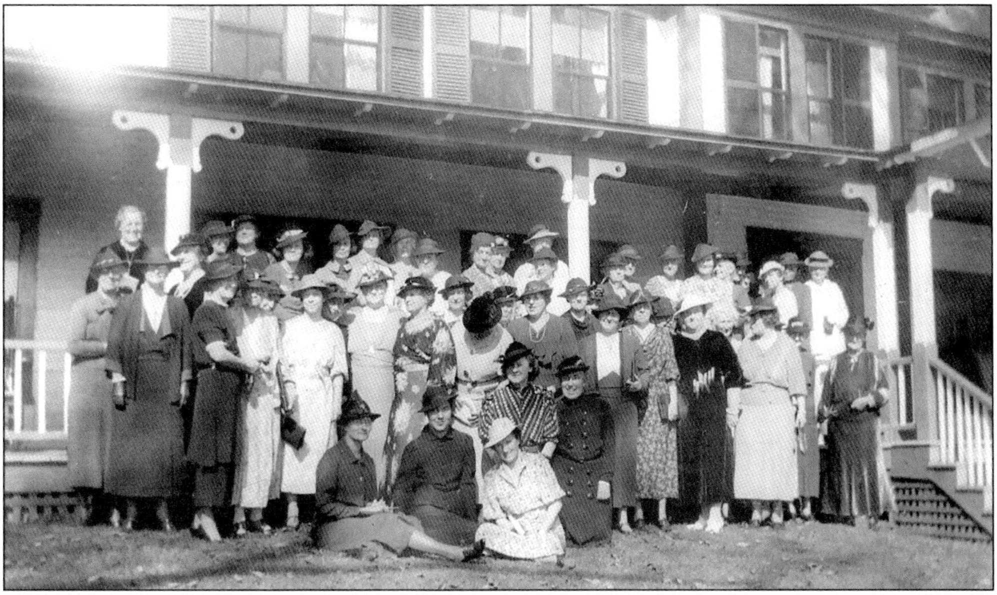

The Women's Club 25th-Anniversary Luncheon, Twin Lake Villa, October 1936. Started in 1911 by Bertha Kidder, this club began with 18 charter members. Its motto is "Good the more communicated, the more abundant grows." The group is involved in many charitable and social activities, including fundraising for the hospital and sponsoring essay contests. (Courtesy of Colby-Sawyer College Archives.)

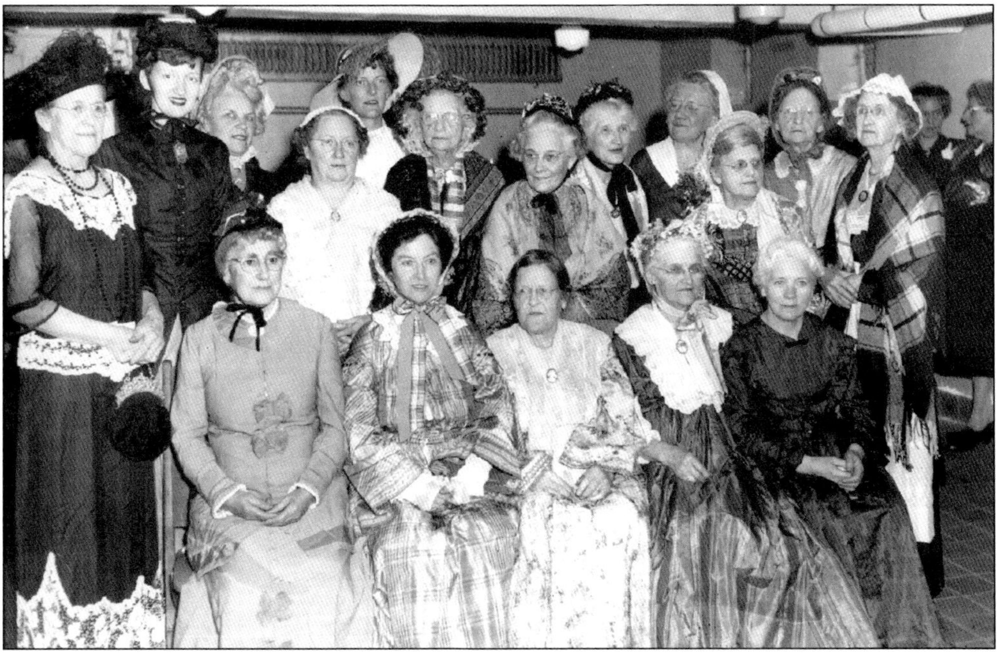

The Women's Club Thanksgiving Party, 1946. Pictured, from left to right, are the following: (front row) Margie Todd, Doris Smith, Eliza Robbins, Martha Sholes, and Verna Granger; (back row) Mary B. Macomber, Adrianne Lauridsen, Eunice Worthen, Mary Lovely, Almina Barton, Esther Crockett, Ella Foster, Julia Todd, Helen Holcomb, Hattie Burpee, Christine Morey, and Mildred Clarke.

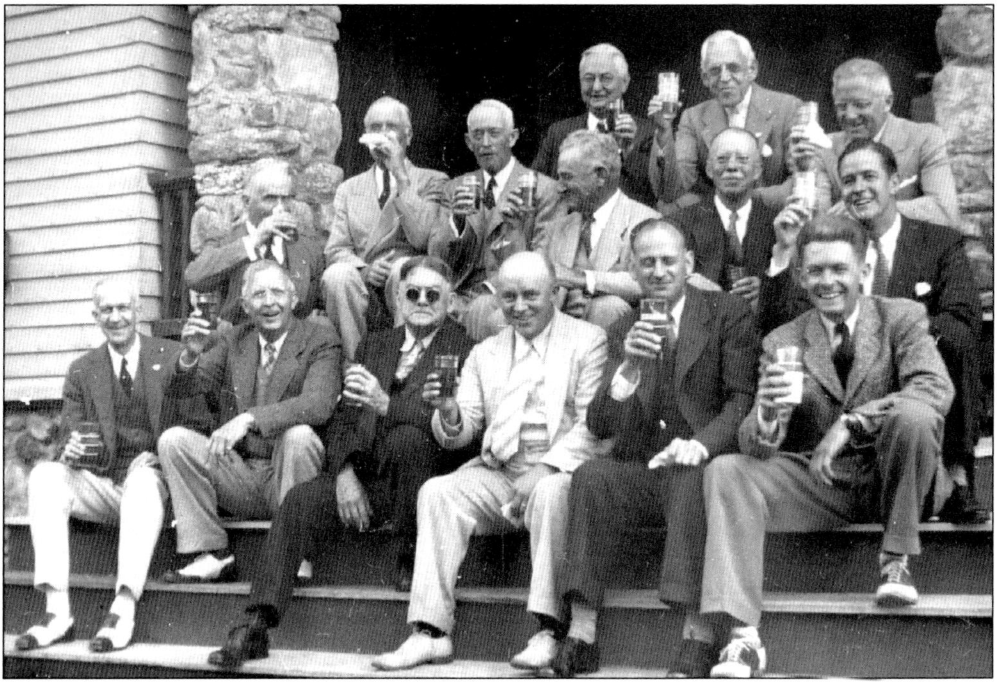

The Boys' Club of New London, September 1940. This club was founded in 1935 in order to bring together year-round and summer residents. The club always held its annual gathering late in the summer.

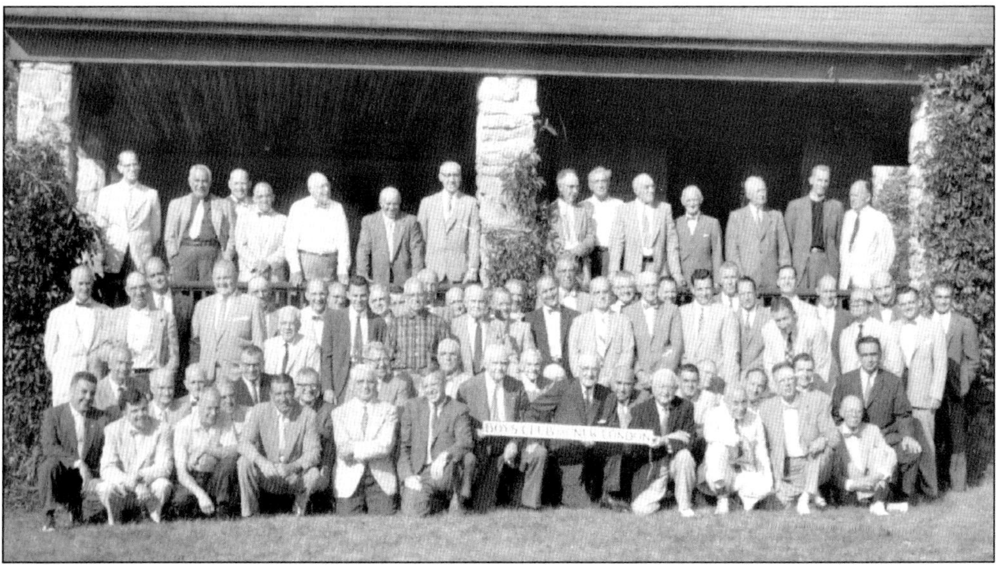

The Boys' Club, 1957. This photograph was taken at the club's annual gathering.

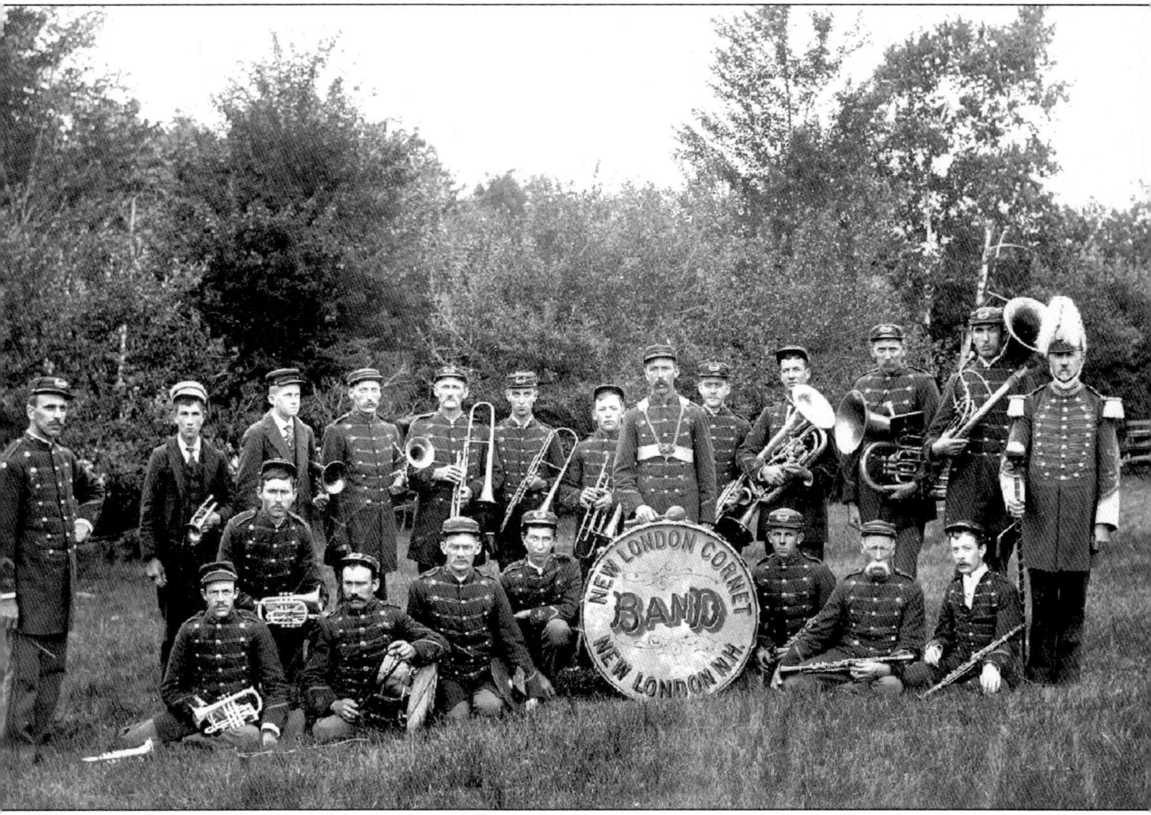

THE CORNET BAND. The New London Cornet Band was started in 1888. The group, renamed the New London Cadet Band in 1897, held concerts at a bandstand near the Colby Academy building on Main Street throughout the 1940s. This photograph was taken on July 4, 1897, at Blodgett's Landing. Pictured, from left to right, are the following: (front row) Ralph Kiel, Herbert Smith, Charlie Weeks, Benjamin Sargent, William P. Clough, Will Leach, Ransom Sargent, and William Cleves; (back row) Herman Adams (leader), Walter Leach, Harry Messer, George French, Edwin Ashby, Elmer Messer, Herman Currier, Luther Ray, Evarts Messer, William Kidder, Henry Quimby, Sidney Smith, and Frank Dow (drum major). (Courtesy of Colby-Sawyer College Archives.)

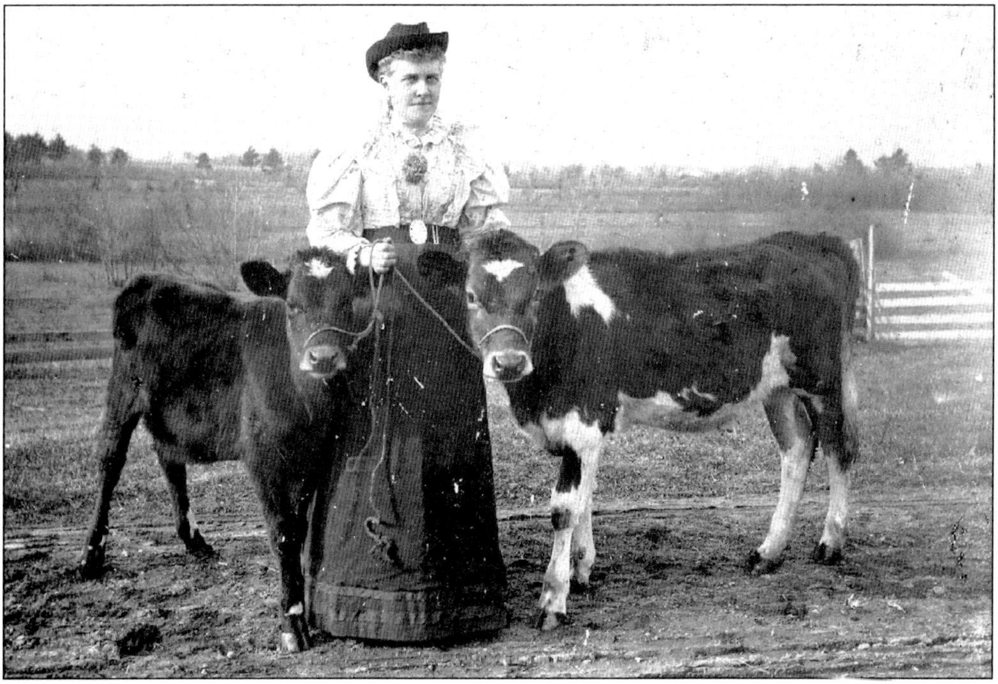

EMMA BARTLETT, C. 1910. Born in Hill, New Hampshire, Emma Bartlett was the town's librarian until 1919. She died in 1921.

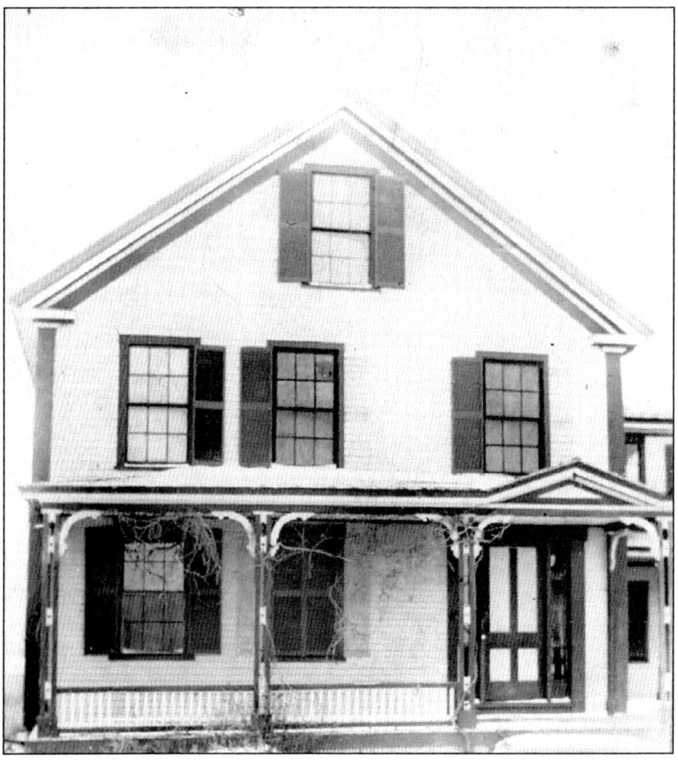

THE JOSIAH BROWN HOUSE. Josiah Brown (1767–1854) was a carpenter who also invented a winnowing mill for cleaning grain. This house was built c. 1793 on Colby Hill. The academy eventually bought the land, and parts of the building were moved to another location.

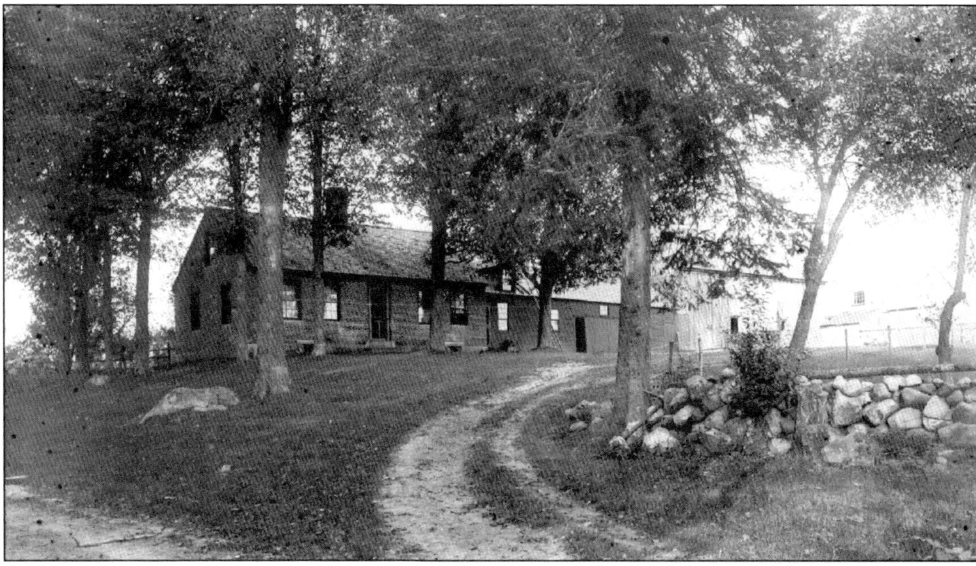

THE BUCKLIN FARM, C. 1900. This farm was located on an area referred to as Bucklin Corner, near the intersections of County Road and Little Sunapee Road.

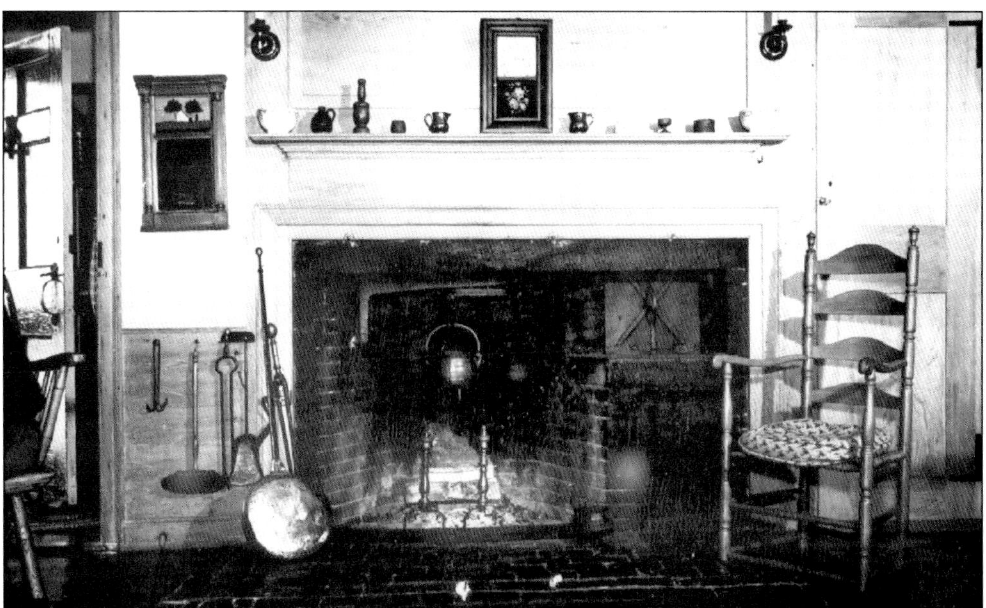

THE BUCKLIN FARM, AN INTERIOR VIEW. Fireplaces such as this one were common in many early New England houses.

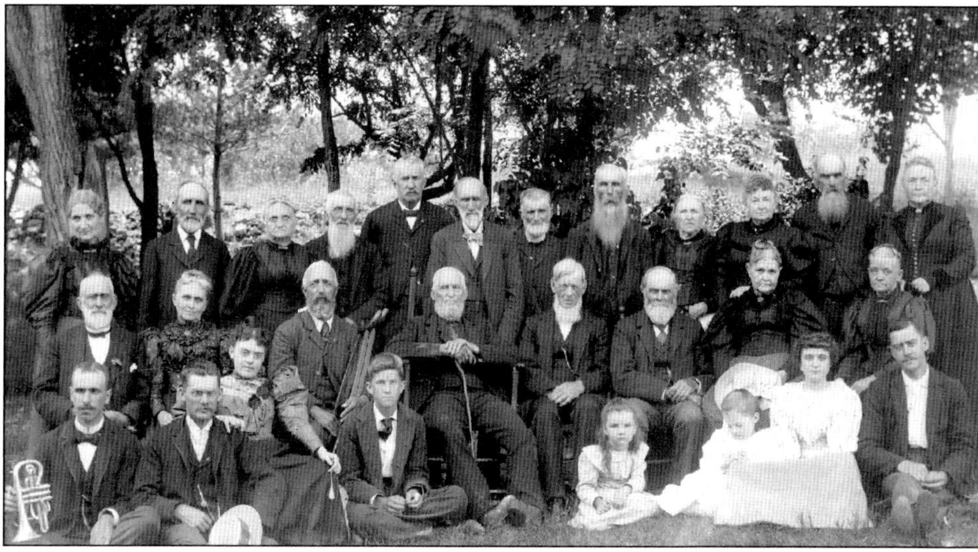

Pleasant Street Friends. This photograph of Pleasant Street residents was taken on July 22, 1895. From left to right are the following: (front row, on grass) Herman S. Adams, Benjamin F. Sargent, Florence G. Sargent, Harry Leroy Messer, Eva E. Dean, Ella Messer, Belle M. Nye, and Evarts W. Messer; (middle row, sitting) Daniel J. Woodward, Susan ?, Solon Cooper, Dennis H. Adams, Charles C. Pingree, David Baldwin, Miriam Dickey Baldwin, and Sarah Clement Littlefield; (back row, standing) Mary Woodward, George Woodward, Mary Hannah Messer, Seth Littlefield, William Alonzo Messer, Marshall J. Woodward, Joseph H. Messer, Stephen J. Dean, Eliza Ann Dean, Sara Jane Sargent, Hiram Sargent, and Judith Messer. (Photograph by E.A. Dean.)

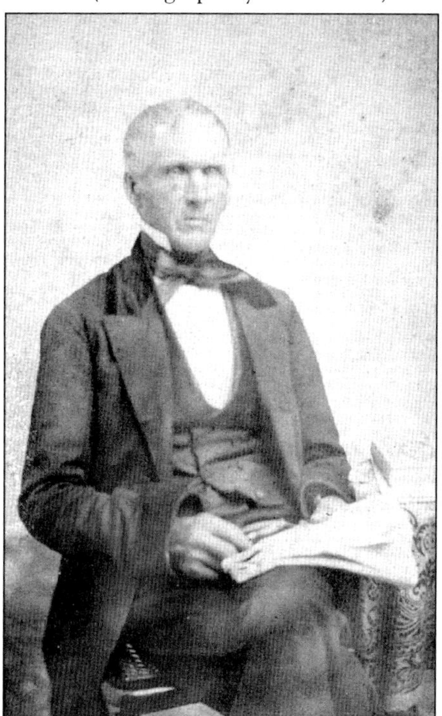

Perley Burpee. Perley Burpee was born in 1790, the son of Asa and Mary Perley Burpee. He married Judith Colby in 1816 and was a captain in the militia, as well as a shoemaker and farmer. He lived in New London until his death in 1865.

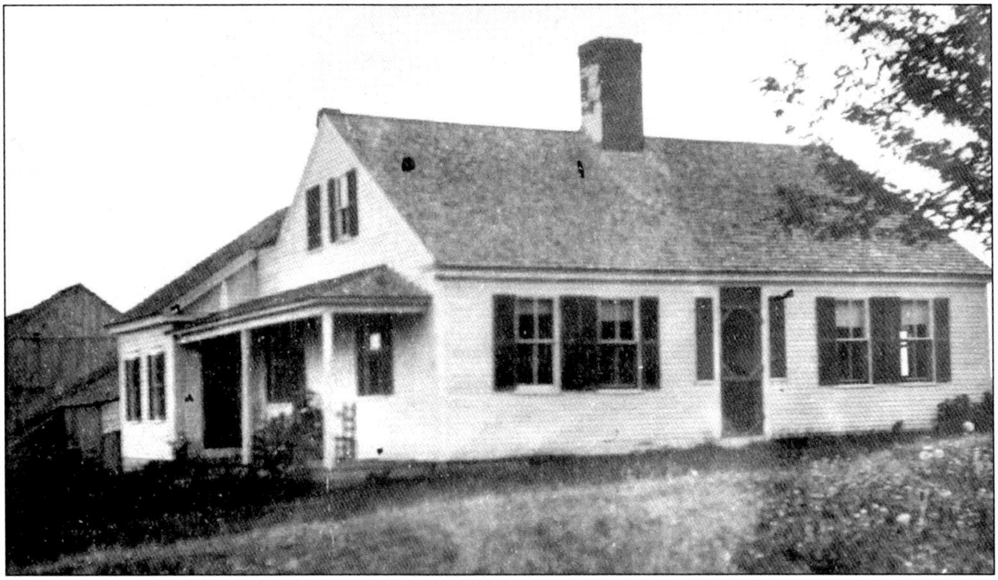

THE BURPEE HOME, 1902. This building was constructed in 1830 on Burpee Hill and was first owned by David Towle.

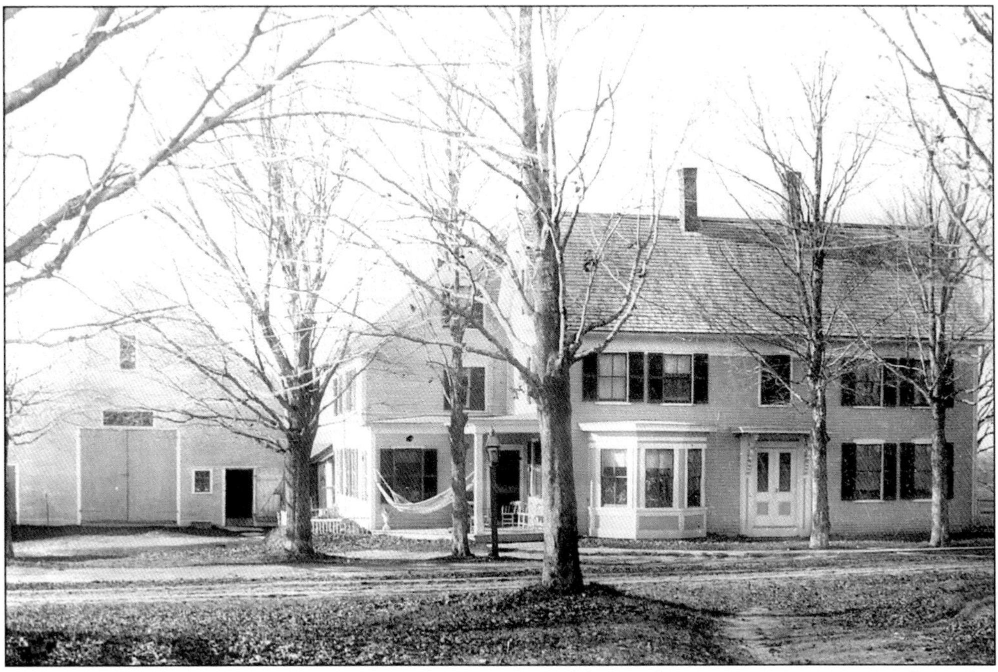

THE BURPEE HOMESTEAD, C. 1900. Built in 1816 and located on Main Street across from the Colby Homestead, this was the home of Perley Burpee and his wife, Judith.

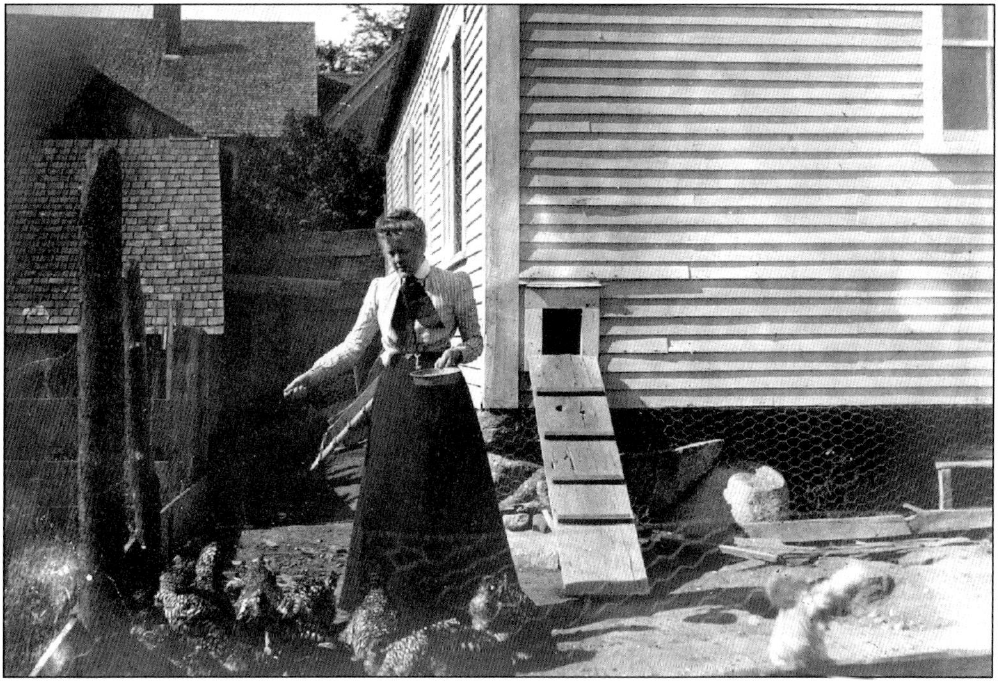

Eliza Burpee (1867–1959). Shown here feeding her chickens at the Burpee Homestead, Eliza Burpee was a lifelong resident of New London. She was active in the Baptist church, the Grange, and the garden club. (Courtesy of Colby-Sawyer College Archives.)

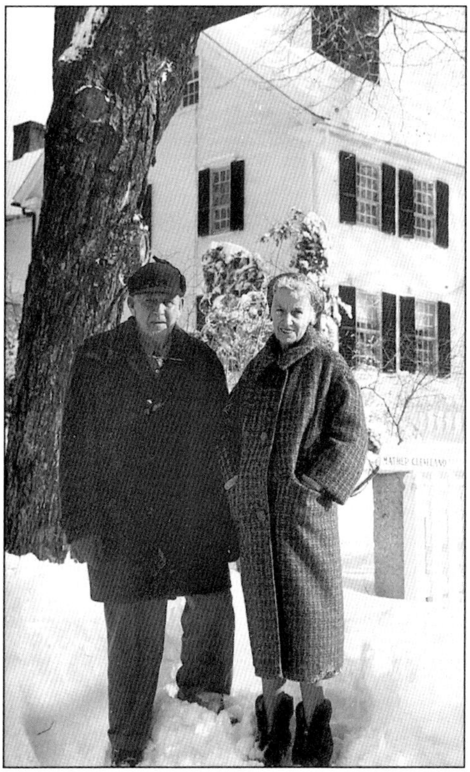

Dr. Mather Cleveland and Susan Cleveland. Mather Cleveland (1889–1979), summer resident for 30 years and a full-time resident for another 20, was an orthopedic surgeon, a soldier, and an author. He served in both world wars and in the Korean War and earned many decorations, including France's Chevalier Legion of Honor. He was the author of *New Hampshire Fights the Civil War*, in addition to several medical articles. His wife, Susan Colgate Cleveland (1891–1967), was also very active, serving as a trustee of Colby Junior College for 30 years and directing the restoration of the Colby Academy building in 1960. In appreciation of her efforts, Colby-Sawyer College named its library and learning center after her. She also helped with the restoration of the Baptist church.

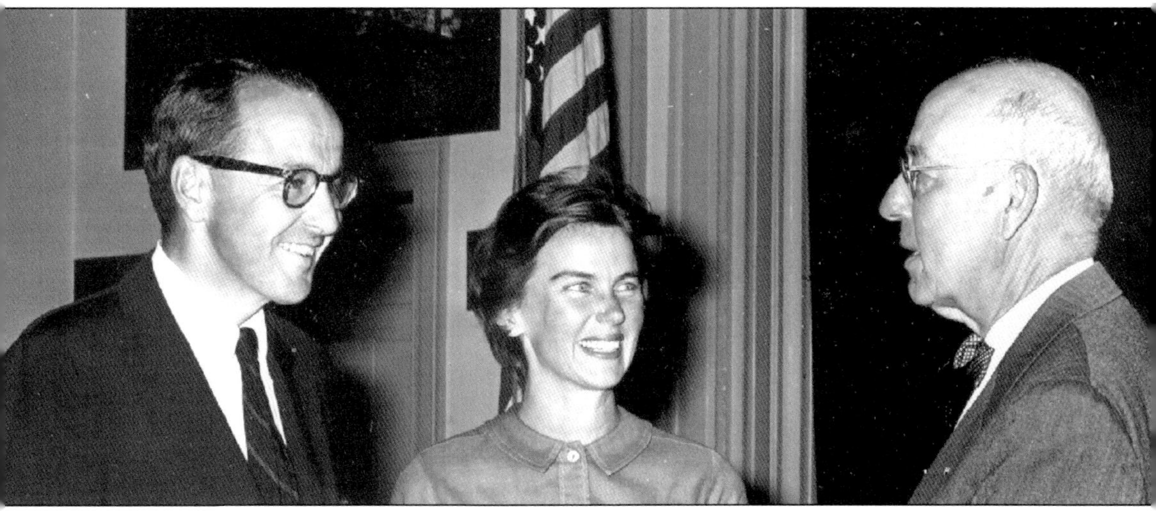

REP. JAMES C. CLEVELAND, HILARY CLEVELAND, AND M. ROY LONDON, C. THE 1960S. The son of Mather and Susan Cleveland, James Cleveland served as a state senator from 1950 to 1962 and as a U.S. representative from 1962 to 1980. He was the author of compromise legislation routing Route 93 through Franconia Notch. He was also the cofounder of New London Trust. His wife, Hilary, has served as town moderator since 1982. She also worked as an associate professor at Colby-Sawyer College from 1955 to 1997. M. Roy London was a longtime teacher, selectman, library trustee, and judge of the New London district court. (Courtesy of Colby-Sawyer College Archives.)

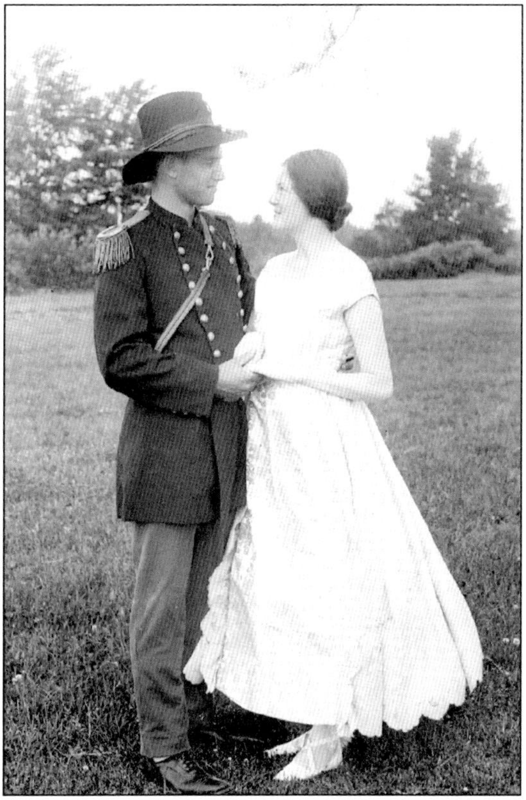

***Hills against the Sky,* August 1929.** Shown here are William Clough Jr. and Helen Kidder portraying Civil War sweethearts in the New London centennial pageant *Hills against the Sky*, written and directed by Leila M. Church. The pageant depicted many scenes from New London history, including the establishment of factories in Hominy Pot and Anthony Colby's election to governor. Many cast members were descendants of the people whose parts they played.

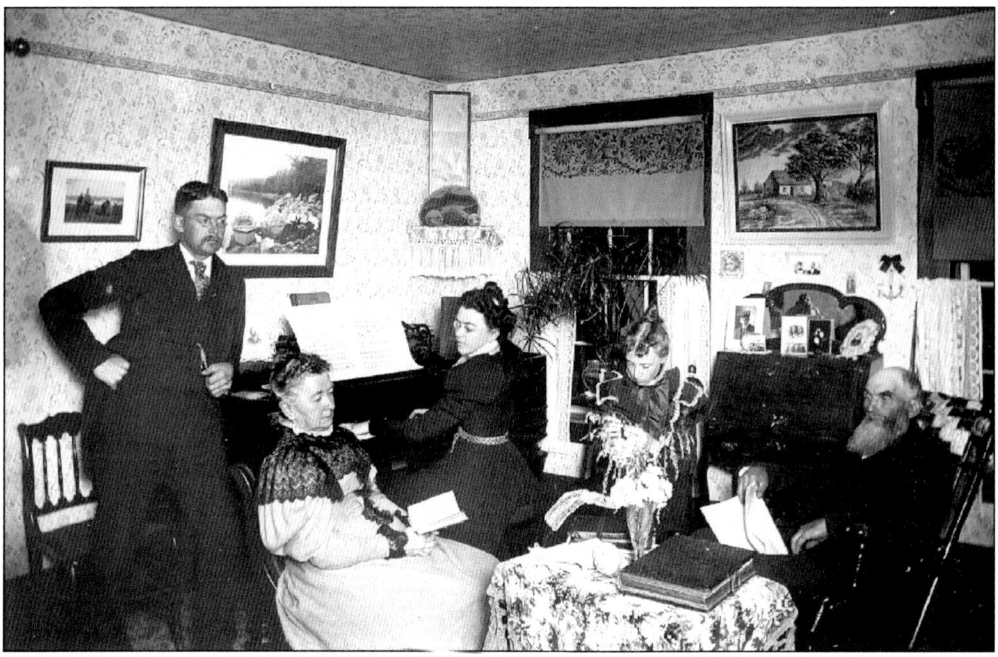

The Sargent Family. Pictured, from left to right, are Benjamin F. Sargent, Sara Whittier Sargent, Florence G. Sargent, Annabelle Pillsbury Sargent, and Hiram Sargent. The Sargents lived on Pleasant Street.

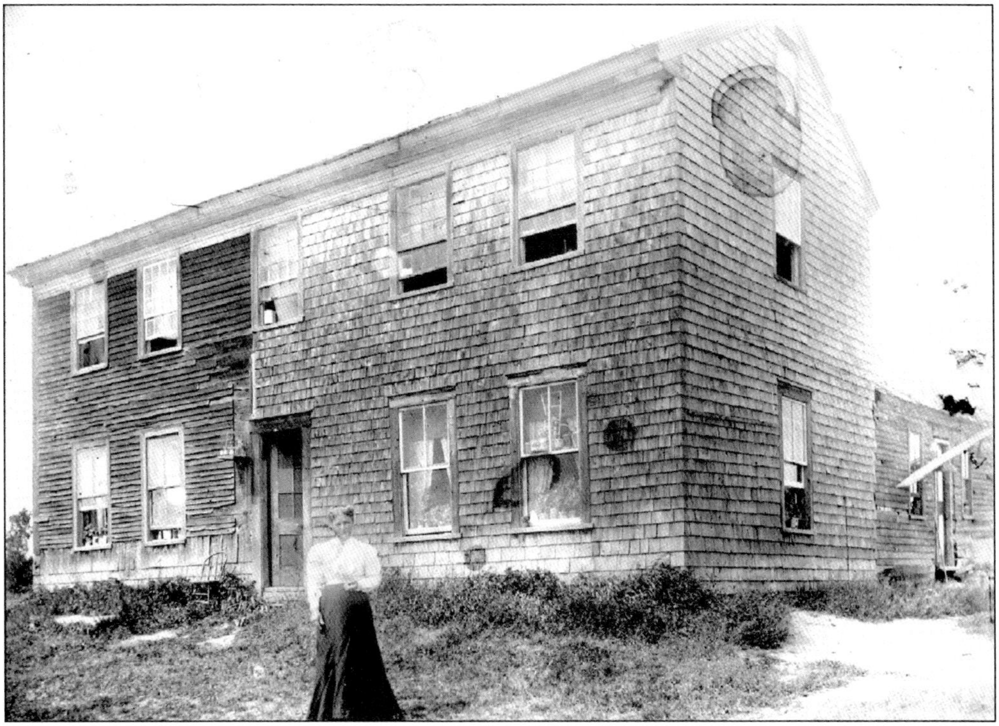

THE JOSEPH COLBY HOUSE. Built in 1788, this house was located on Seamans Road. It was the home of Joseph Colby, New London's 13th settler. This house was also the birthplace of Sarah, Anthony (who became the governor of New Hampshire), and Judith Colby. It was destroyed by fire sometime in the 1920s.

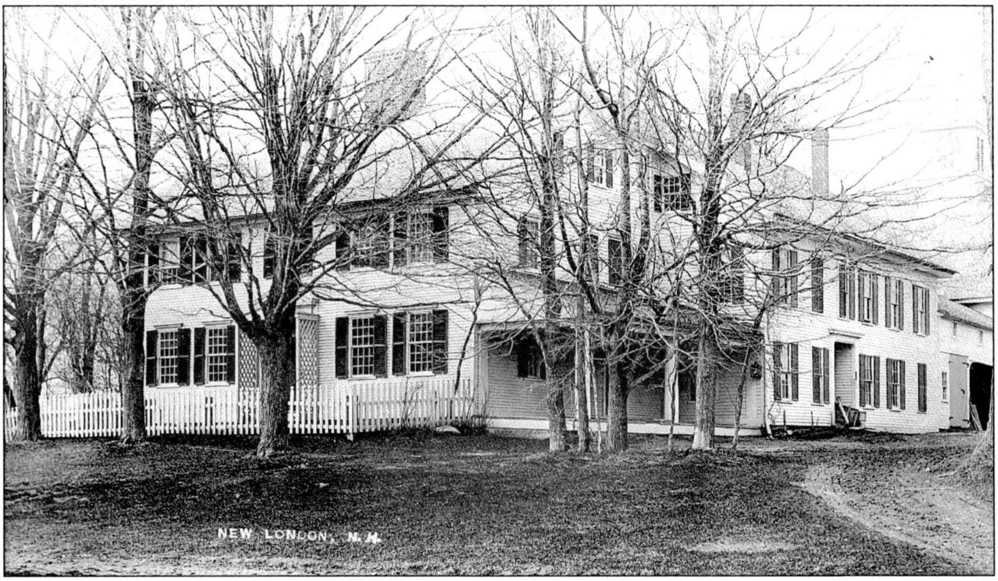

THE COLBY HOMESTEAD. Joseph Colby, the first storekeeper in town, moved to the Colby Homestead in 1800. The property was sold to Colby Junior College in the early 1970s, and its barns are now Colby-Sawyer College's library, with the ell connecting the barns to the homestead that serves as the school's Archives Reading Room.

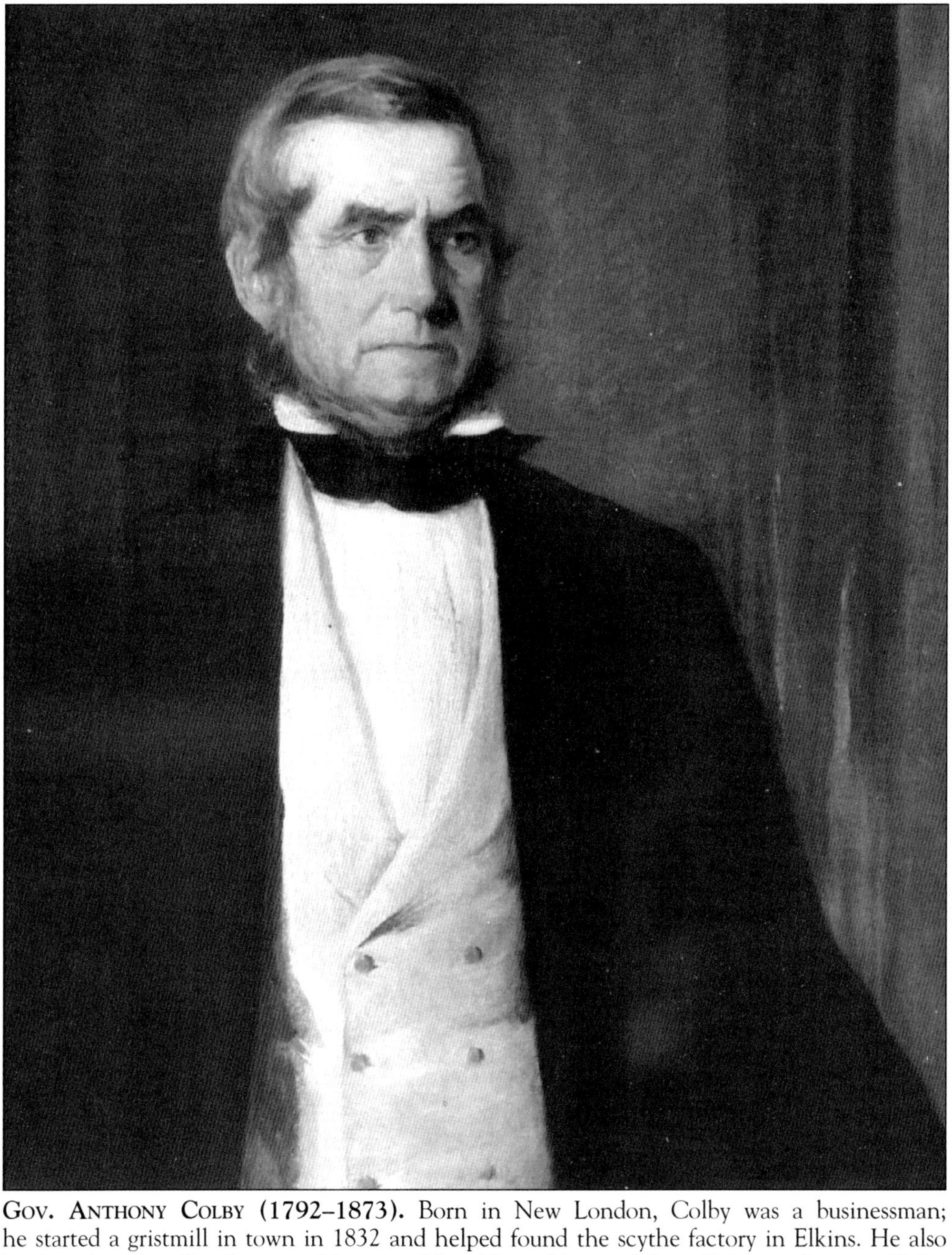

GOV. ANTHONY COLBY (1792–1873). Born in New London, Colby was a businessman; he started a gristmill in town in 1832 and helped found the scythe factory in Elkins. He also instituted a stage line between Hanover, New Hampshire, and Lowell, Massachusetts. Colby was successful in the state militia, rising through the ranks to become a major general in 1837. He served as a state representative from 1828 to 1832 and again from 1837 to 1839. He was the Whig party's nominee for governor four times before finally winning the election, defeating Democrat Jared Williams. He served as governor for only one year in 1846, while the nation was at war with Mexico. In addition to his political activities, Colby was instrumental in founding the New London Academy (later renamed Colby Academy in his honor) and served as a trustee of Dartmouth College for 20 years. (Courtesy of Colby-Sawyer College Archives.)

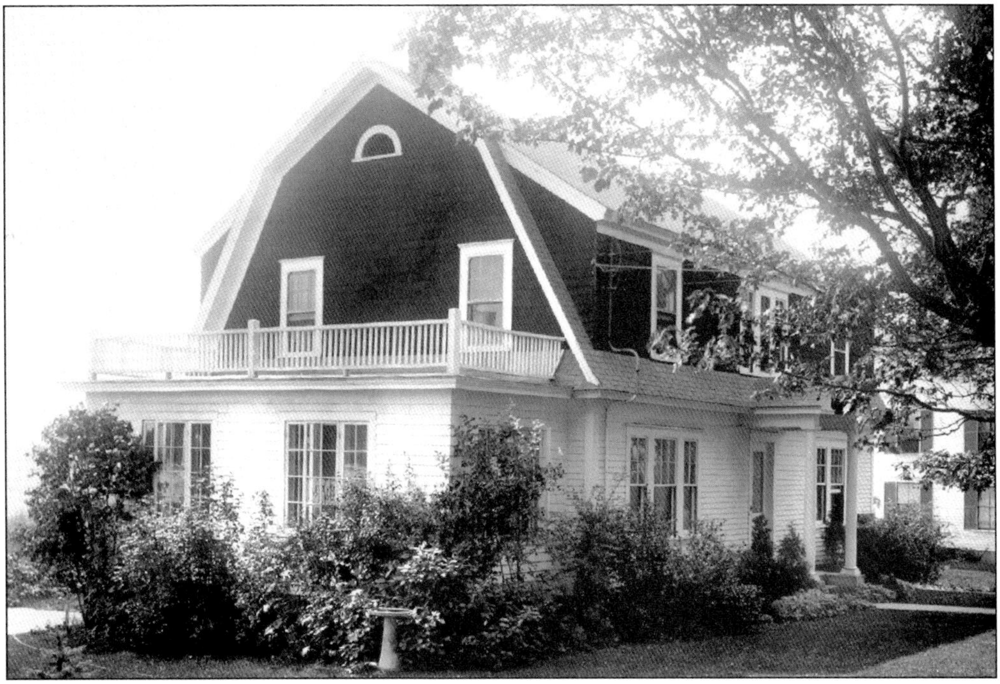

The Emma L. Colby House. Emma Colby was a teacher at various schools and taught at Colby Academy for three years. She also served on the school board in New London for 25 years. The house was later bought by Colby-Sawyer College and used for a short time as a dormitory called Heidelberg House.

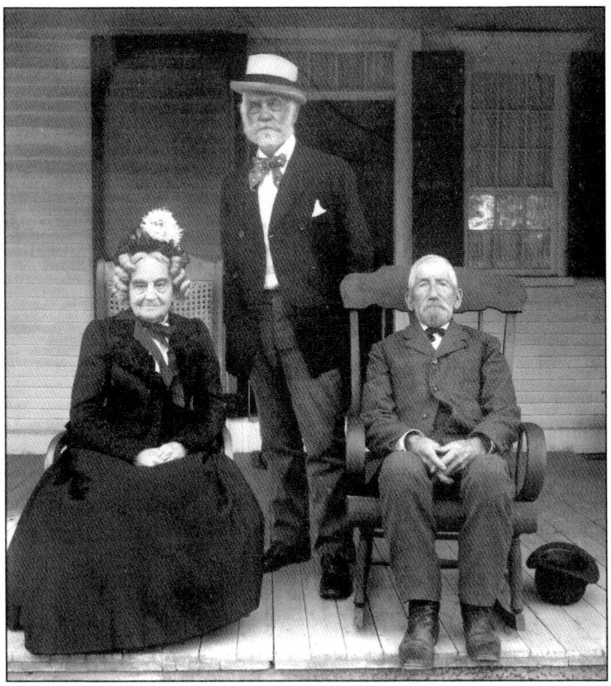

Susan Colby Colgate, Robert Colby, and Anthony Burpee, 1901. This photograph was taken on the porch of the Colby Homestead. Susan Colby (1817–1919) was the daughter of Gov. Anthony Colby and the first woman principal at the New London Academy. She married James Colgate in 1851 and served as a trustee of the academy. Her brother Robert Colby (1822–1904) was a graduate of Dartmouth College and worked as a lawyer in Concord and New York. Their cousin Anthony Burpee (1817–1905) was a partner in Nahum Greenwood's store, a colonel in the militia, a state legislator, and an academy trustee; he led the church choir for 50 years. (Courtesy of New London Town Archives.)

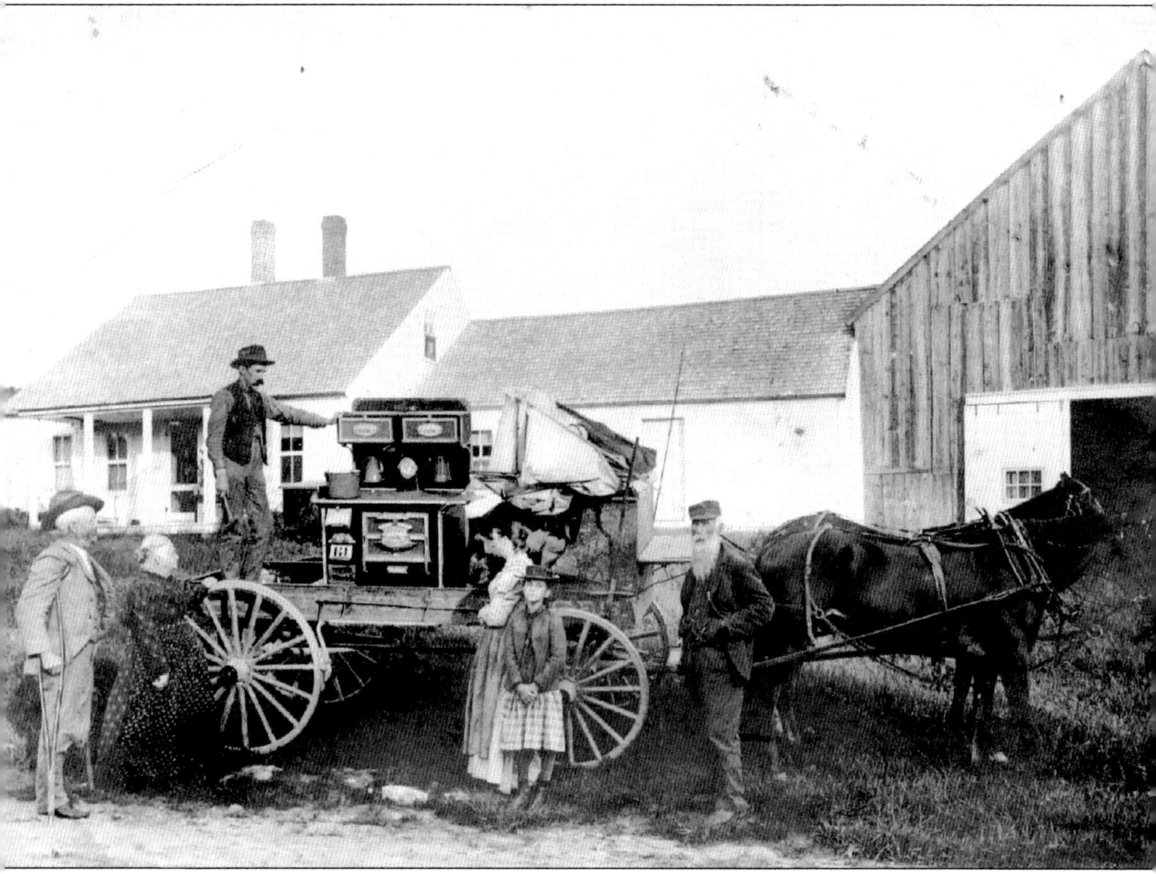

The Arrival of a New Stove. This photograph was taken at the Cooper farm, located on Pleasant Street. Pictured, from left to right, are Solon Cooper, Hannah Cooper, unidentified, Janet McCallum Dean, Eva Dean, and Stephen J. Dean.

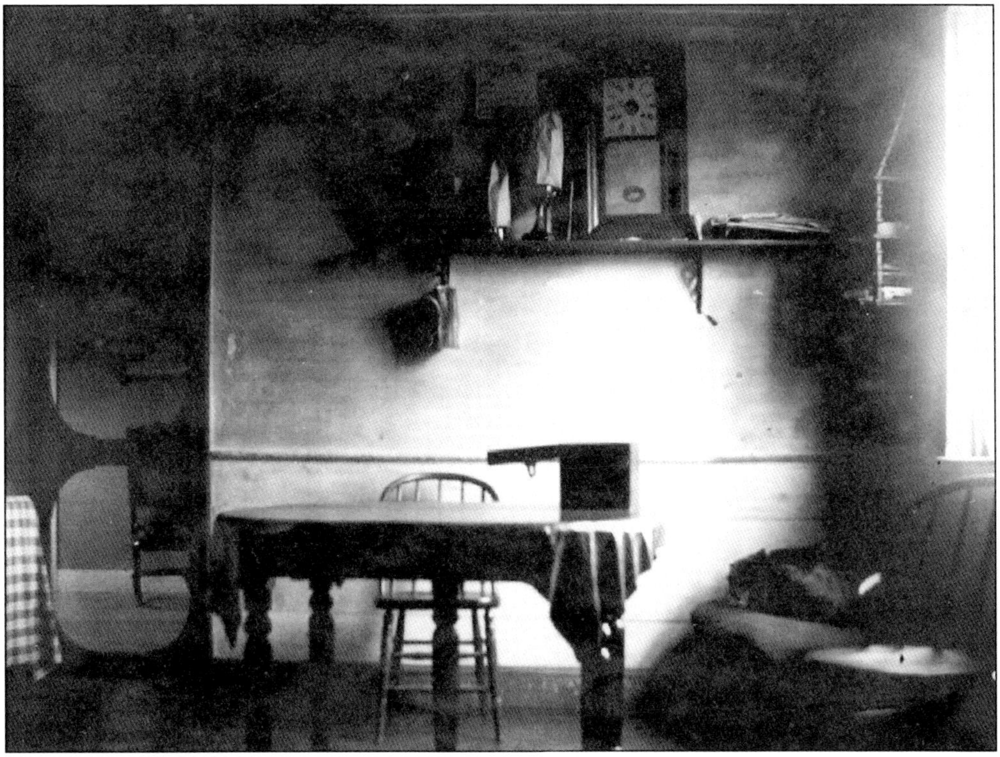

THE INTERIOR OF ROBERT DAVIS'S HOME. Robert Davis was a carpenter who lived almost his entire life in New London. He built several cottages around town. He married Emma Jewett in 1877, and they lived in this house, located on Old County Road near King Hill, in the western part of town.

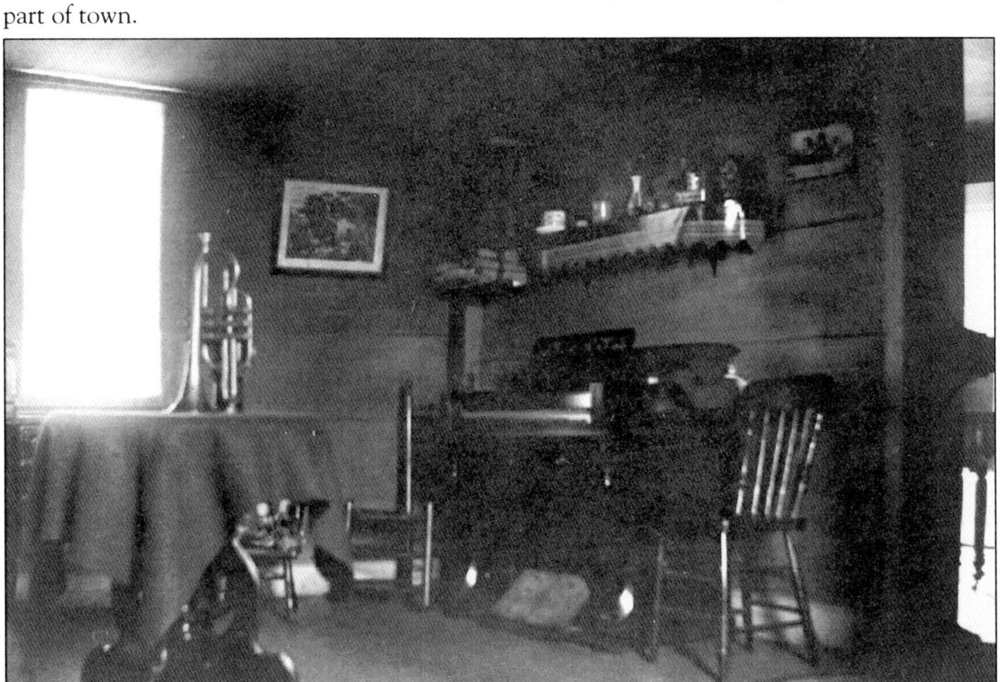

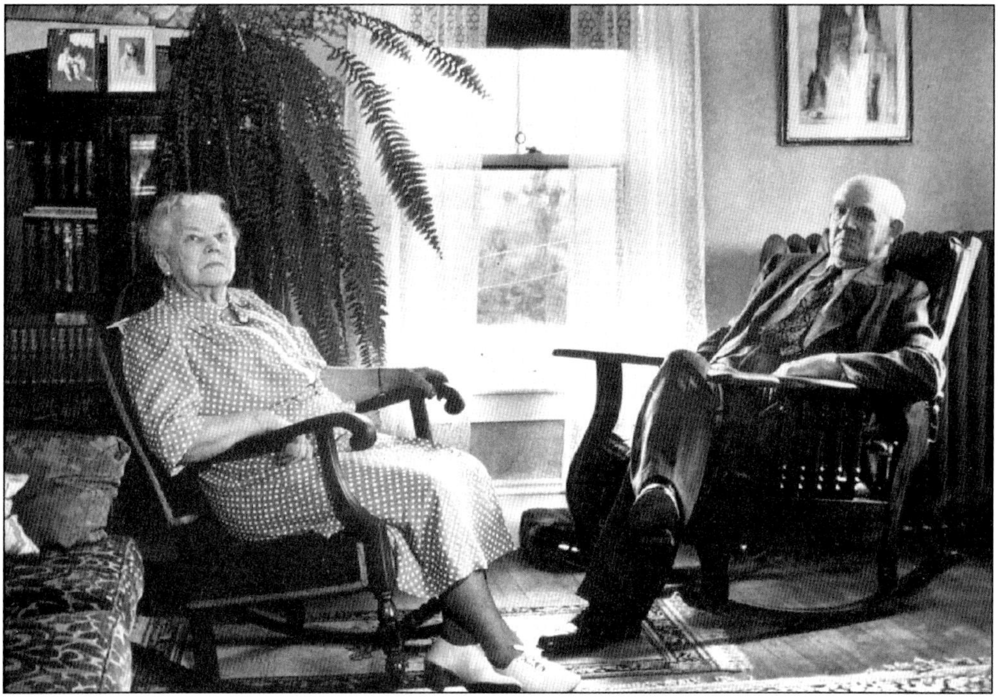

Martha and Joseph Cutting. The Cuttings were very active in town affairs. Martha attended Colby Academy and was a longtime library trustee. Her husband, Joseph, was a selectman for 12 years, as well as a partner in Kidder Garage for 17 years.

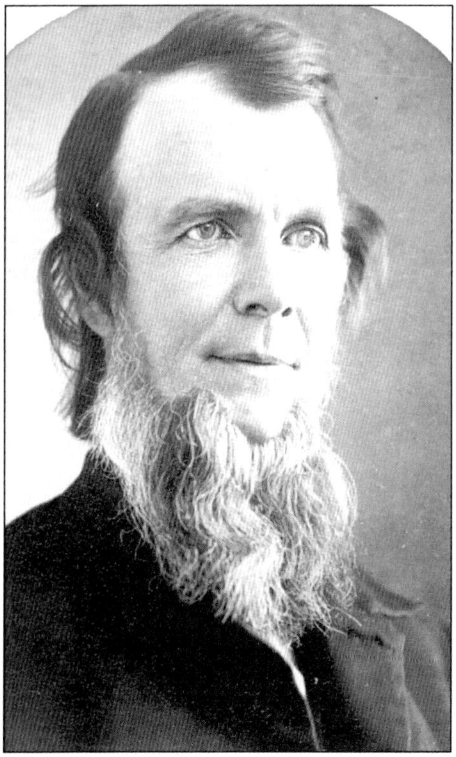

Ebenezer Dodge. A graduate of Brown University and Newton Theological Seminary, Dodge was the well-liked pastor of the New London Baptist Church from 1849 to 1853. He left New London to teach at Madison (now Colgate) University, where he served as president from 1868 until his death in 1890. (Courtesy of Colby-Sawyer College Archives.)

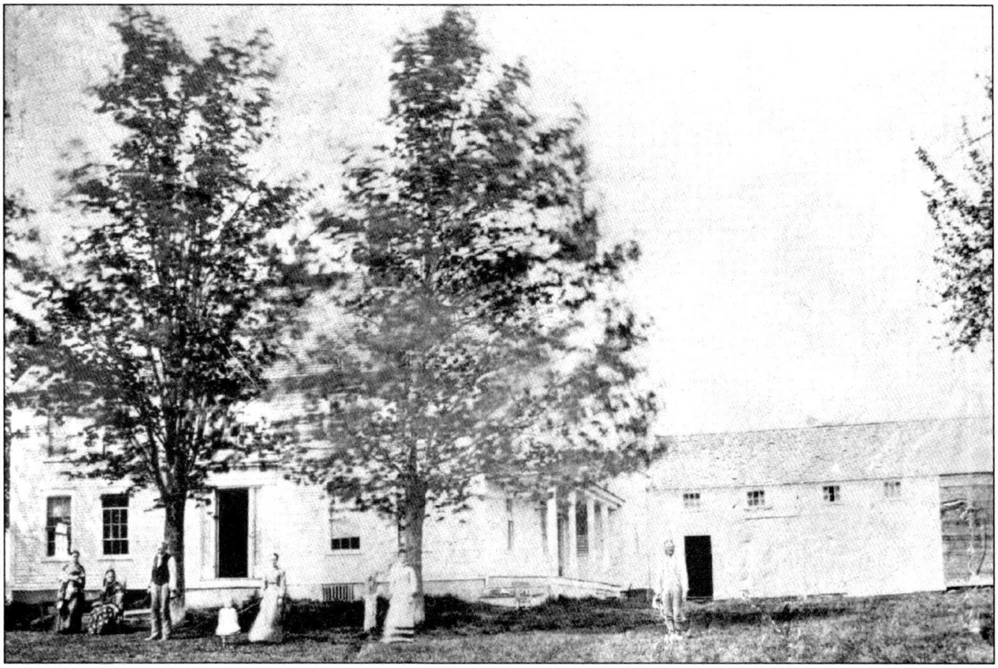

THE DAVID EVERETT FARM. This photograph was taken prior to 1885. Built between 1815 and 1825, the house was later occupied by James Morgan and Capt. Jack Sargent. Its barn, located across Main Street, became the Barn Playhouse. The house was destroyed by fire in 1905.

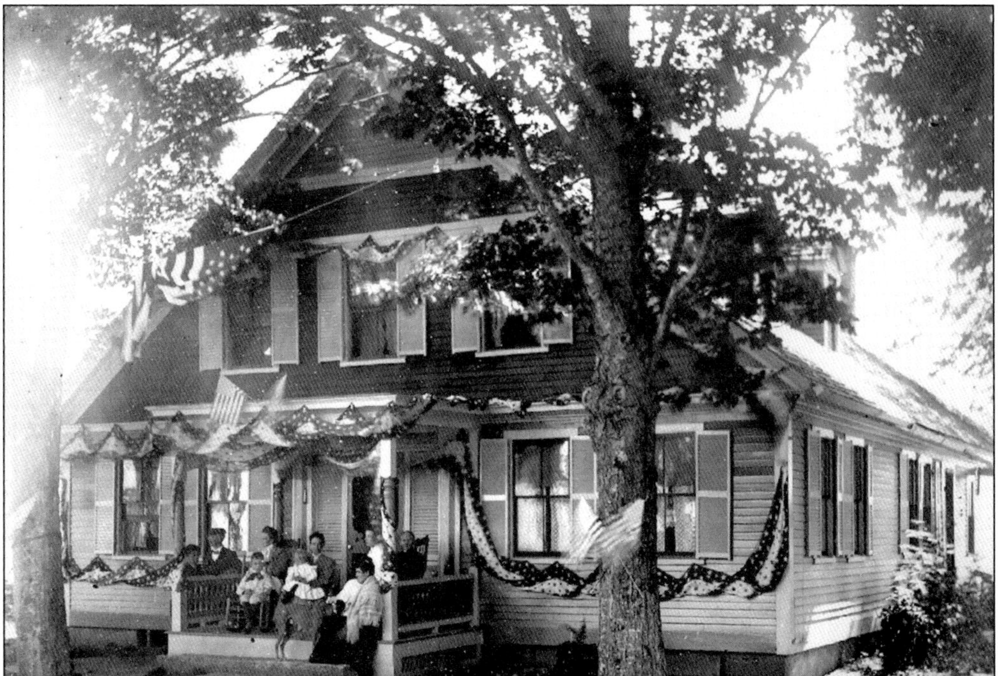

THE JONATHAN EVERETT JR. HOUSE. Built *c.* 1836, this home was located on Main Street near the barn that became the Barn Playhouse. The photograph was taken in 1905.

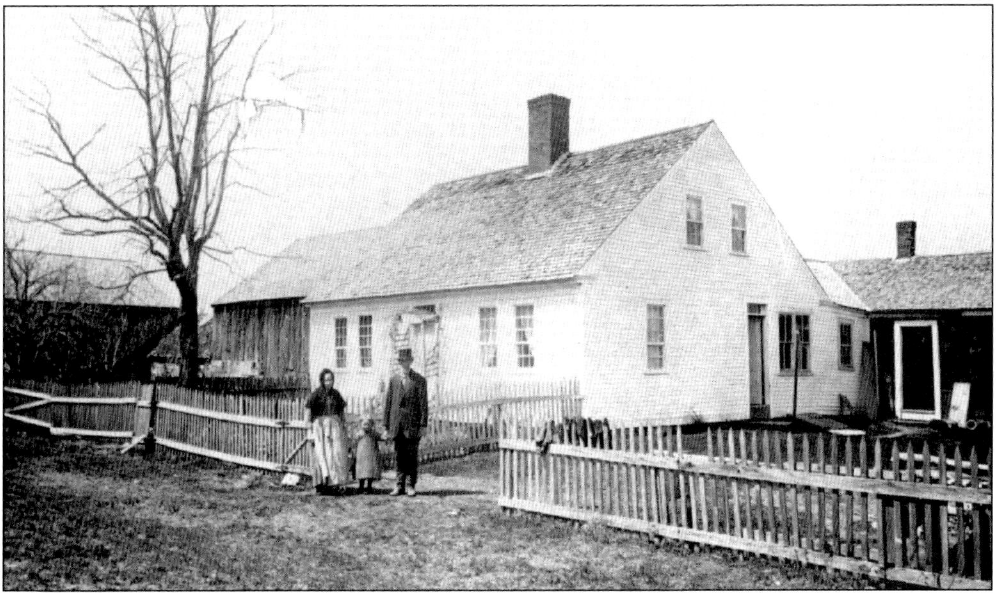

THE GRIFFIN HOUSE, 1888. This Cape Cod–style home was located on Old Main Street.

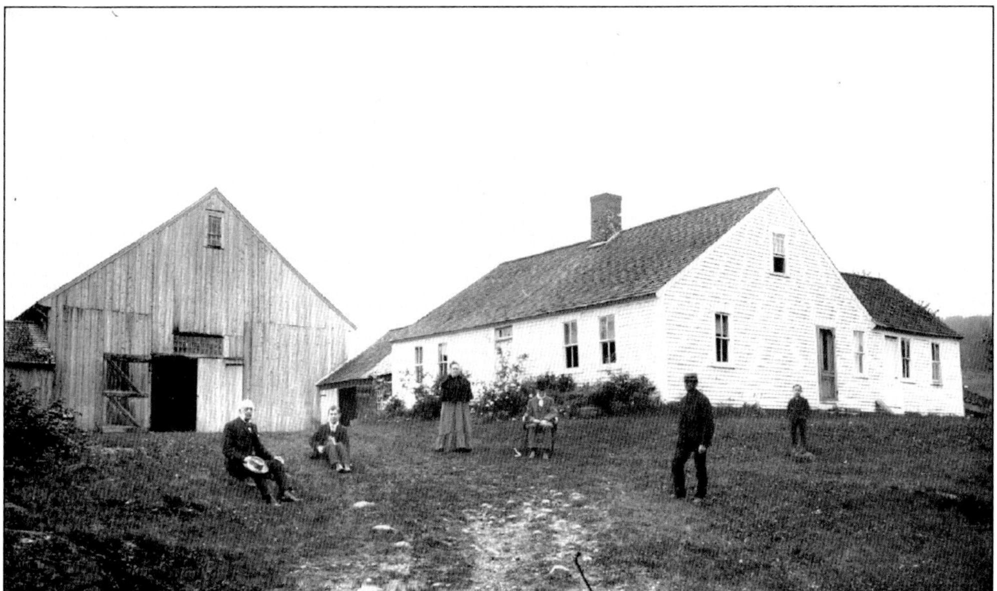

THE PINGREE-HAYES HOUSE, 1900. This house was built by Jeremiah Pingree Jr. in 1824 just northwest of Pleasant Lake on what is now appropriately called Pingree Road.

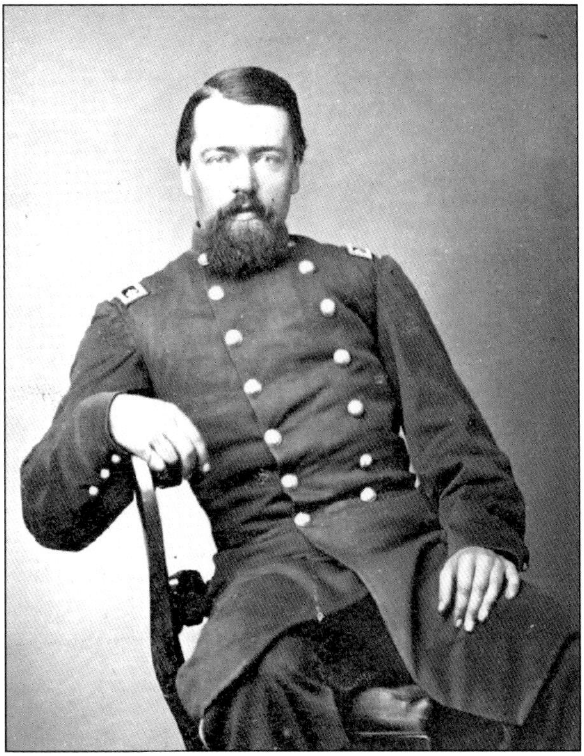

GEORGE H.W. HERRICK. Herrick attended the New London Academy, Harvard Medical School, and Jefferson Medical College. He was a surgeon and major in the 1st Massachusetts Infantry. During his service in the army, his wife and young son died while living in the Herrick Homestead, on Main Street. He eventually settled in Charlestown, Massachusetts, and started a medical practice there. He died at age 38 in 1877.

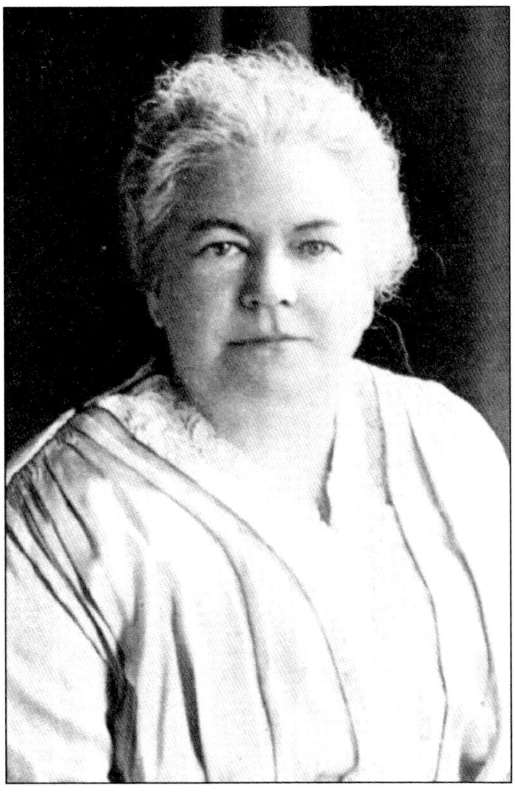

JULIA M. GAY. Graduating from Colby Academy in 1890, Julia Gay was a teacher and the preceptress at the academy from 1908 until her death in 1923. During that time, she influenced many New London lives, since at that time the academy served as the modern-day equivalent of the local high school. According to the inscription on her memorial plaque at the school, she "inspired her students toward ethical conduct and lifelong learning, holding no compromise with mediocrity."

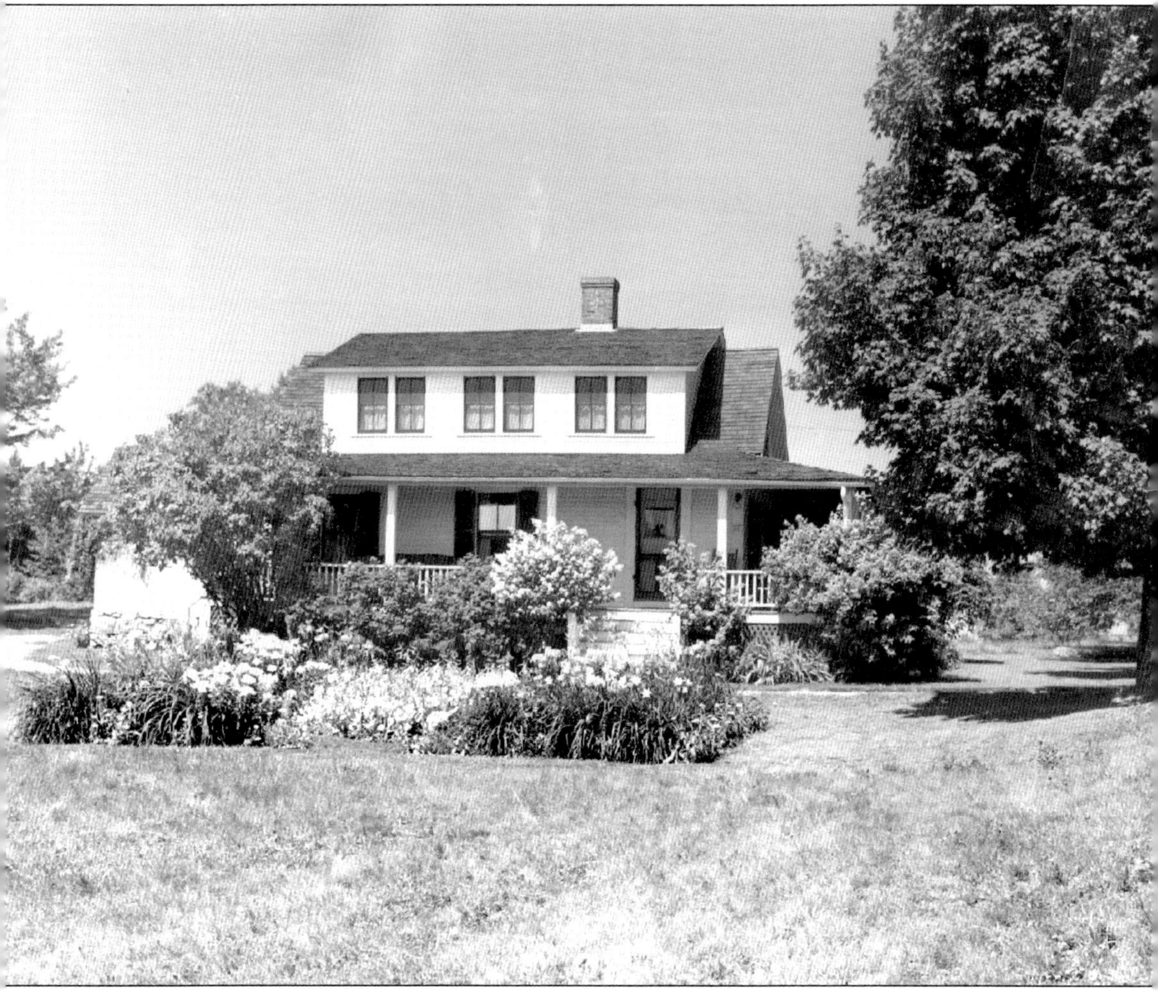

THE JARDINE HOME, 1952. Ruth Jardine returned every summer for more than 60 years to this house, also known as Summer Rest, located on Knight's Hill.

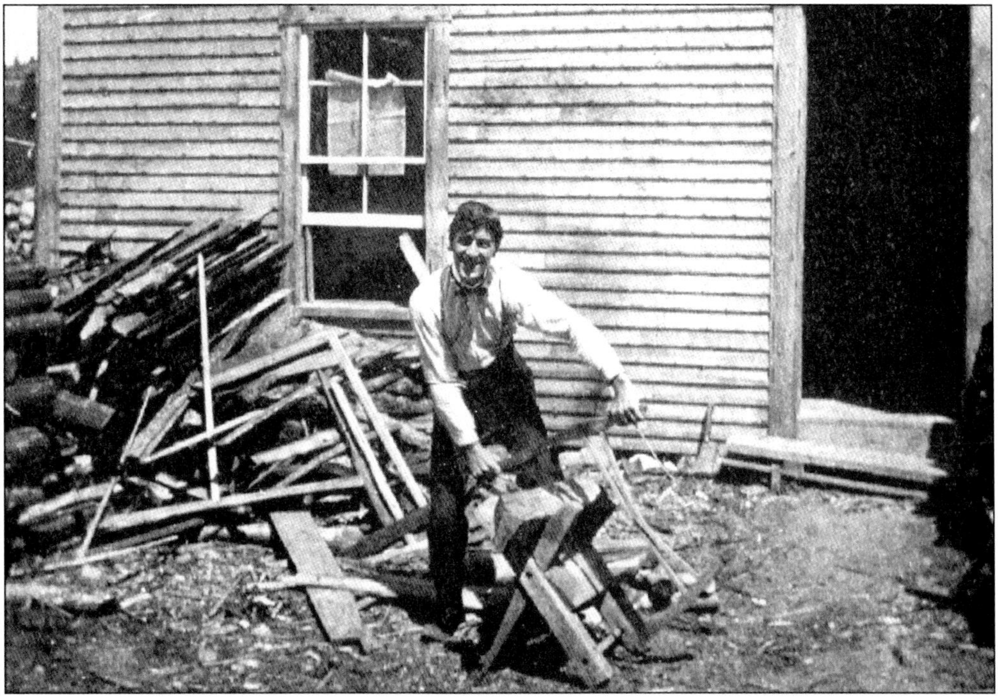

WILL KIDDER. Kidder attended Colby Academy and was active in town affairs, serving as town clerk before and after an almost four-year stint in the services during World War II. He owned Kidder Garage at Four Corners and helped found the New London Trust with James Cleveland and Wayne Wheeler.

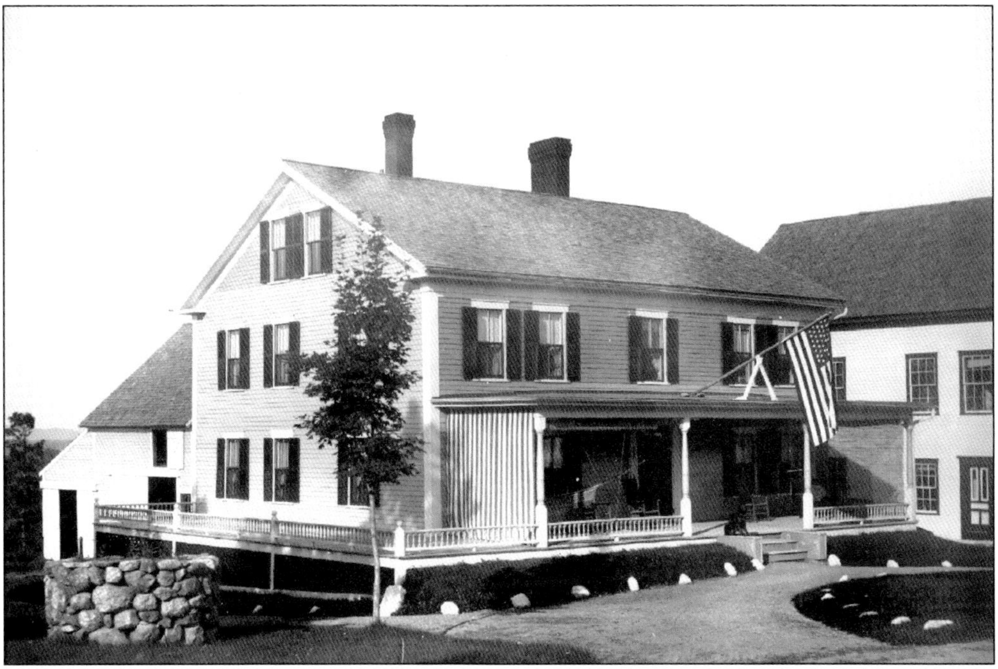

THE LAMSON HOUSE. Formerly known as the Gile House, this building was destroyed by fire in 1918. It was located across from the Baptist church.

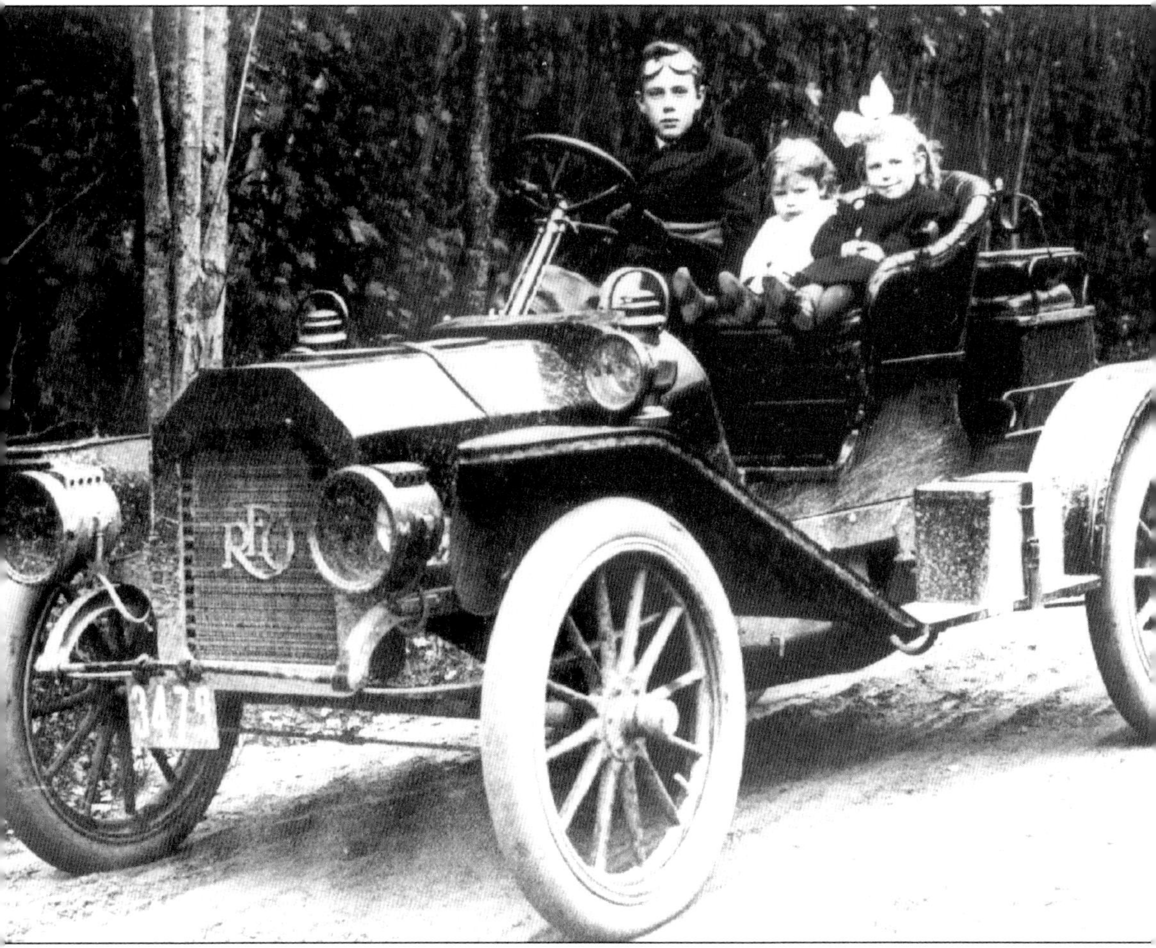

The Lamson Children. Pictured, from left to right, are Donald, Seth, and Dorothea Lamson. Donald moved to Bristol, New Hampshire, in 1920. His children Donald Jr. and Dorothea Bette were the first set of twins born at New London Hospital. Seth was a resident of New London for almost 65 years. Dorothea worked as a kindergarten teacher before her marriage.

EPHRAIM KNIGHT. Professor Knight worked as an associate principal and chair of mathematics at the New London Literary and Scientific Institution (later renamed Colby Academy) for 20 years. He retired in 1873, after the death of his only daughter, and died himself in the spring of 1878.

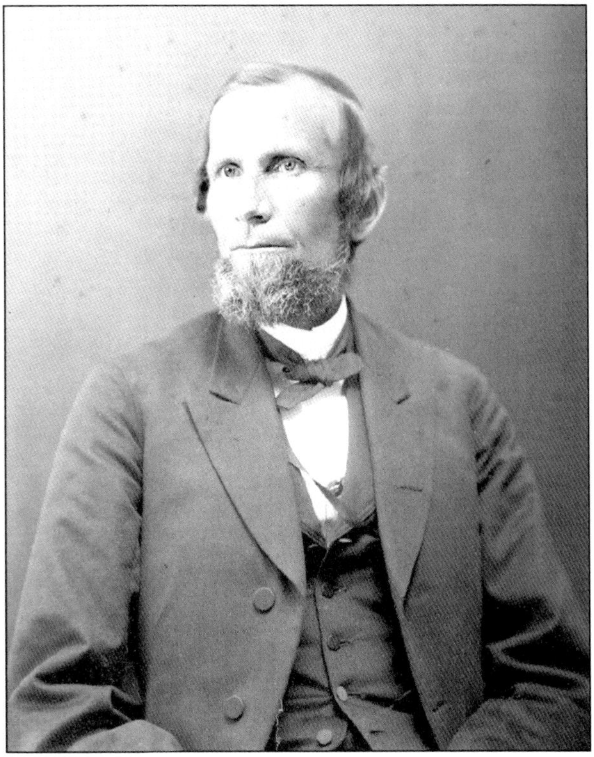

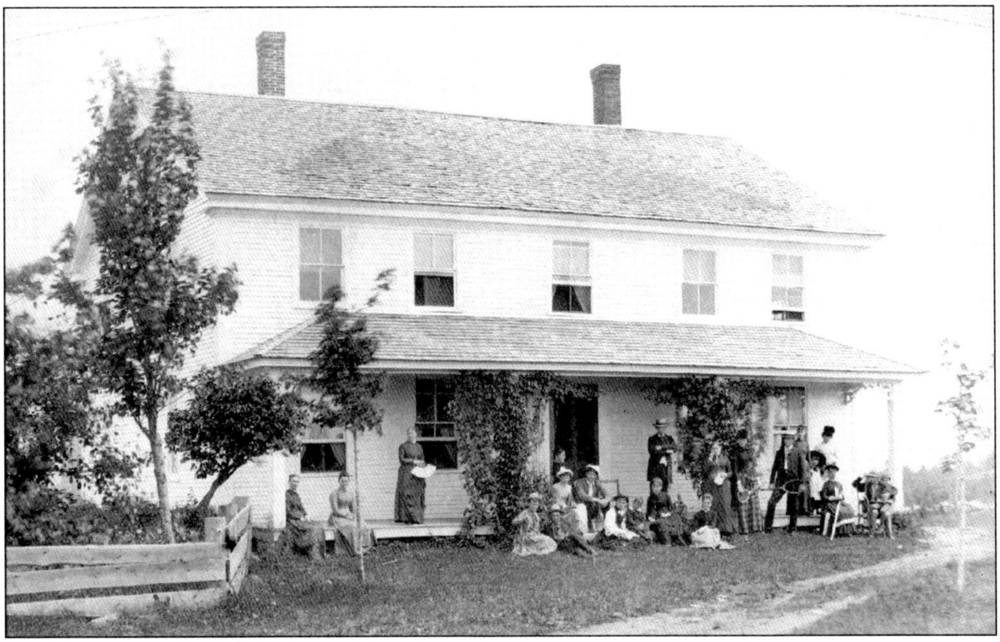

THE KNIGHT-GORDON HOUSE. This building is located on Knight's Hill to the north of Messer Pond.

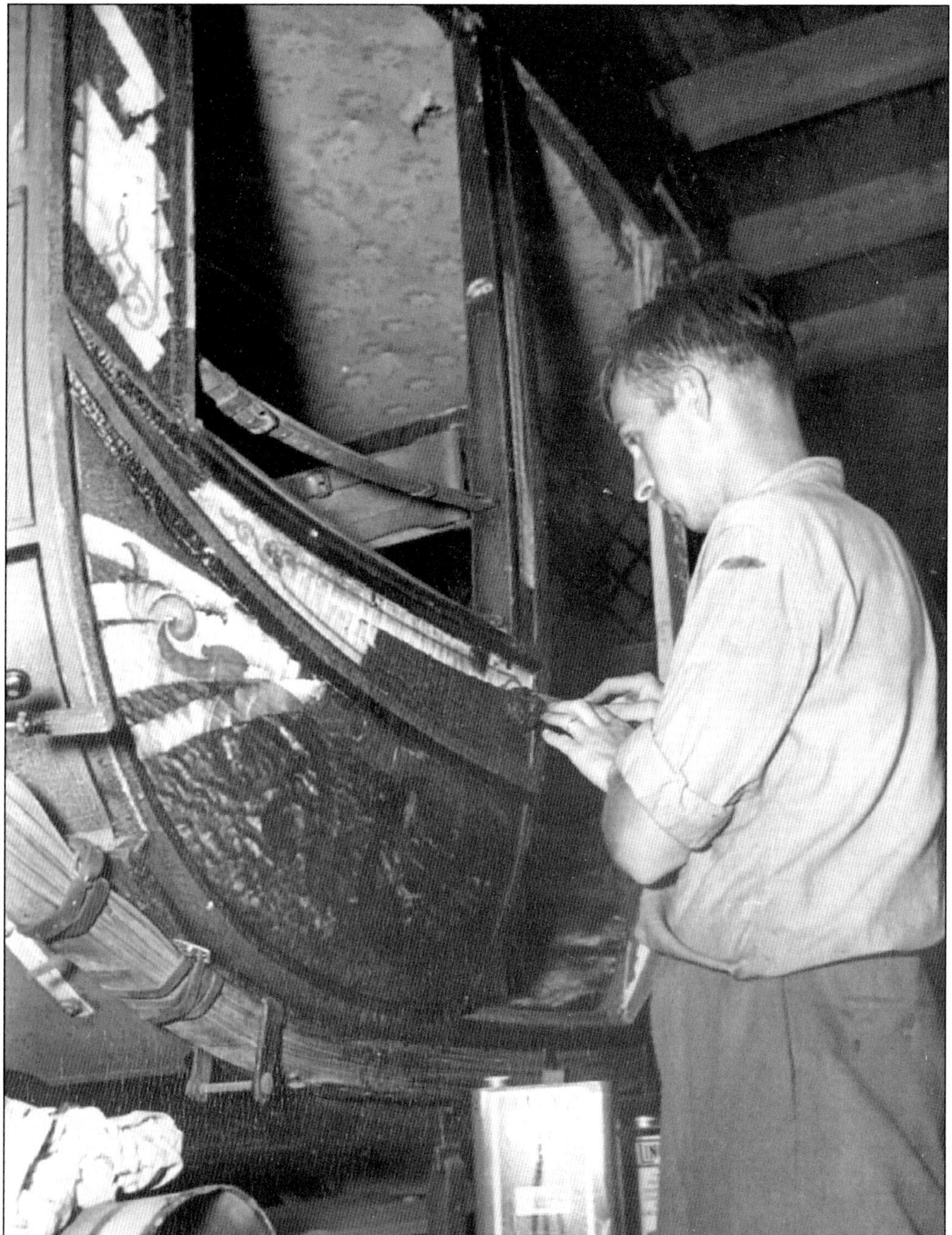

"BUD" LAURIDSEN. A resident since 1945, Laurids "Bud" Lauridsen is very involved in town activities, especially the ski school and historical society. He is a still-life artist and is shown here restoring a Concord coach for the historical society in 1946.

DR. ANNA LITTLEFIELD. A graduate of Colby Academy and the Women's College of Pennsylvania, Littlefield was one of the earliest practicing women doctors in the state of New Hampshire. She started her medical practice in New London in 1896 and also worked as an anesthetist at New London Hospital until 1940.

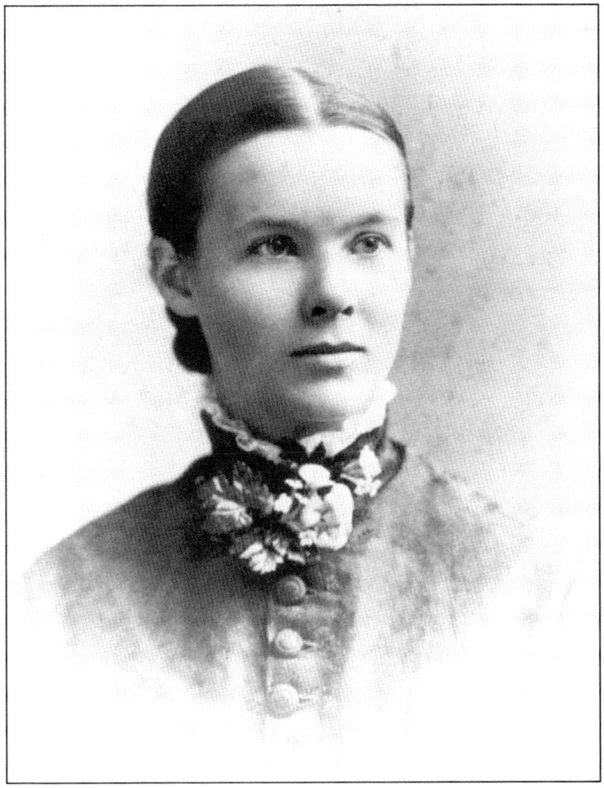

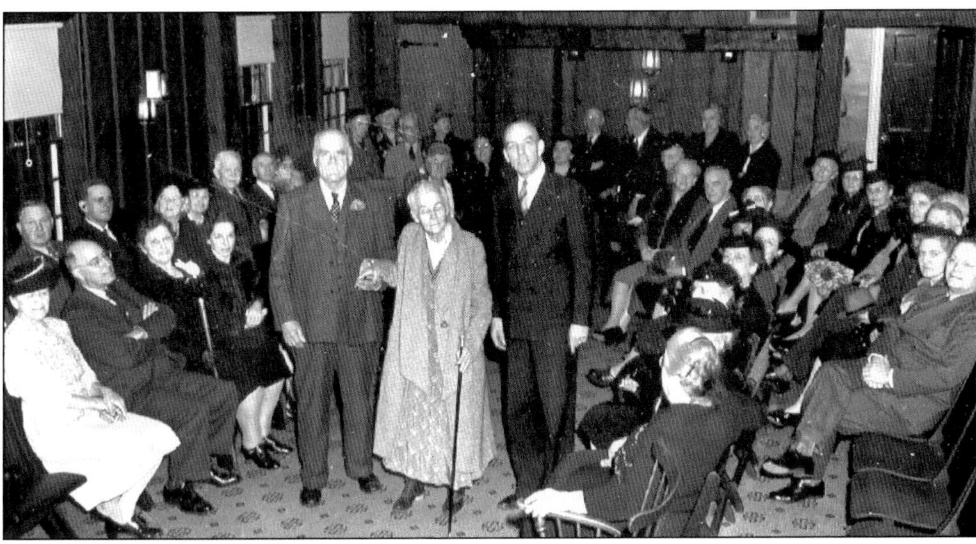

A PORTRAIT DEDICATION, 1947. For Dr. Anna Littlefield's 87th birthday, a portrait of her was dedicated and hung at the Tracy Memorial Library, where she worked when the building was used as a hospital in the 1920s. The portrait is now hung in the New London Hospital wing that bears her name. Pictured in the center are, from left to right, Ira Littlefield, Dr. Anna Littlefield, and Rev. H.W. Buker.

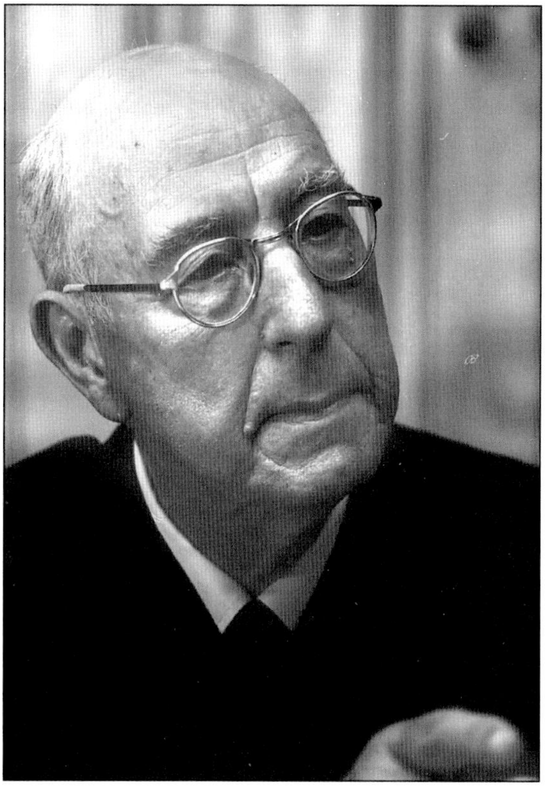

M. Roy London (1890–1974). Milo Roy London earned degrees from Beacom College and Rider College before starting his career as a teacher. He taught at Colby Academy from 1915 to 1918 and at Colby Junior College from 1928 to 1958, when he served as chair of the Secretarial Science Department. After his retirement in 1958, he served as a Republican representative in the state legislature until 1967. Throughout his entire life, he was active in community service. He was particularly active in the Boys' Club of New London and the Boy Scouts and held a variety of positions in the town of New London, including moderator and selectman. (Courtesy of Colby-Sawyer College Archives.)

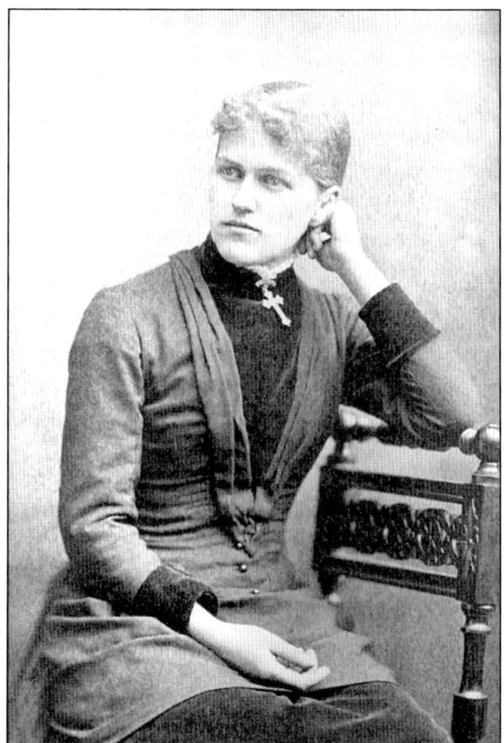

Mary Burpee Macomber (1863–1952). A graduate of Colby Academy and a special student at Radcliffe College, Macomber traveled extensively and was a Red Cross worker in both world wars. She served for 40 years as a library trustee and was a trustee of Colby Academy and Colby Junior College from 1905 to 1952. (Photograph by W.G.C. Kimball, courtesy of Colby-Sawyer College Archives.)

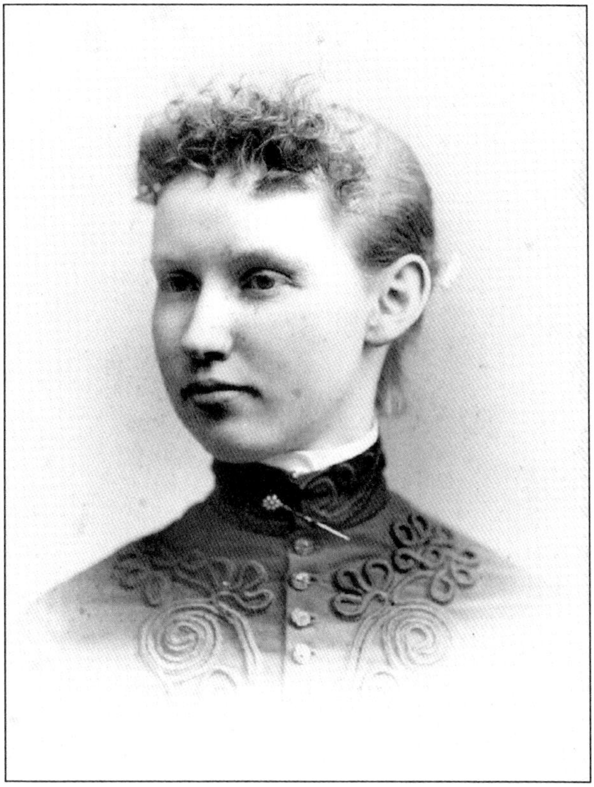

Gertrude Messer (1871–1950). A resident of New London all her life, Messer was co-proprietor of one of the summer boardinghouses in town.

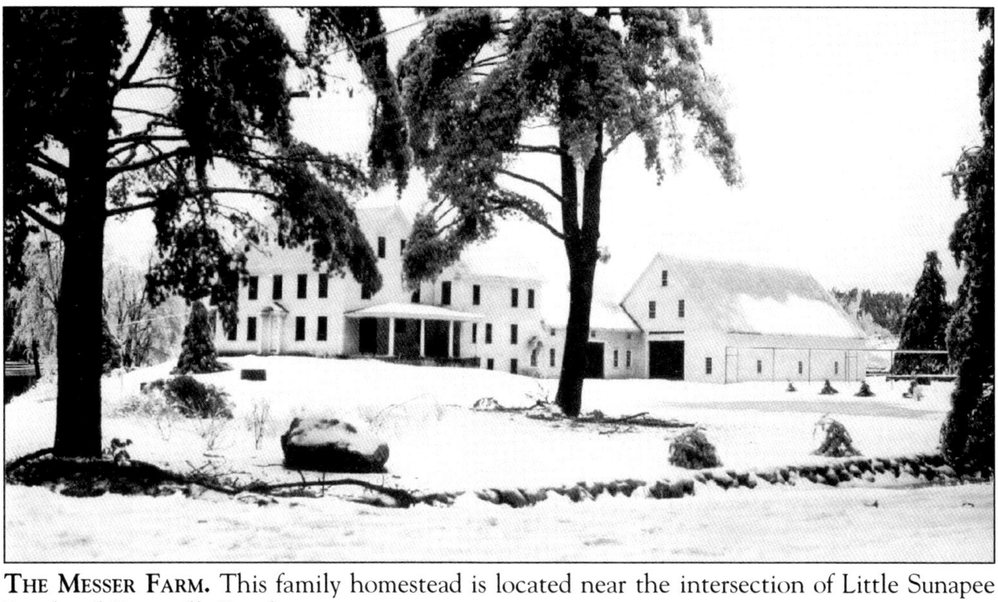

The Messer Farm. This family homestead is located near the intersection of Little Sunapee Road and Otterville Road.

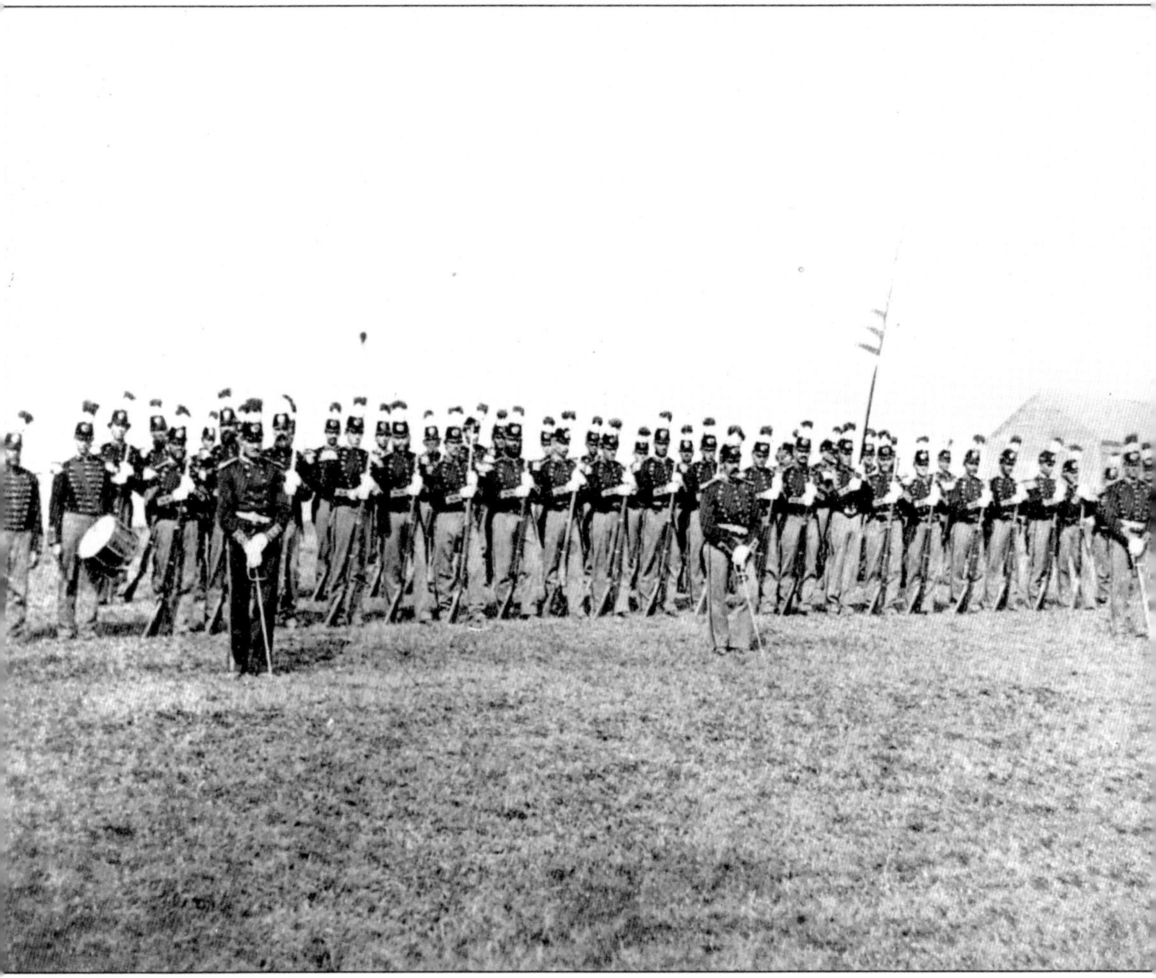

MESSER'S RIFLES, C. 1865–1870. This volunteer military company was the result of the reorganization of the McCutchins Guards, which began in 1858. The Rifles instituted an annual reception every winter. (Courtesy of Colby-Sawyer College Archives.)

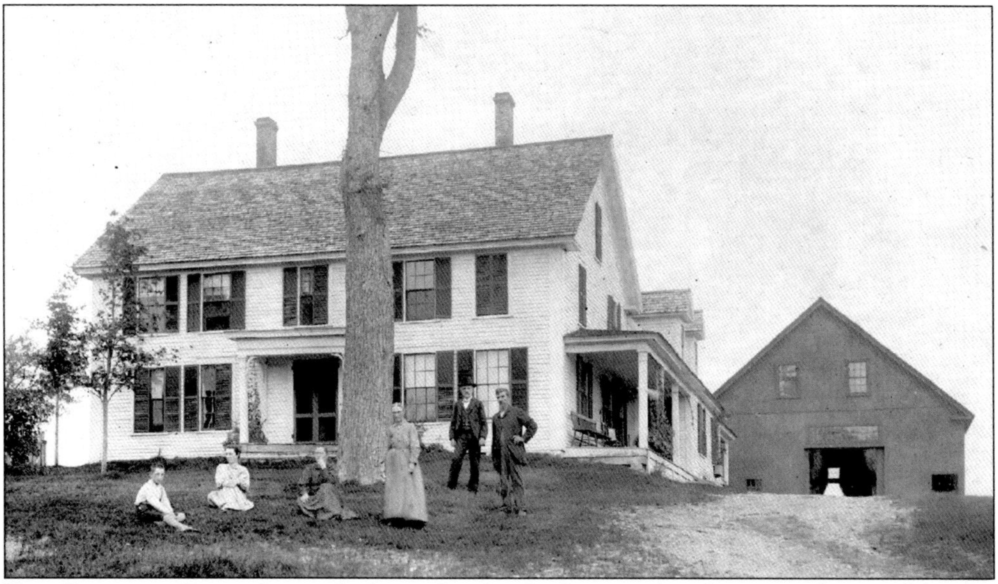

THE PRESCOTT FARM. Located above Crockett's Corner, this farm was destroyed by fire in 1912.

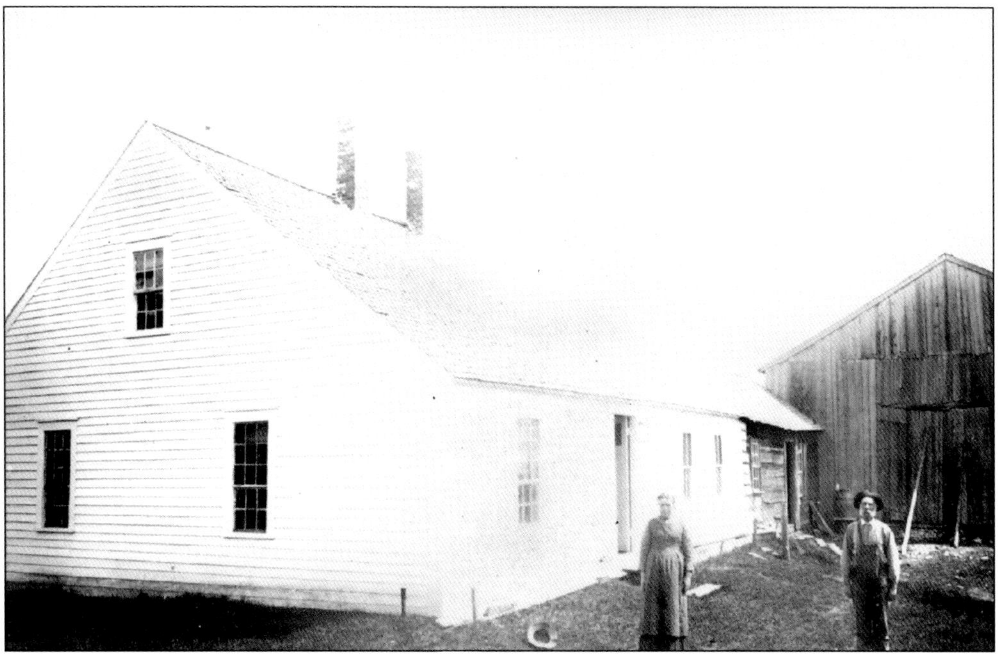

THE PINGREE HOUSE, 1881. Shown here are Nancy and Walter Pingree. This house was built prior to 1800 and was moved to modern-day Pingree Road in 1813. Walter Pingree fought and was wounded in the Civil War with the 11th New Hampshire Volunteers.

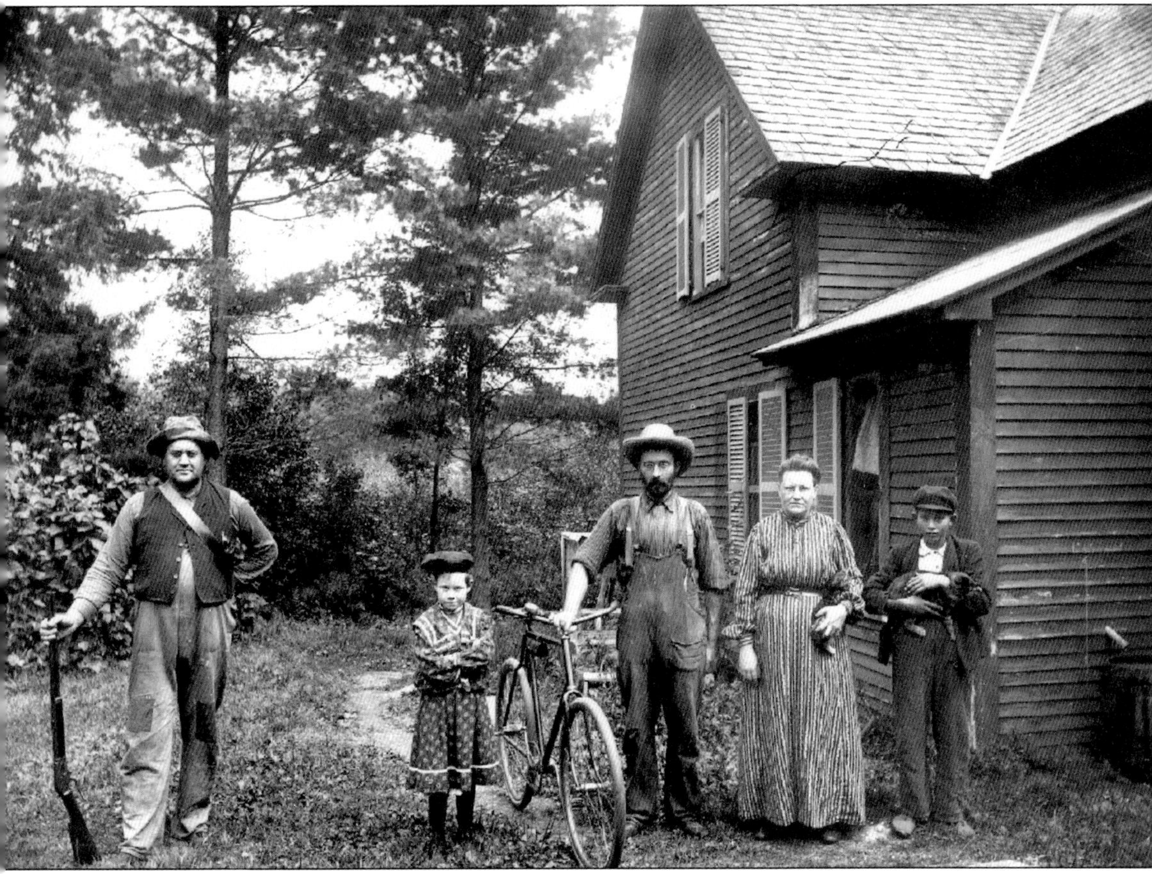

The Piper Family in Elkins, c. 1905. Pictured, from left to right, are an unidentified person, Mary Piper, Fred Piper, Pamelia Piper, and Walter Piper.

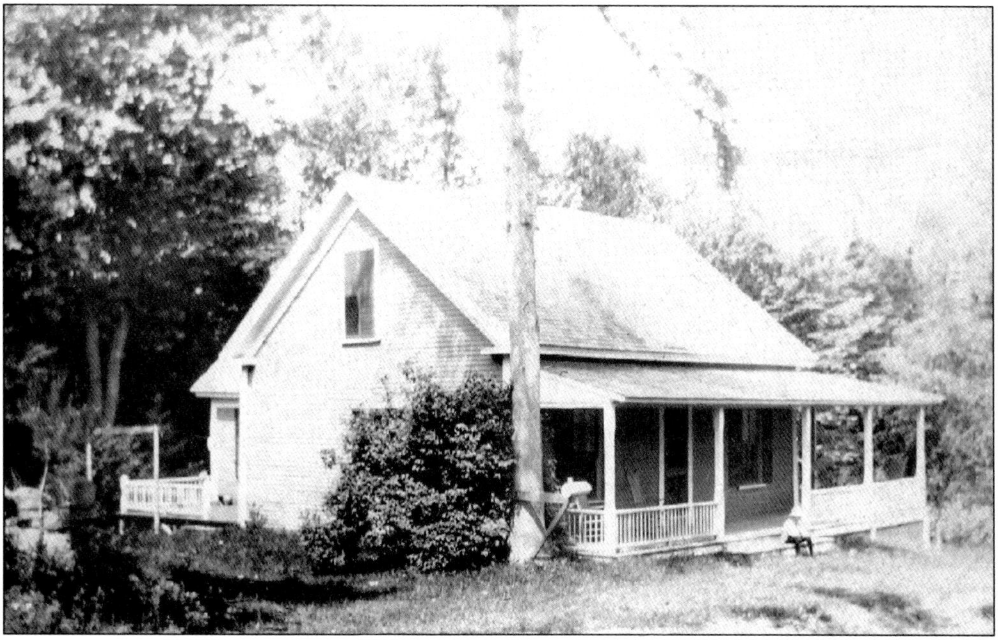

Ray Cottage. This cottage was built by Asa Ray (1816–1879) near Bucklin Beach c. 1839. Ray was a blacksmith and also had a shoe shop.

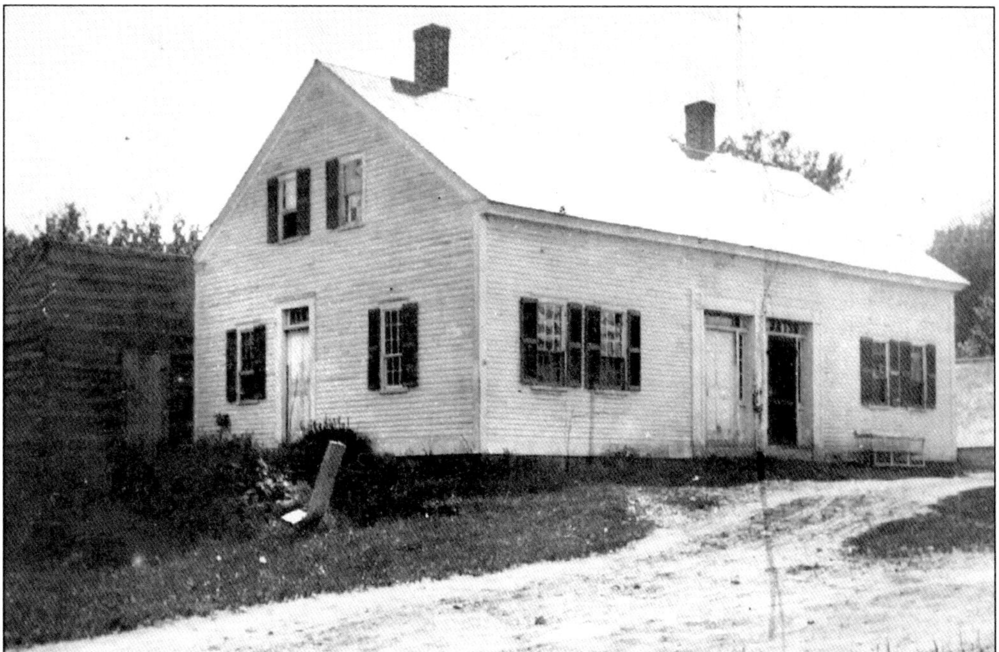

A Scythe Company House. This building, constructed between 1835 and 1840, was one of many used by the New London Scythe Company, located in Elkins.

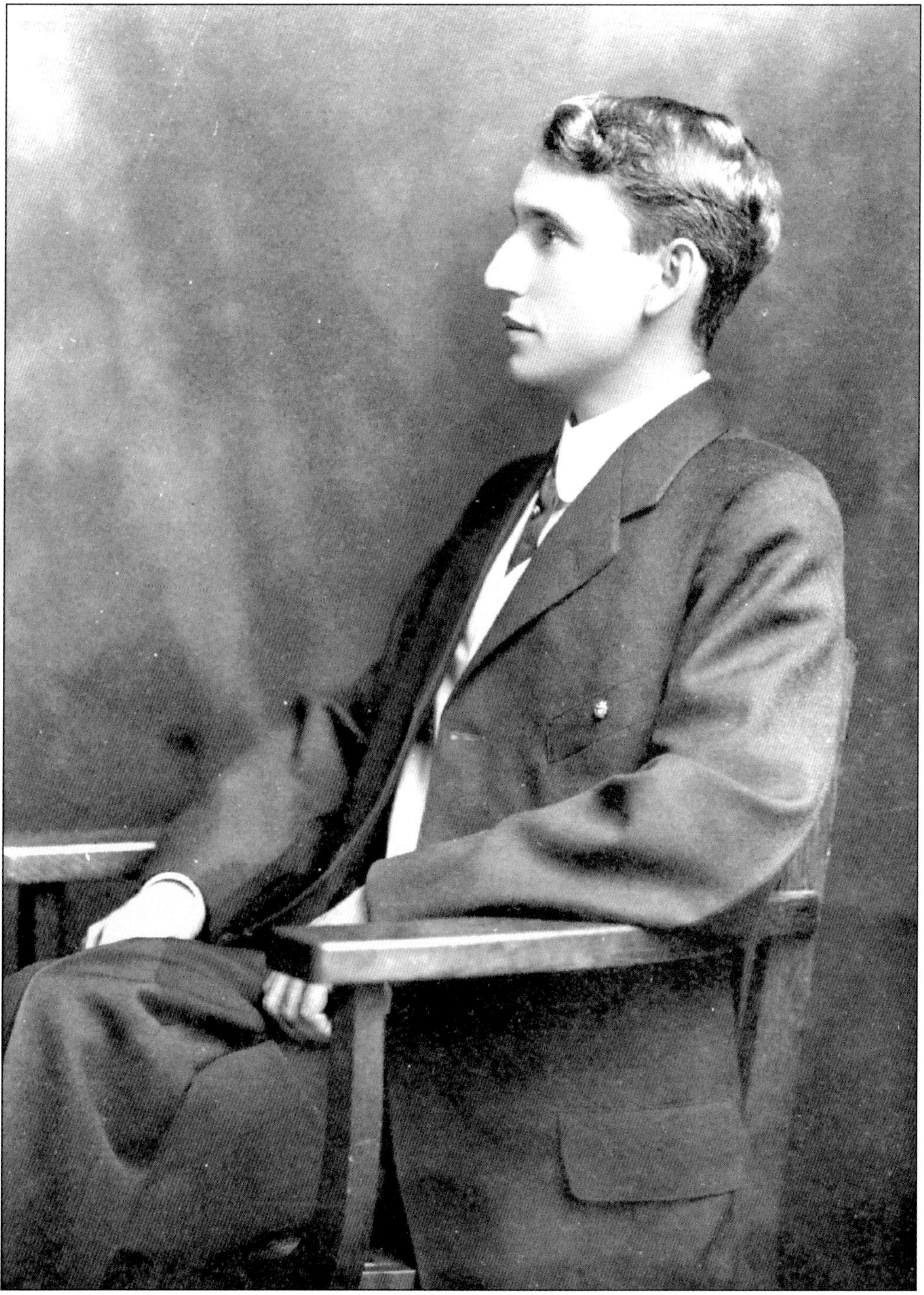

AUSBON SARGENT (1891–1988). Sargent graduated from Colby Academy in 1910 and worked as a house painter. He also worked on the maintenance crew at Colby Junior College for many years. He is remembered for spending his life savings to buy three acres of land on Main Street and donating it to the town. This piece of land is now known as Sargent Common. (Courtesy of Colby-Sawyer College Archives.)

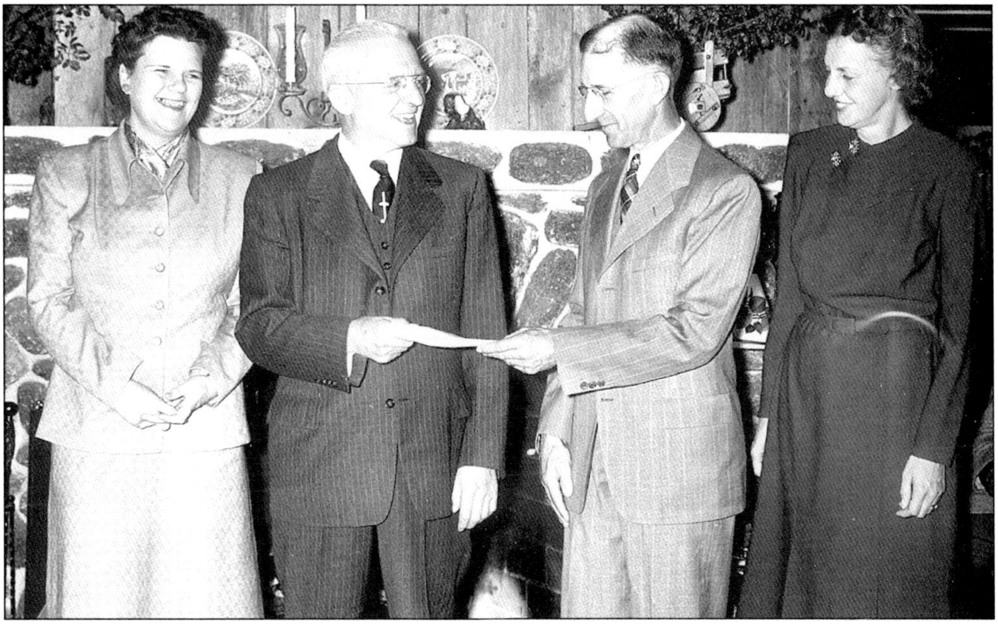

New London Gives $5,805 to Colby Advancement Program, 1951. Relations between the town and the college have always been close; each realizes that its success depends on the well being of the other. Pictured, from left to right, are Charlotte D. Meinecke (resident director of the fund), H. Leslie Sawyer (president of the college), Erwin P. Edmunds (selectman), and Harriett Kidder (chairwoman of town campaign). (Photograph by Don Sieburg, courtesy of Colby-Sawyer College Archives.)

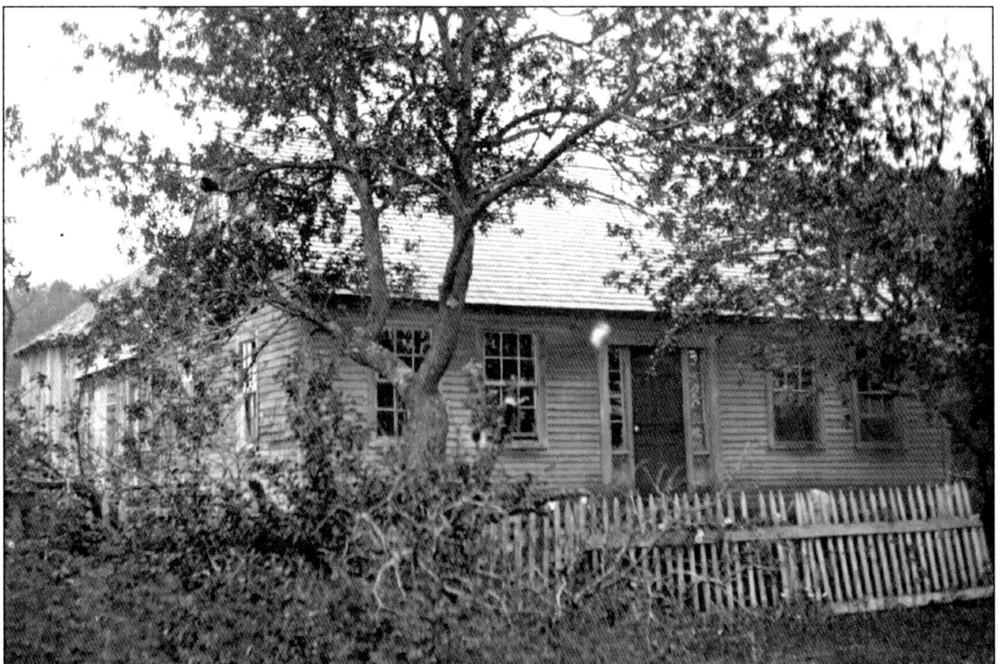

The Gray-Lauridsen House. This house was originally located on Knight's Hill Road but was moved to the historical society site in 1992 and renamed the Lauridsen Acquisitions building.

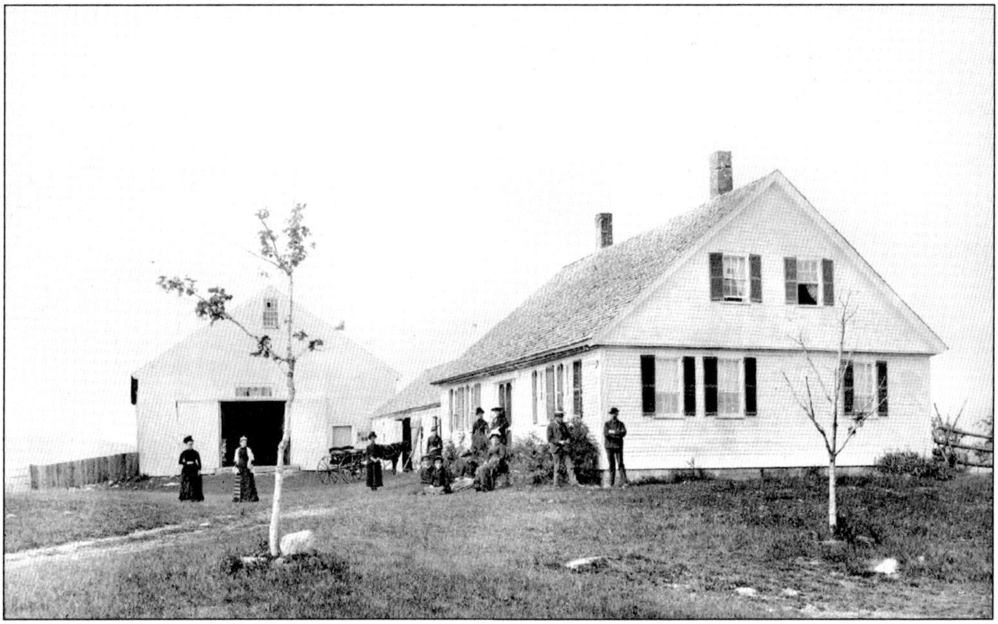

THE SHOLES HOUSE. This house, located on Knight's Hill, burned in the 1890s.

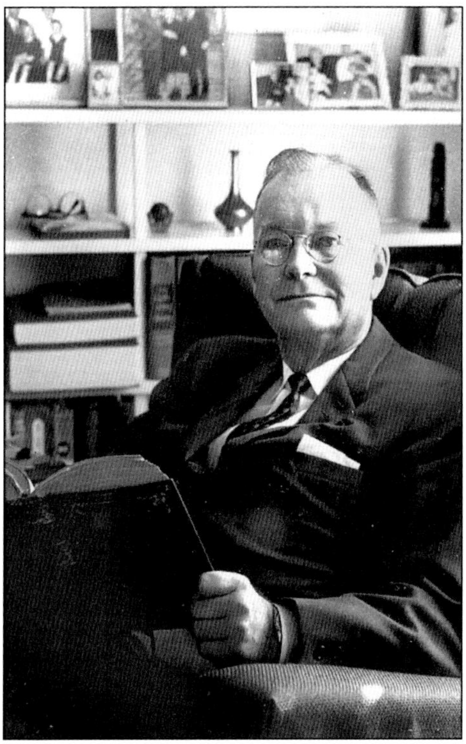

DR. J. DUANE SQUIRES (1904–1981). After earning his doctorate from Harvard in 1933, Squires moved to New London to teach history at Colby Junior College. He served as chairman of the Social Studies Department from 1935 until his retirement in 1970. Squires was a prolific history writer, as well as a lecturer and lay preacher. His books include *Mirror to America: A History of New London, N.H. 1900–1950; The Granite State of the United States 1623–1955;* and *British Propaganda at Home and in the United States from 1914 to 1917.* He gave an estimated 2,000 lectures and sermons throughout the state on a variety of historical and theological topics. Squires was involved with New London Hospital, the New London Service Organization, and the New Hampshire Council of Churches and Religious Education. He was chairman of the New Hampshire Civil War Centennial Commission and a member of the board of directors of the American Revolution Bicentennial Administration. (Courtesy of Colby-Sawyer College Archives.)

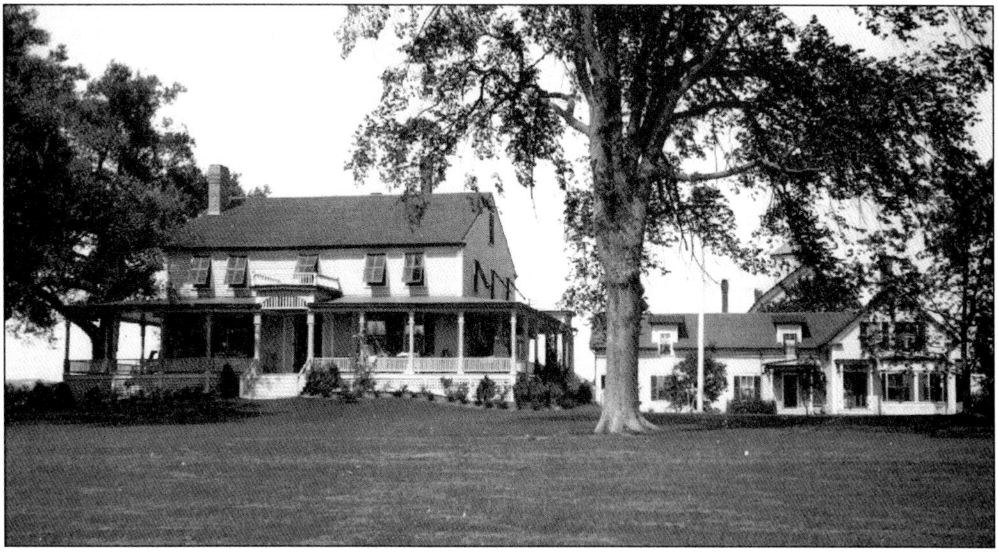

The Willow Farm. Located in the West Part on what is now Tracy Road, the Willow Farm building was erected sometime before 1820. This farm has also been called Tracy Farm after its inhabitants, Mr. and Mrs. James Tracy, who opened a nine-hole golf course on the property in 1909. The golf course was in operation for the public from the 1930s until 1942.

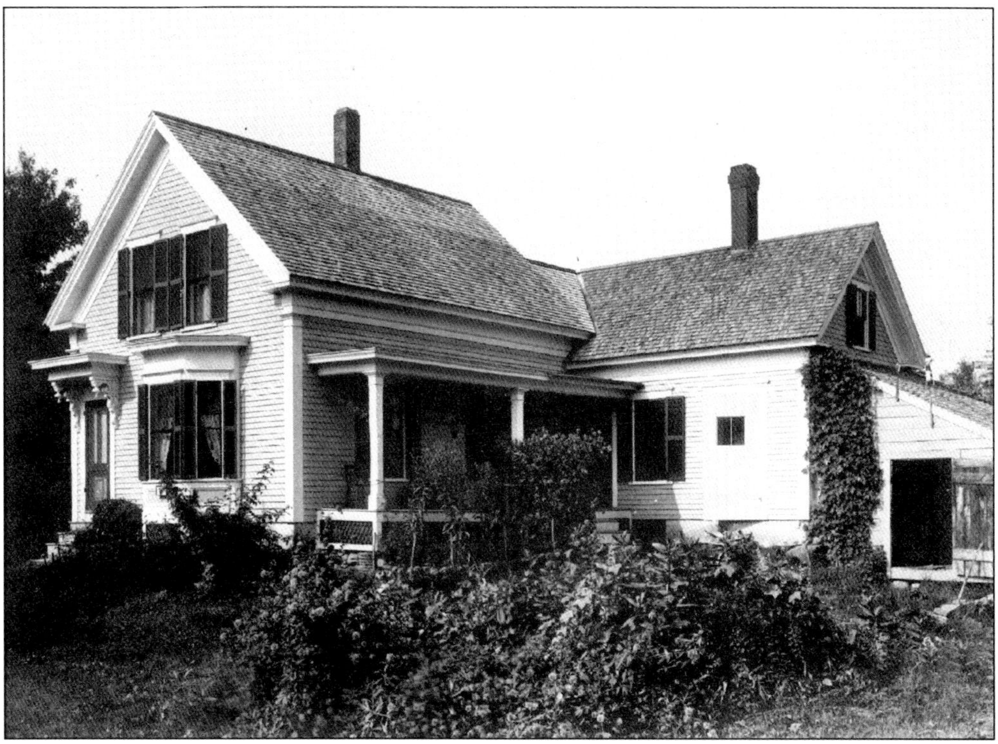

The Whitcomb House. This house is located in Elkins Village.

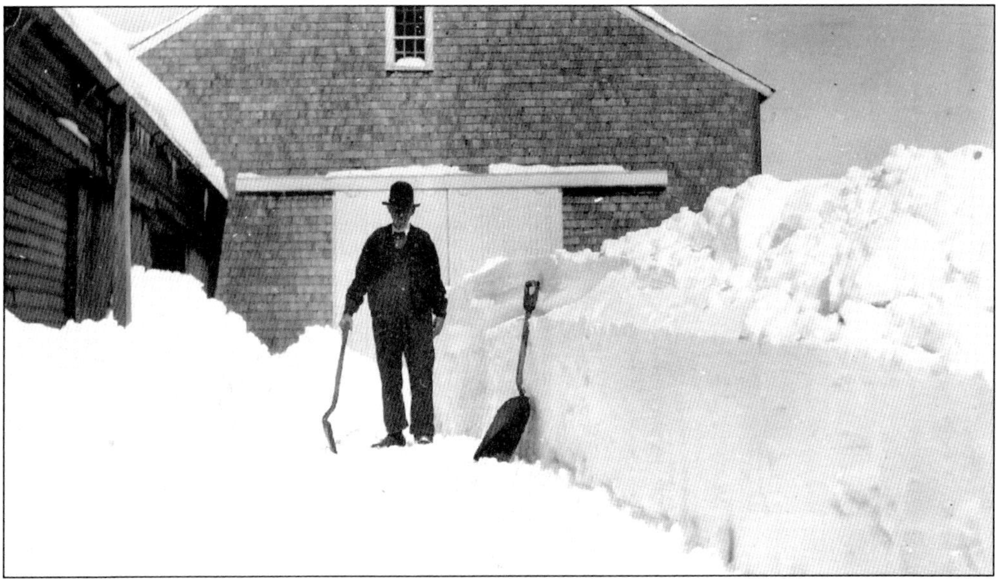

Harrison Williams (1845–1920). This home, located next to the Burpee Hill School, burned down in March 1916. Harrison Williams lived his whole life in New London and worked as a farmer and teamster.

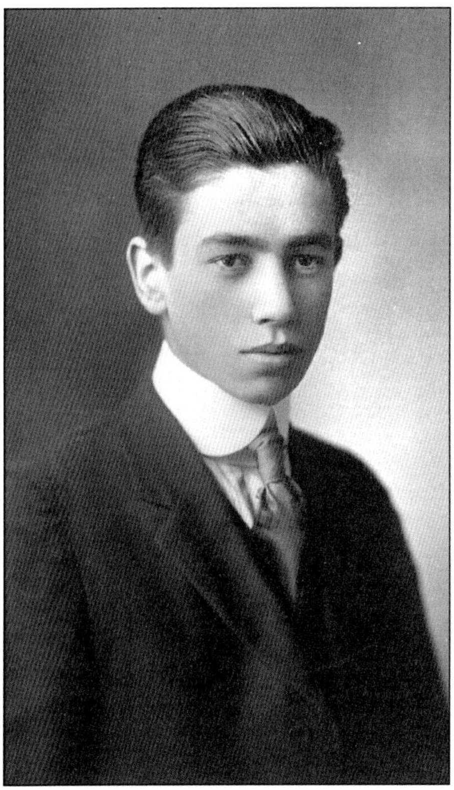

Harry Woods. A graduate of Colby Academy in 1915, Woods was a composer of many songs, such as "When the Red, Red Robin Comes Bob, Bob, Bobbin' Along," made famous by Al Jolson, and "I'm Looking over a Four Leaf Clover." One of his most famous compositions was about Mount Kearsarge: "When the Moon Comes over the Mountain," which became a Kate Smith signature song in 1931. (Courtesy of Colby-Sawyer College Archives.)

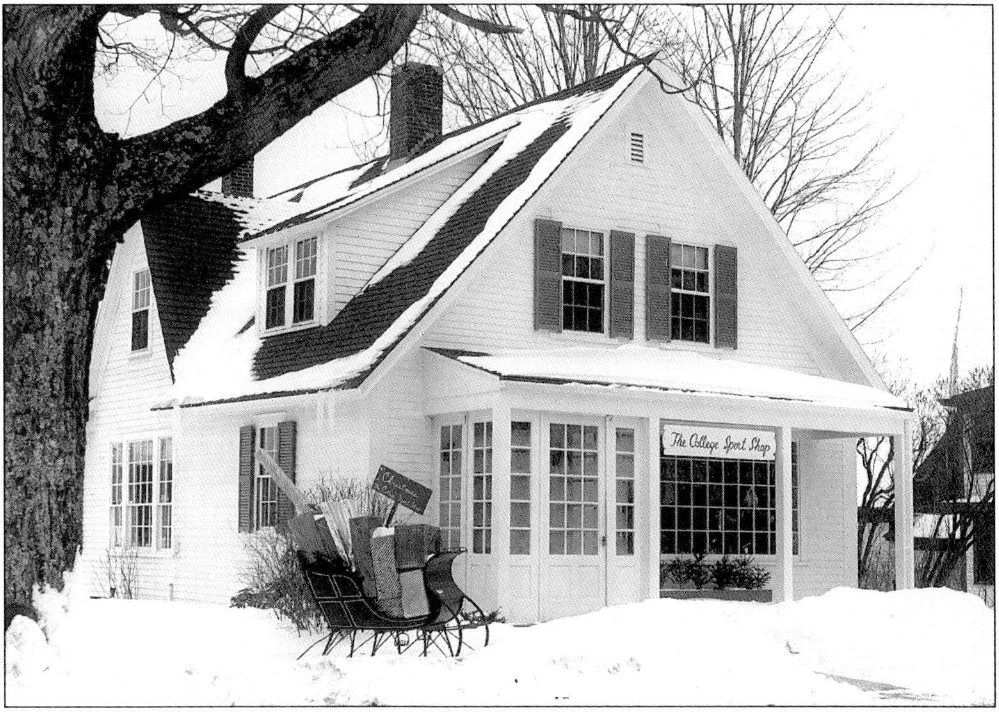

STIMSON COTTAGE. Now known as the College Sport Shop, this cottage on Main Street was used by Augusta Knight after her husband's death. The photograph was taken in 1981. (Photograph by Thompson Photo, courtesy of Colby-Sawyer College Archives.)

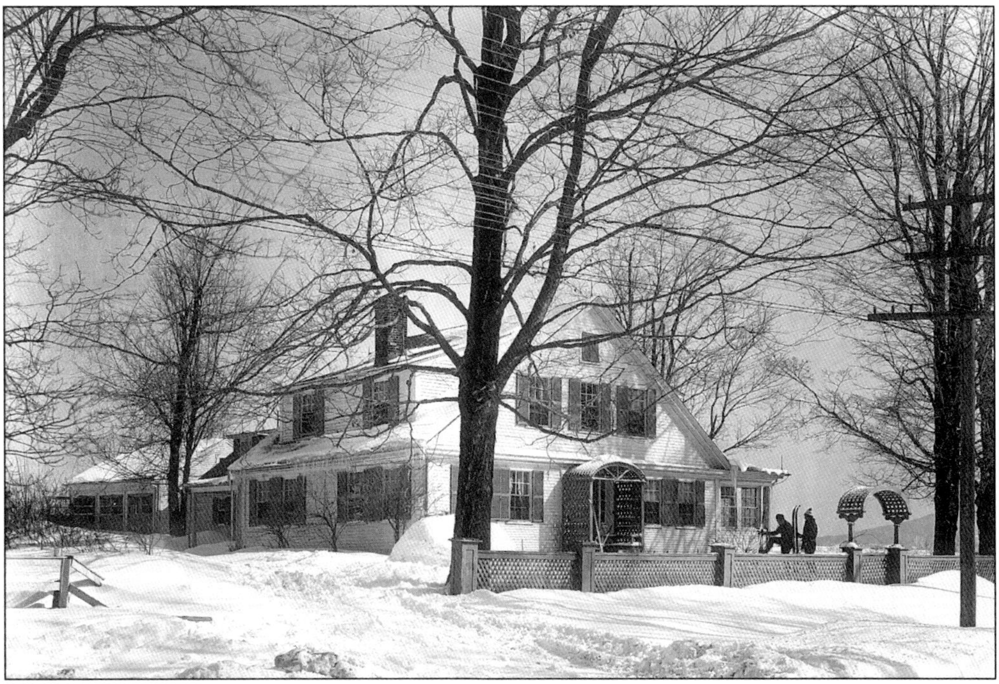

APPLETREE COTTAGE. Located across from the Burpee Homestead on Main Street, this building suffered a minor fire in January 1940. (Courtesy of Colby-Sawyer College Archives.)

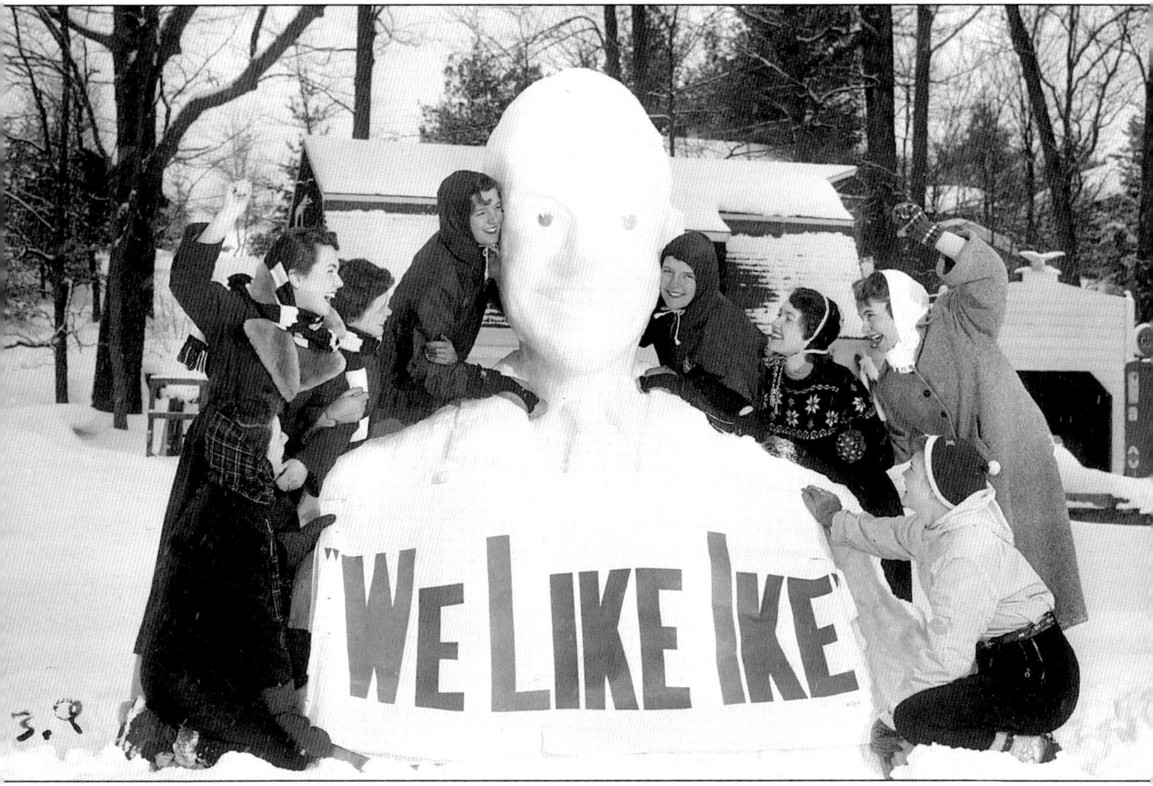

"We Like Ike." Students at Colby Junior College show their support for their candidate, Dwight D. Eisenhower, in an unorthodox fashion in 1952. (Courtesy of Colby-Sawyer College Archives.)

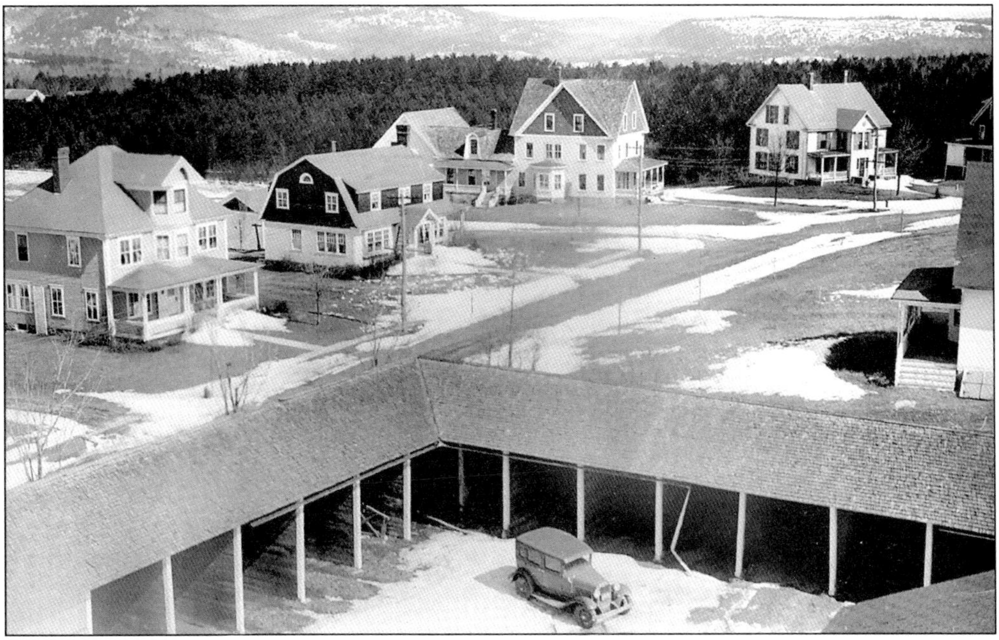

A View of Seamans Road from the Belfry of the Baptist Church, 1944. Pictured, from left to right, are the Kidder, Gould, Quimby, and Henry Sargent homes. (Courtesy of Colby-Sawyer College Archives.)

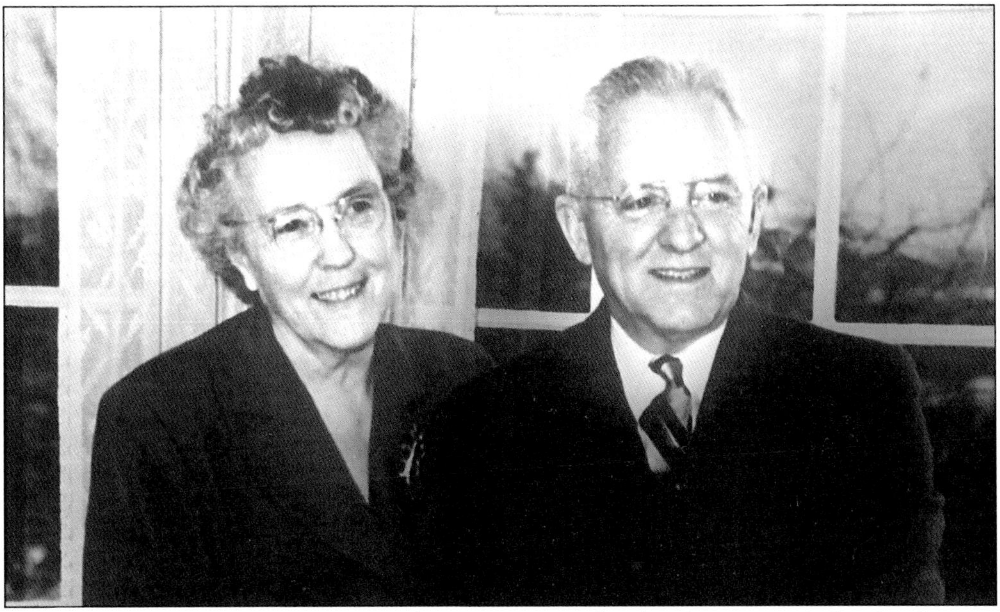

Emma and H. Leslie Sawyer. H. Leslie Sawyer started as headmaster at Colby Academy in 1922 and stayed for 33 years. During his long tenure, the school developed from a coeducational preparatory school into a junior college for women. When Colby Junior College further expanded its programs to a four-year baccalaureate institution, the school was renamed Colby-Sawyer College to honor Dr. Sawyer's commitment to the school while differentiating it from Colby College in Maine. This photograph is from 1947, Dr. Sawyer's 25th anniversary at Colby. (Courtesy of Colby-Sawyer College Archives.)

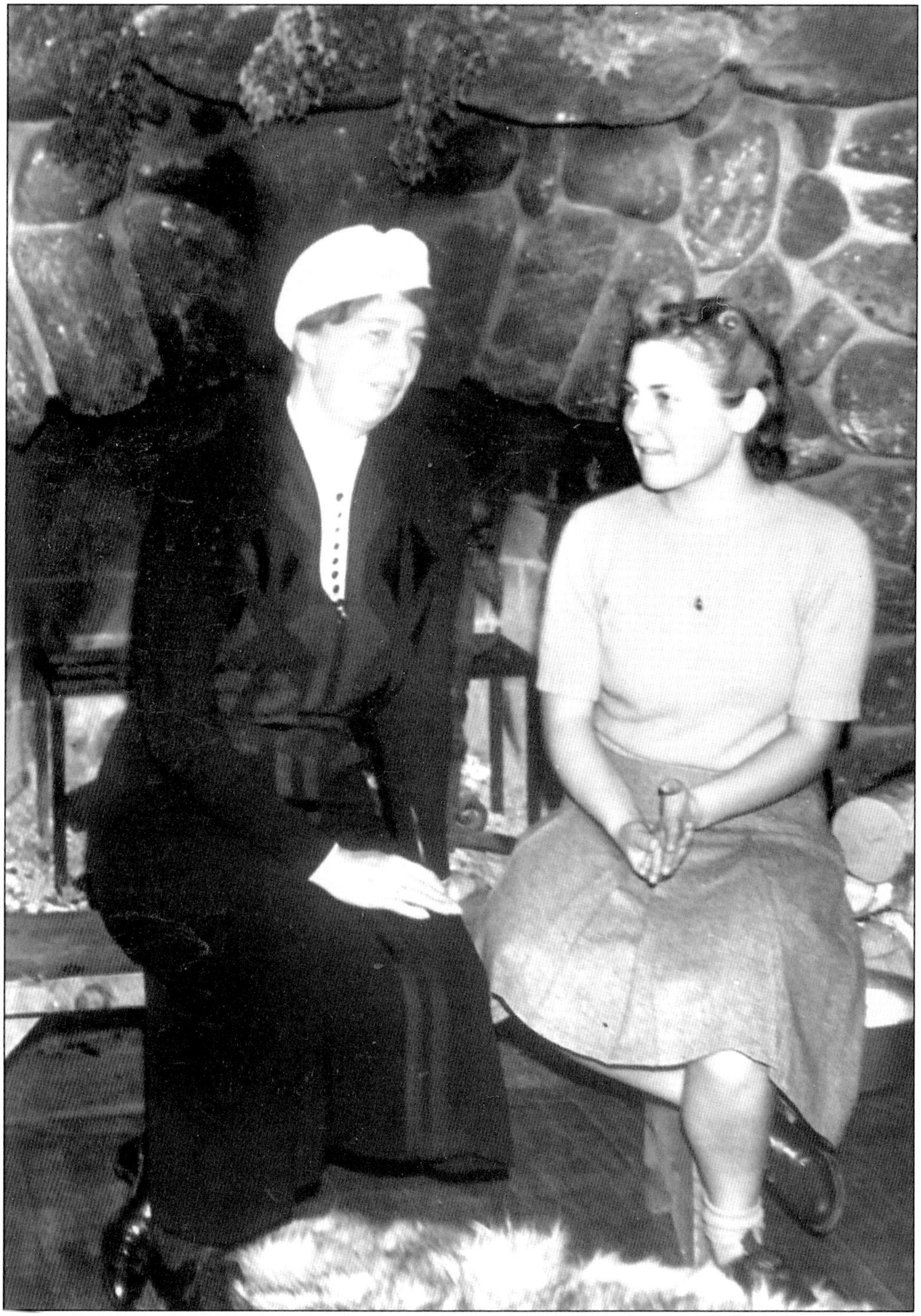

ELEANOR ROOSEVELT VISITS NEW LONDON, 1941. Seven hundred residents packed into the Baptist church on October 8, 1941, for a lecture given by the First Lady about the war in Europe. Roosevelt (left) is pictured here with Constance Ernst, a student from Colby Junior College, who organized the event. (Courtesy of Colby-Sawyer College Archives.)

Three

Agriculture and Industry

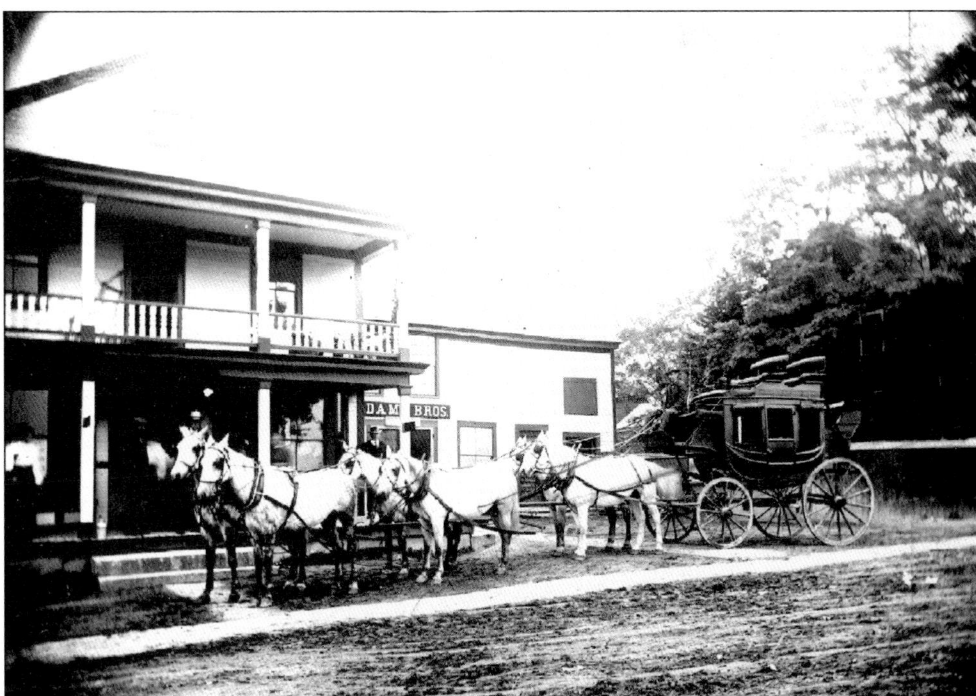

A Stagecoach at Four Corners. The stagecoach to the Potter Place train station in Andover and New London took roughly an hour each way, depending on the weather and road conditions. Two round trips were made daily in the winter and three in the summer.

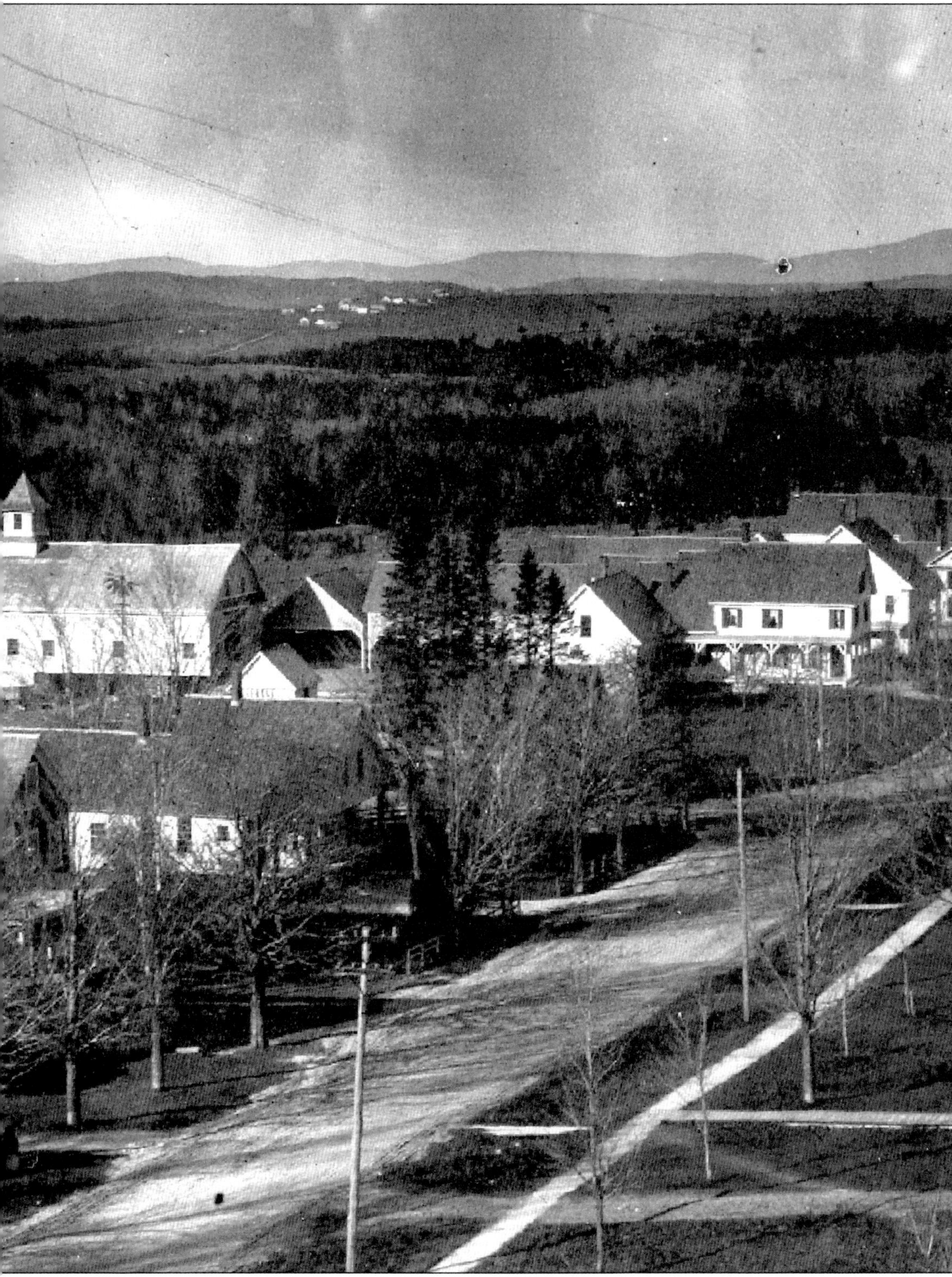

A VIEW OF MAIN STREET FROM THE BELFRY OF THE BAPTIST CHURCH, C. 1900. This view looks

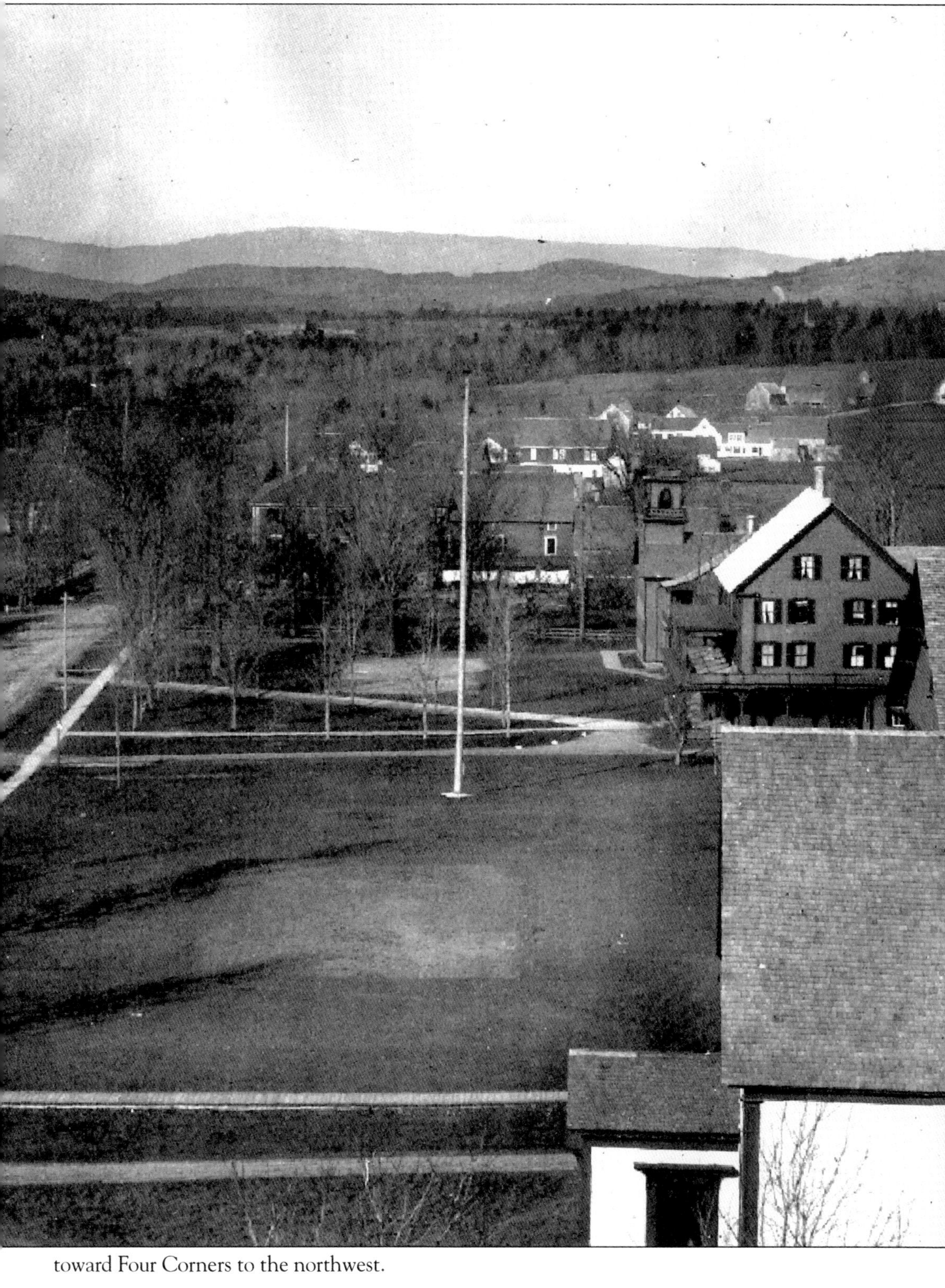

toward Four Corners to the northwest.

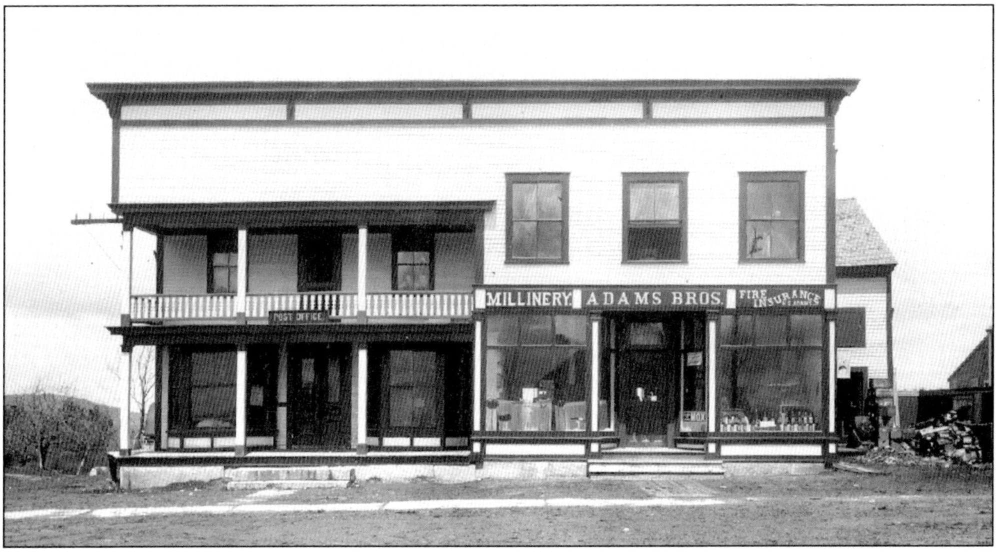

FOUR CORNERS. The intersection of Main and Pleasant Streets was and is an important social and business center in town. The Adams Brothers store opened in 1897. For a time, this building also housed the post office. It was destroyed by fire in August 1949.

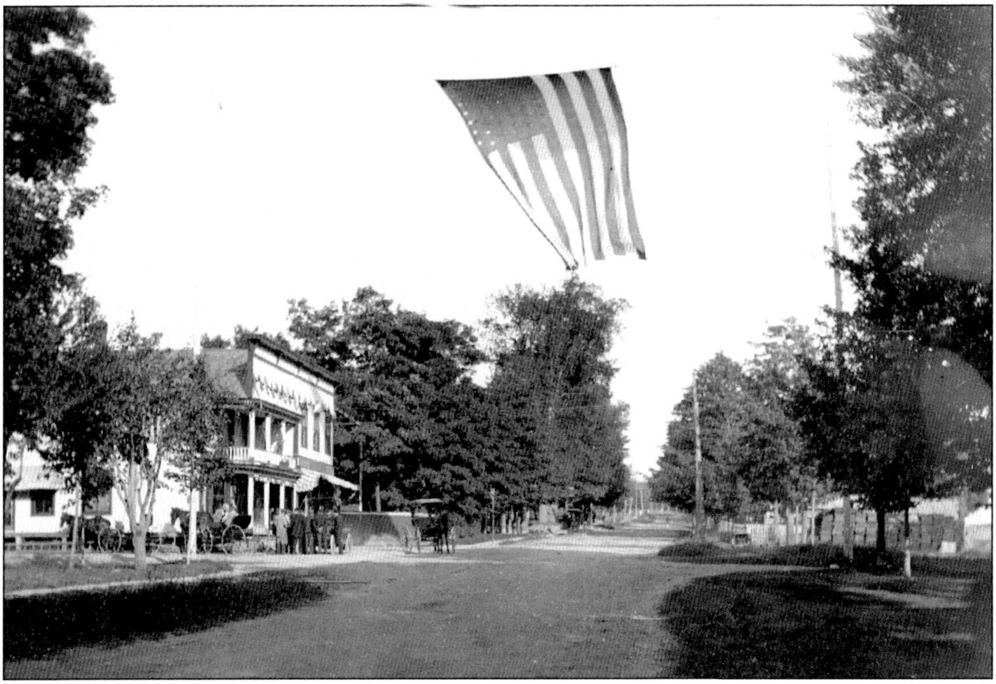

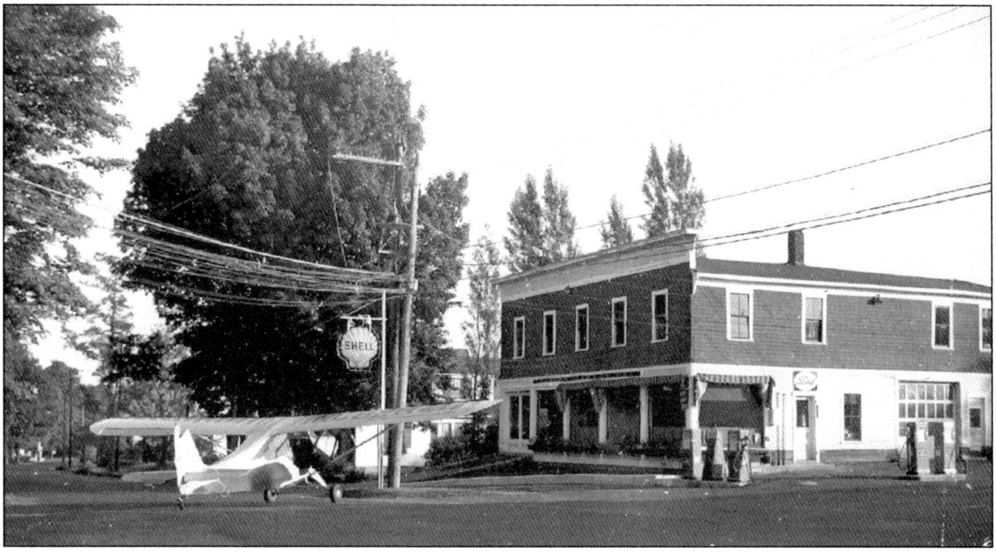

AN UNEXPECTED VISITOR AT KIDDER GARAGE, 1951. An airplane piloted by Harold Buker makes an emergency landing on Main Street. Kidder Garage was built in 1911 by William M. Kidder, after the Kidder homestead was destroyed by fire in 1906. The garage continued operation until 1991.

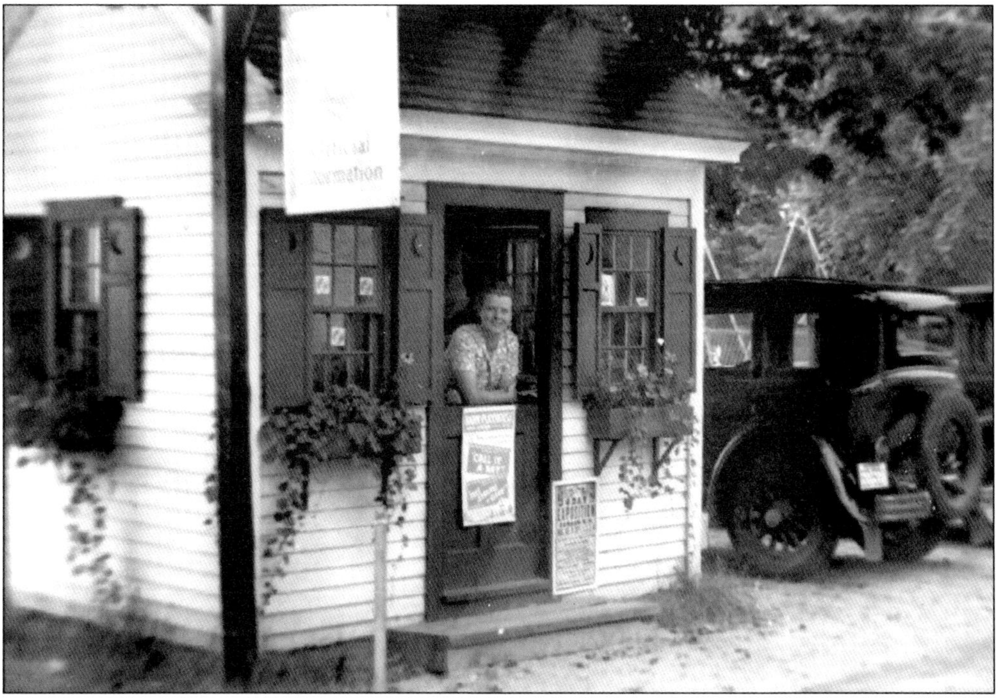

THE INFORMATION BOOTH. Still in operation, the New London information booth was erected on Main Street by the Lake Sunapee Board of Trade in 1929, just in time for the sesquicentennial.

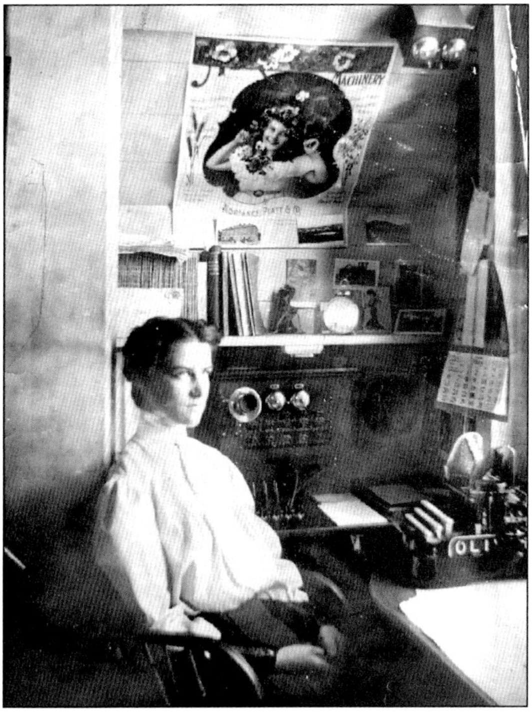

The Early Telephone Company, c. 1900. Alice Moore is watching the switchboard at Knight, Palmer, and Chase's store, located on Main Street near the Cranehurst Inn. The store ceased operations in 1904, and the building was torn down and used by Arthur Roberts to build a home at Hominy Pot.

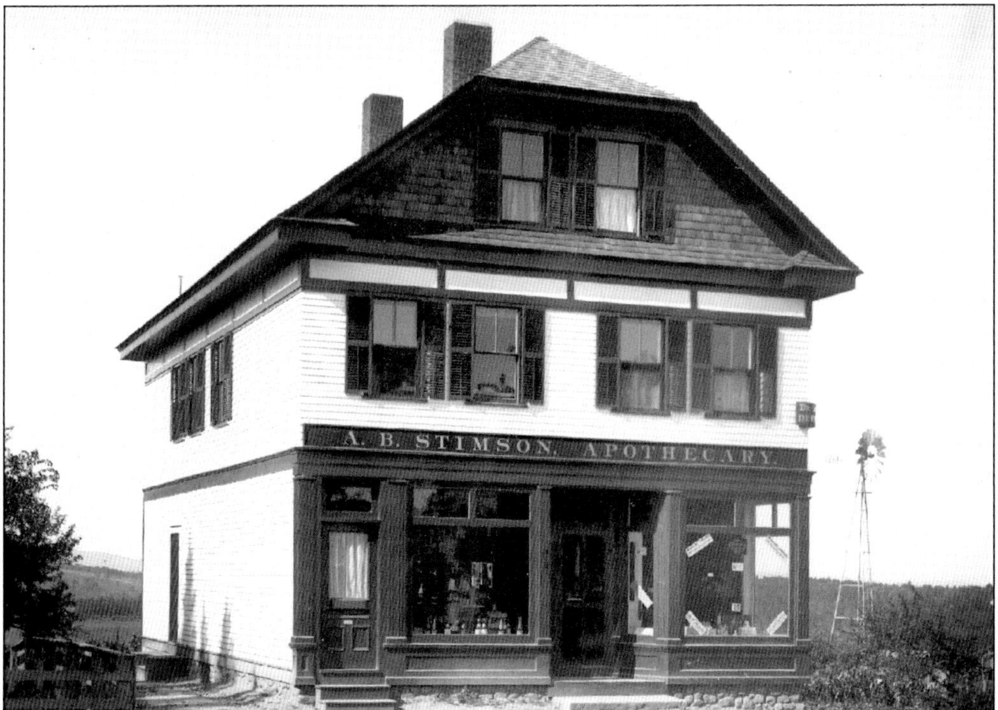

The Stimson Drugstore. Owned by A.B. Stimson, this drugstore was in operation from 1910 to 1924. It was then renamed New London Pharmacy and remained as such until 1999. The building now houses Aesthetics, a beauty shop.

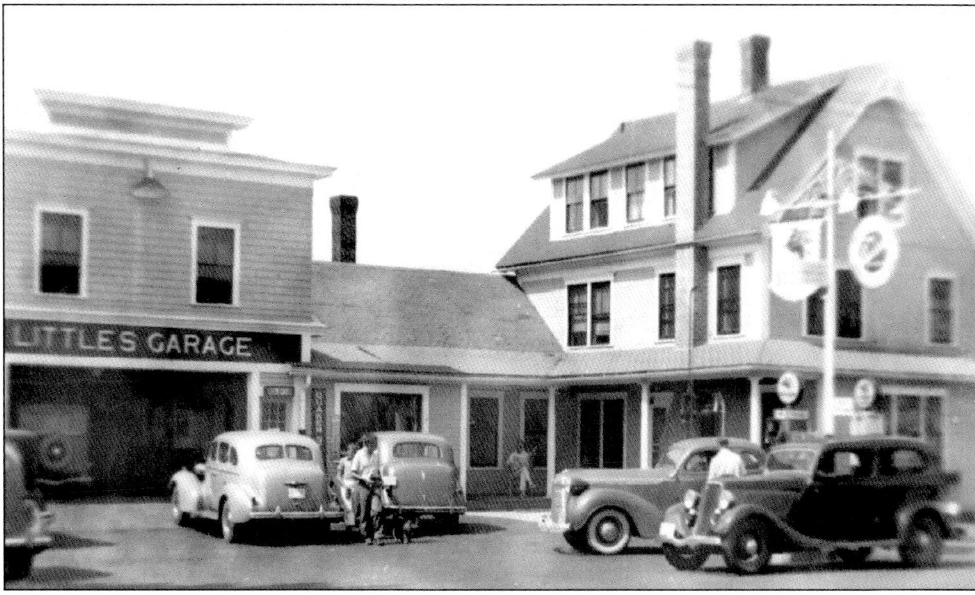

LITTLE'S GARAGE. Located at Shepard's stables, the garage was started in 1917 by Charles Shephard's son-in-law A. Stanley Little.

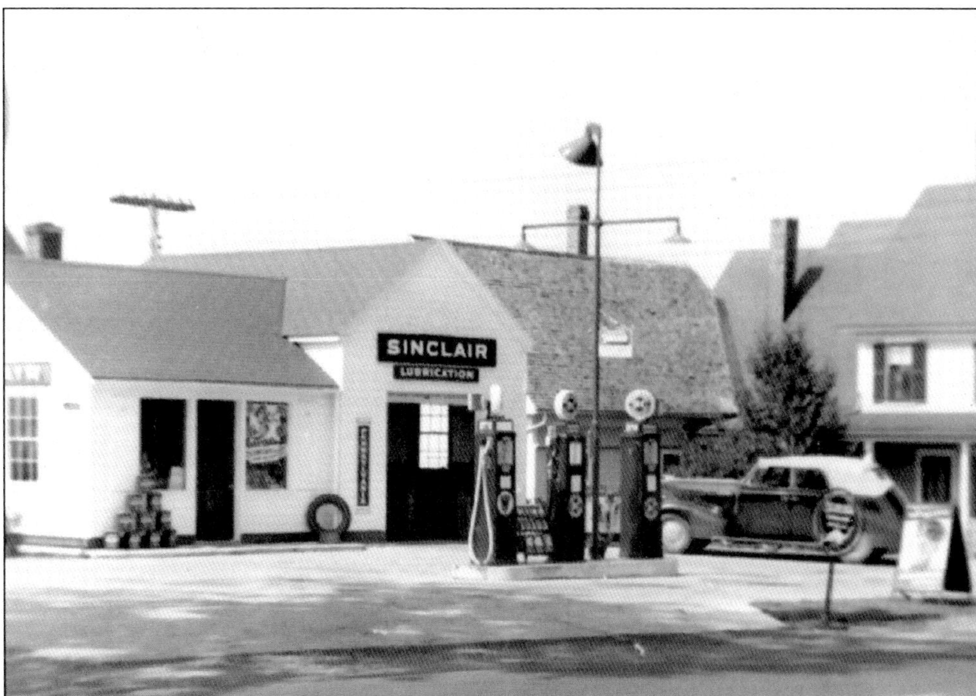

THE TEXACO STATION, 1947. This station was located near Shepard's stables on Main Street. There is still a Texaco station on that site today.

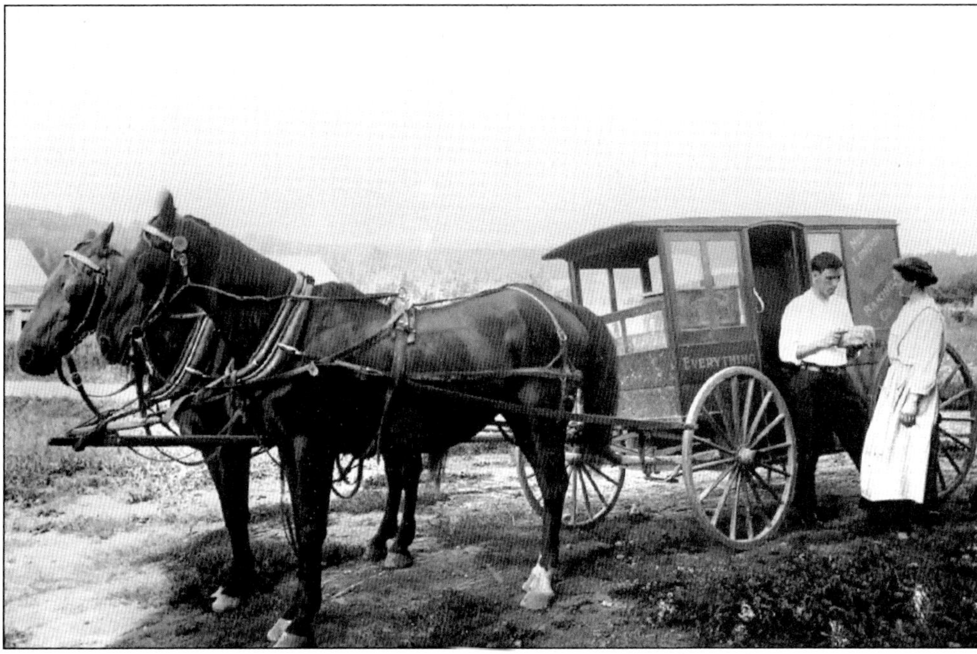

A Bakery Delivery Van. Sylvester Allen started the New London Baking Company in 1909 on Pearl Street. Pictured here is deliveryman Tom Rodman on his rounds.

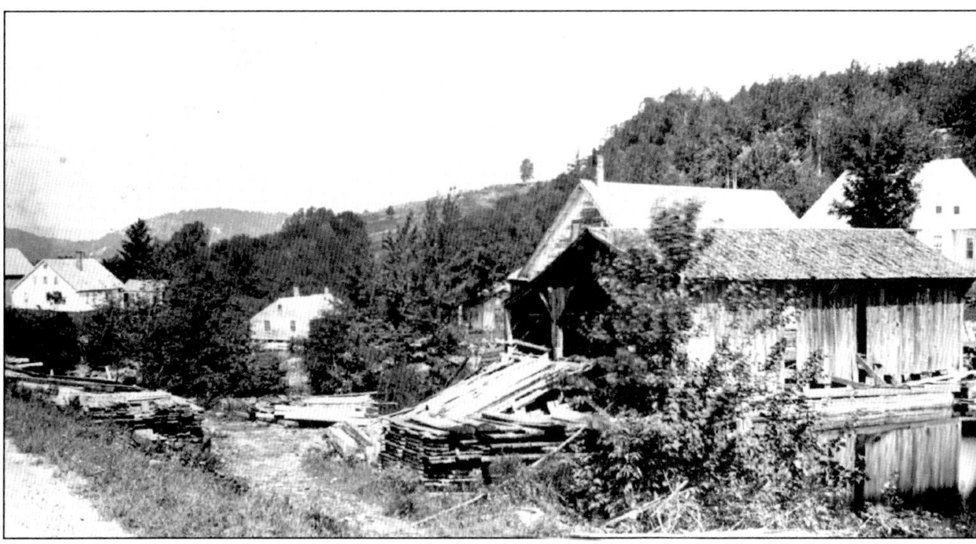

Eastman's Sawmill, c. 1900. Located in Otterville (the area of town to the west of Little Lake Sunapee), this mill was owned by Hiram Eastman and produced unfinished lumber. By 1950, it was in operation only part time.

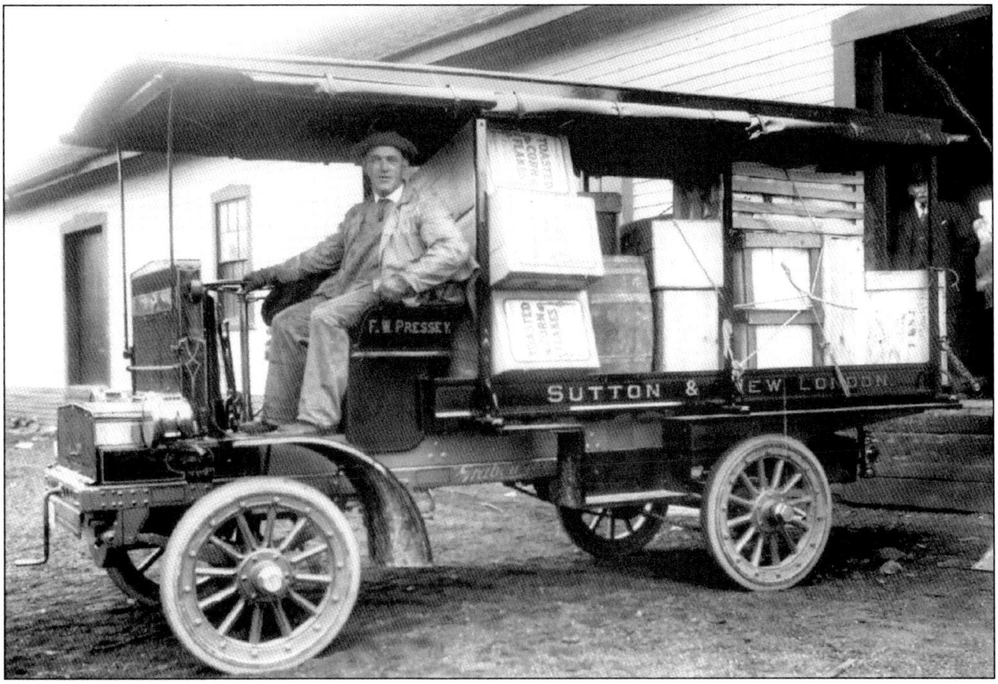

THE BRADFORD STAGE. Fred A. Pressey is shown here delivering goods between Sutton and New London. Pressey also drove shuttle buses between Bradford and New London in addition to operating the Four Corners store and working as an undertaker.

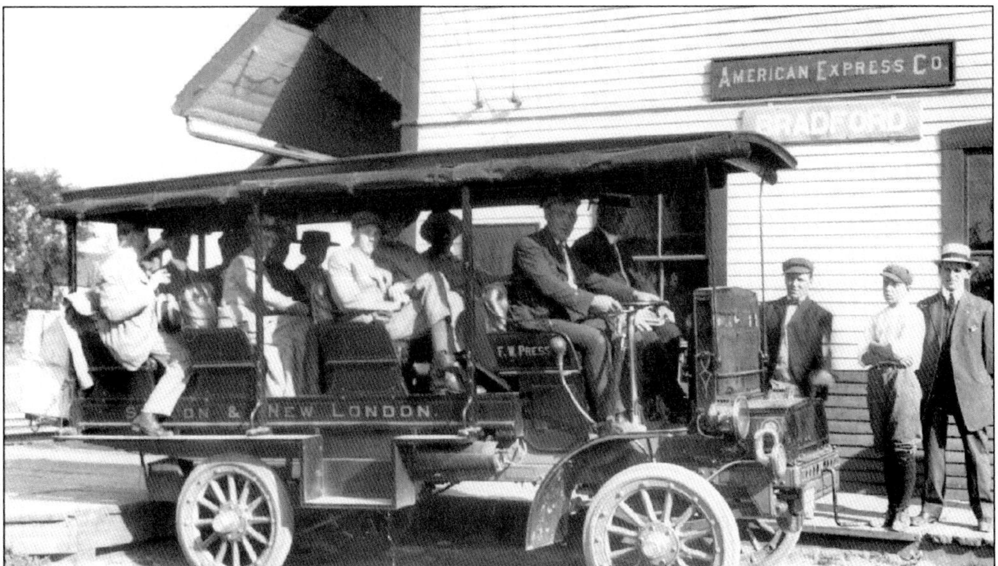

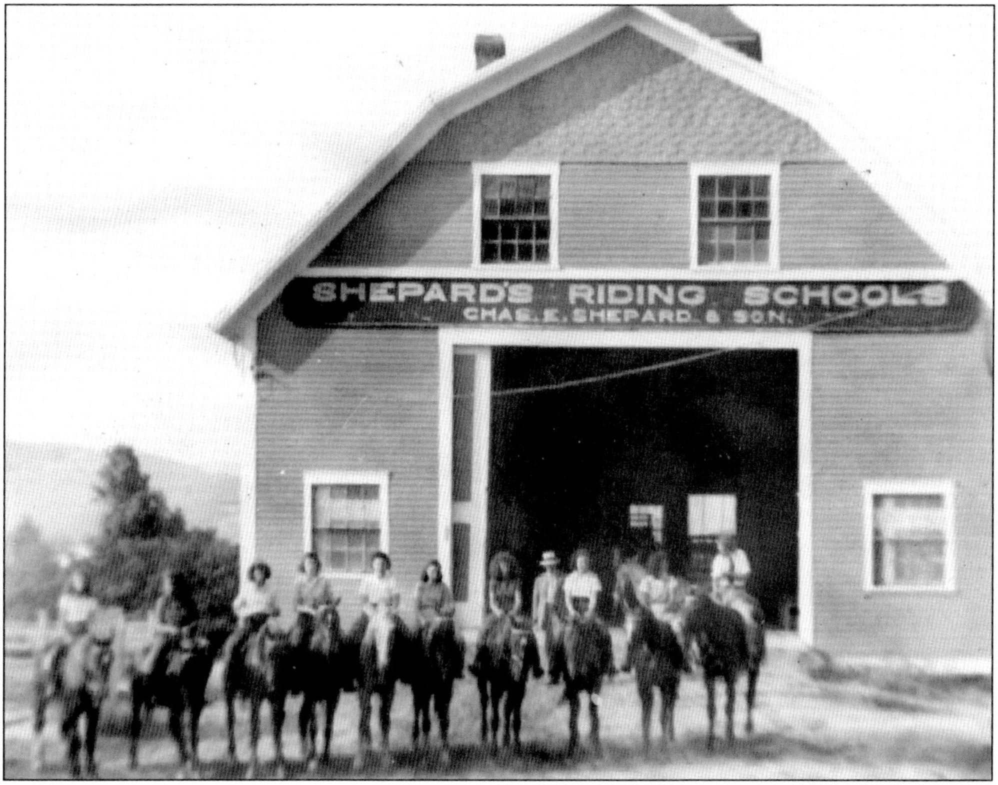

SHEPARD'S RIDING SCHOOLS. Located on Main Street, the riding school started holding horse shows in 1925 in conjunction with Hospital Day in the summer. By the end of World War II, the stables went out of business, and the building was sold to Colby Junior College in 1947.

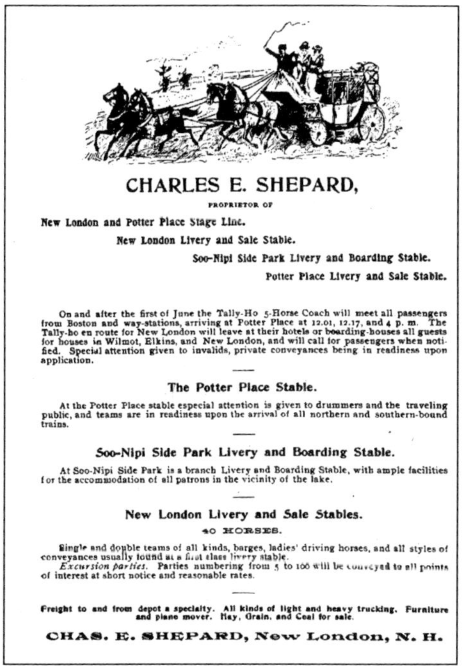

A SHEPARD LIVERY ADVERTISEMENT, C. 1898. Before the age of automobiles, horses and stagecoaches were necessary to get around. (Courtesy of Colby-Sawyer College Archives.)

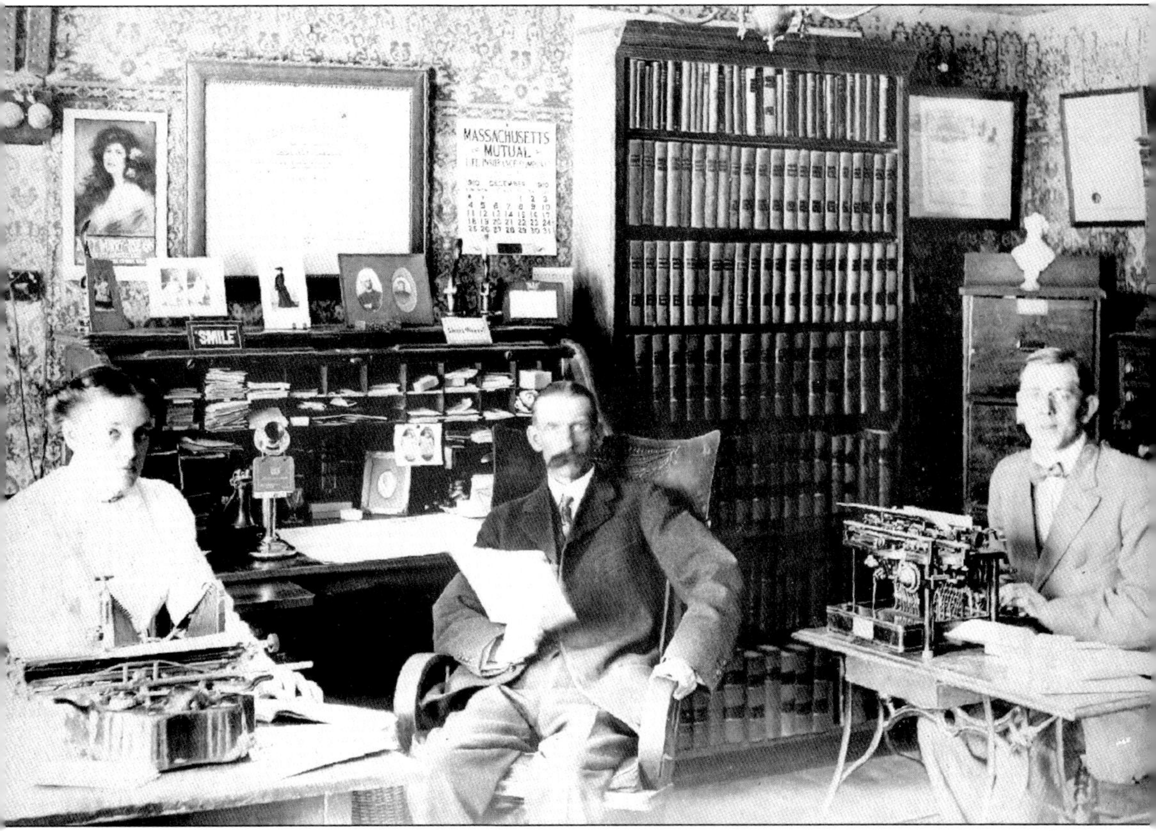

Nathaniel Colby Law and Insurance, 1910. This office provided insurance policies and legal advice to the citizens of New London. Pictured, from left to right, are Ethel Williams, Nathaniel Colby, and Richard Doyle.

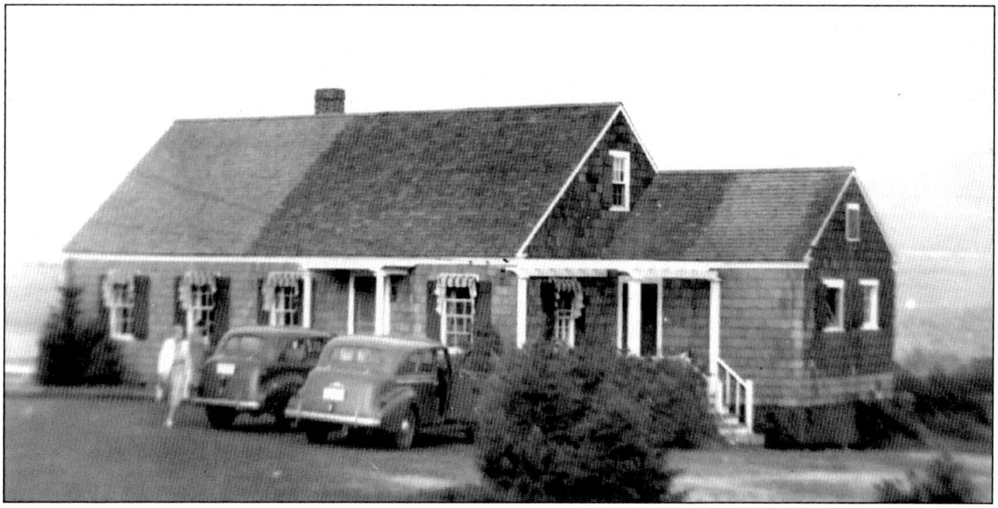

The Gray House Ice-Cream Stand. Located at Crockett's Corner, the Gray House was built in 1932 by Dura and Dorothy Crockett and is still in operation as the Four Corners Grille and the Flying Goose Brew Pub.

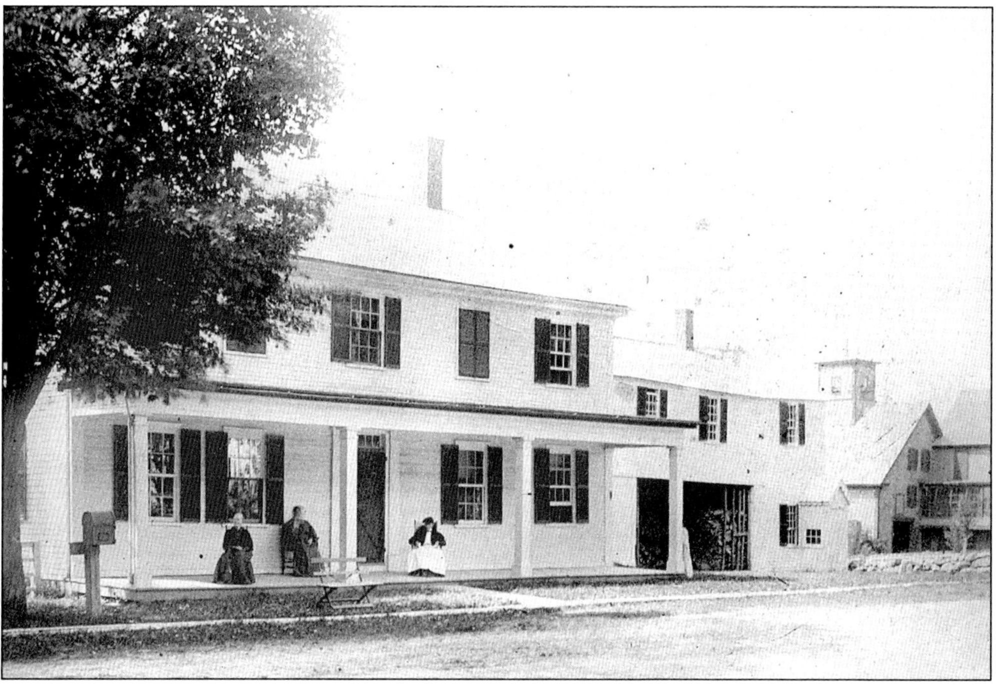

The Herrick Tavern, c. 1895–1900. Built in 1812 for Jonathan Herrick Jr., this building has also been known as the Colby Lane House. Herrick ran a tavern and store here. Starting in 1832, the stagecoach stopped here on its run between Lowell, Massachusetts, and Hanover, New Hampshire. The Nahum Greenwood house is in background. (Courtesy of Colby-Sawyer College Archives.)

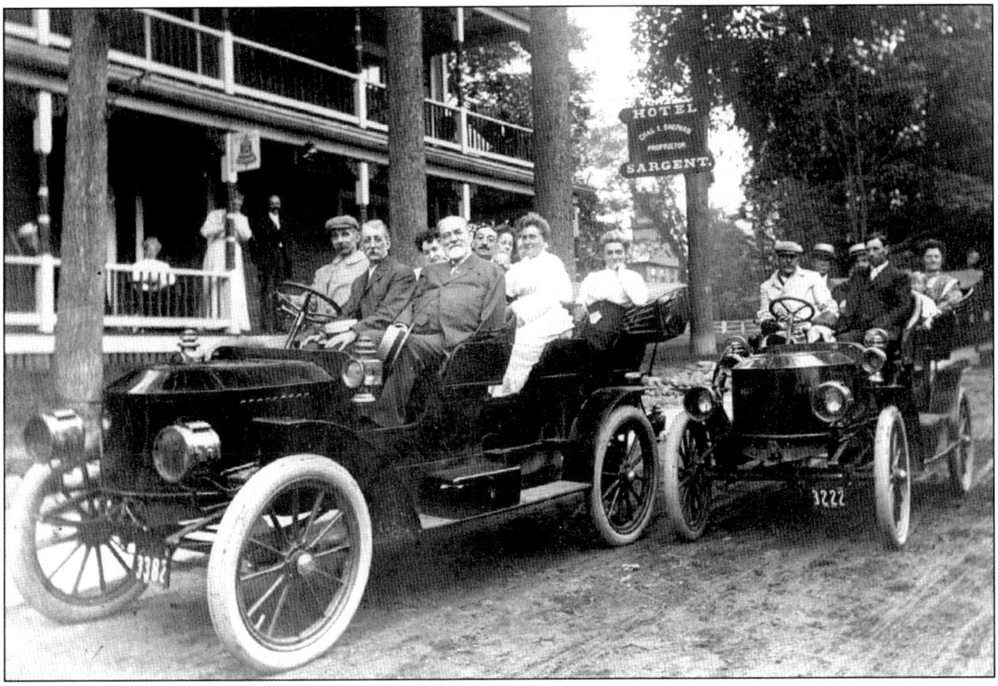

HOTEL SARGENT CAR RENTALS, 1908. In addition to providing lodging for visitors, the Hotel Sargent rented five- and nine-passenger cars for excursions around the area.

PRICES OF AUTOMOBILE TRIPS

	Nine Passenger Car	Five Passenger Car
Newport	$10.00	$ 6.00
Claremont	15.00	8.00
Around the Lake	10.00	6.00
Dartmouth College	20.00	15.00
Warner	10.00	6.00
Henniker	15.00	8.00
Hookset	25.00	20.00
Bristol and New Found Lake	25.00	20.00
Woodstock, Vt	25.00	20.00
Concord	20.00	15.00

Nine Passenger Car		Five Passenger Car	
Per day	$25.00	Per day	$20.00
Half day	15.00	Half day	10.00

Per hour, $5.00 first hour, $3.00 for each additional hour.

Per hour, $3.00 first hour, $2.00 for each additional hour.

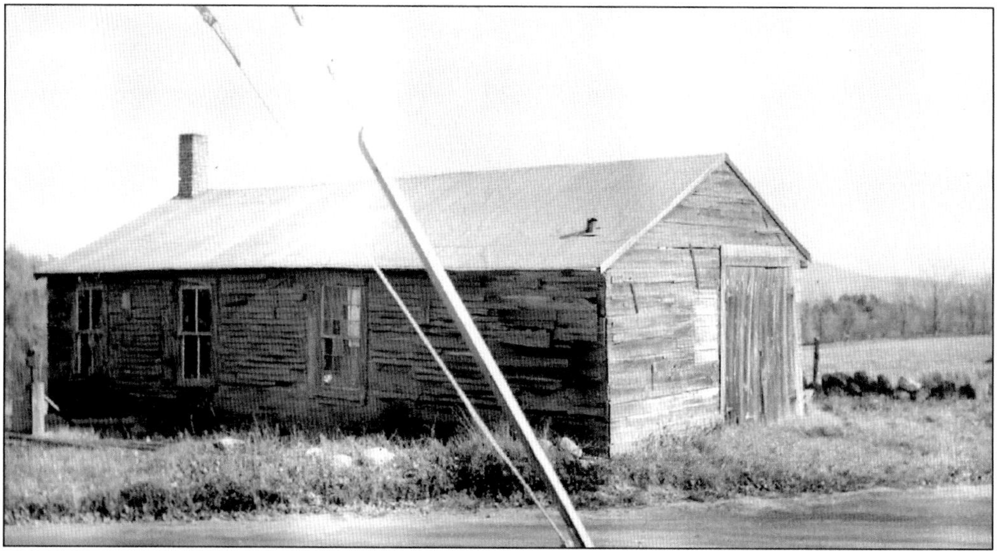

Dow's Blacksmith Shop. Once automobiles eliminated the demand for blacksmithing, this shop, located on Old Main Street, was used as a paint shop by John Edmunds.

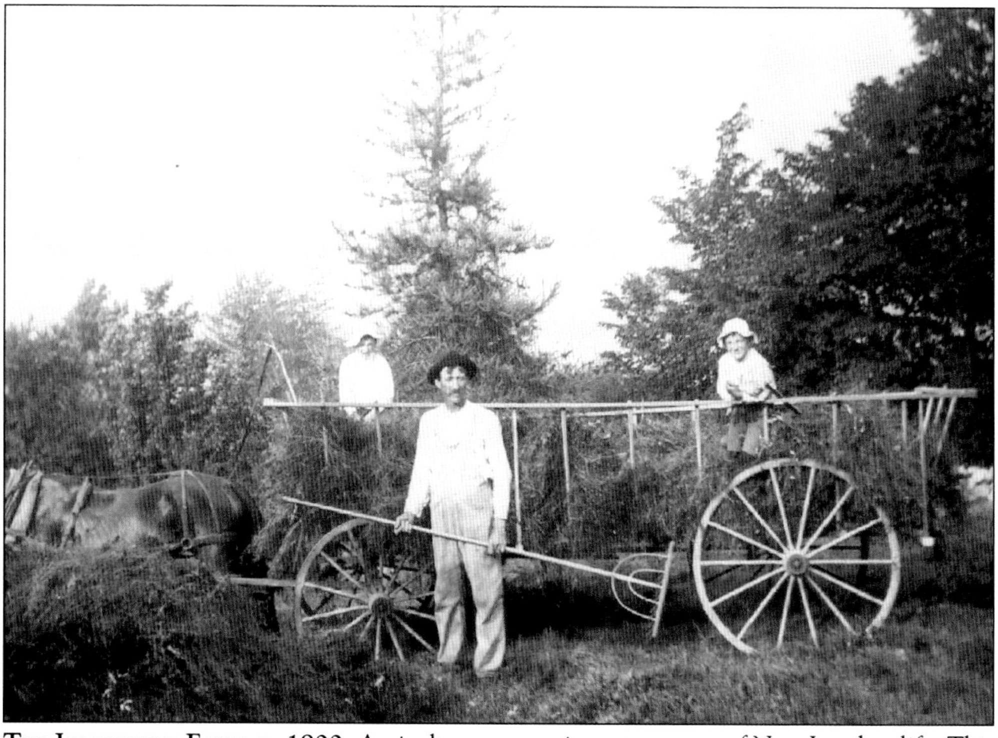

The Littlefield Farm, c. 1900. Agriculture was an important part of New London life. This farm was located on Pleasant Street.

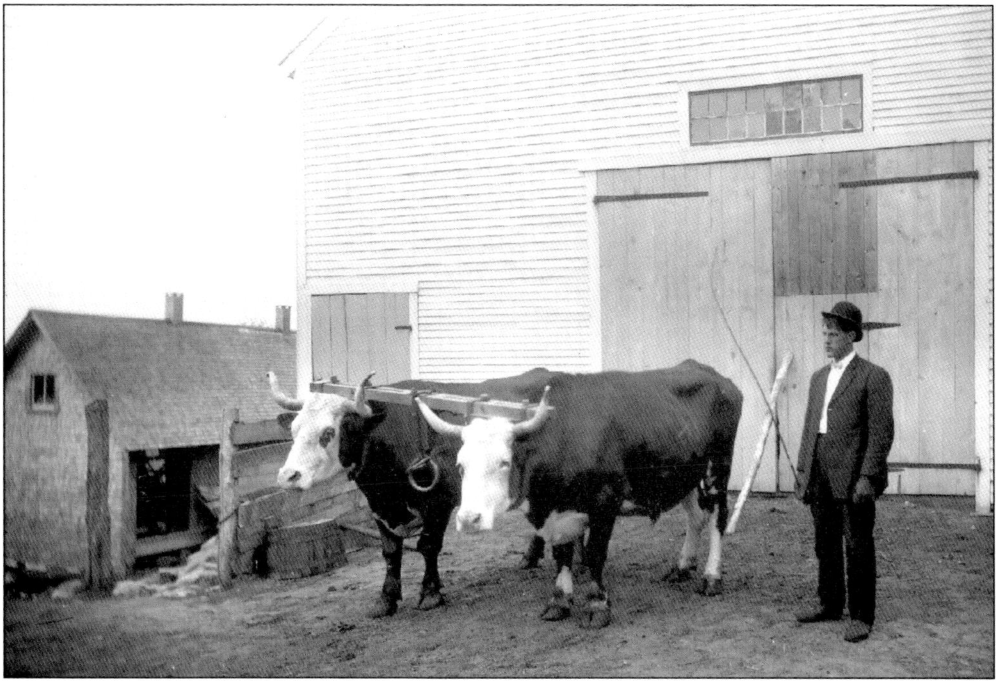

THE KNOWLTON FARM, c. 1900. This farm was located across the road from the West Part schoolhouse.

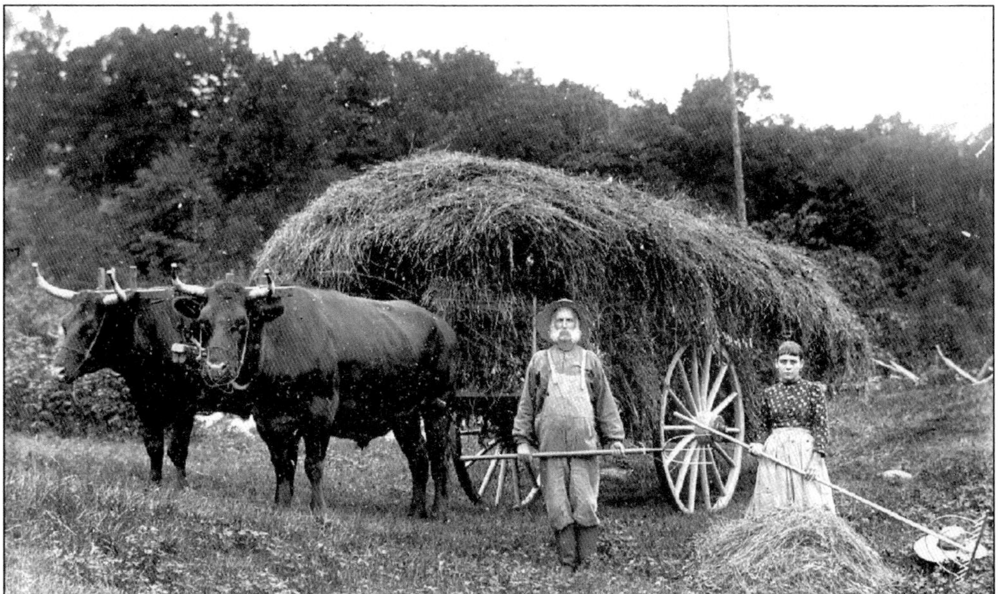

THE PINGREE FARM, MAY 1894. Here, Walter E. Pingree and his daughter-in-law Delia are bringing in the hay. This farm was located to the east of Morgan Hill. (Photograph by E.A. Dean.)

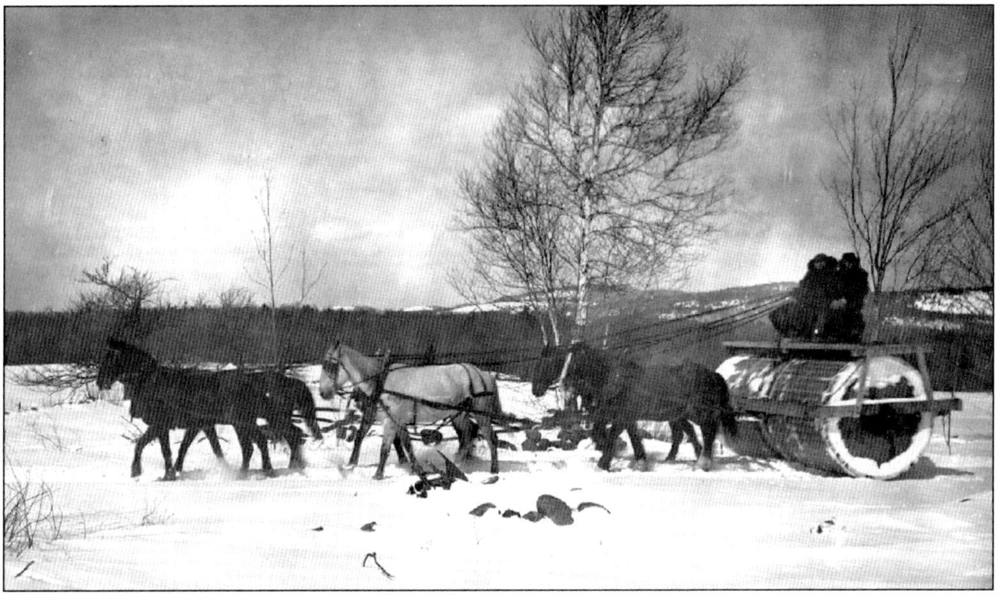

A Snow Roller. Before the days of snowplows and paved roads, it was easier to tamp down the snow to make the roads passable for sleighs. The snow roller weighed approximately one to two tons and was used in New London until the winter of 1926–1927.

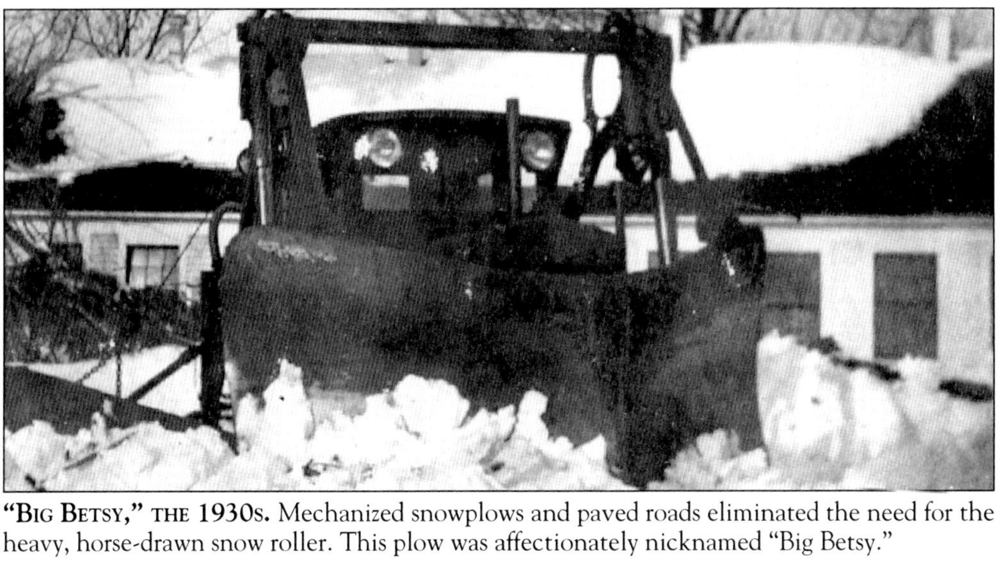

"Big Betsy," the 1930s. Mechanized snowplows and paved roads eliminated the need for the heavy, horse-drawn snow roller. This plow was affectionately nicknamed "Big Betsy."

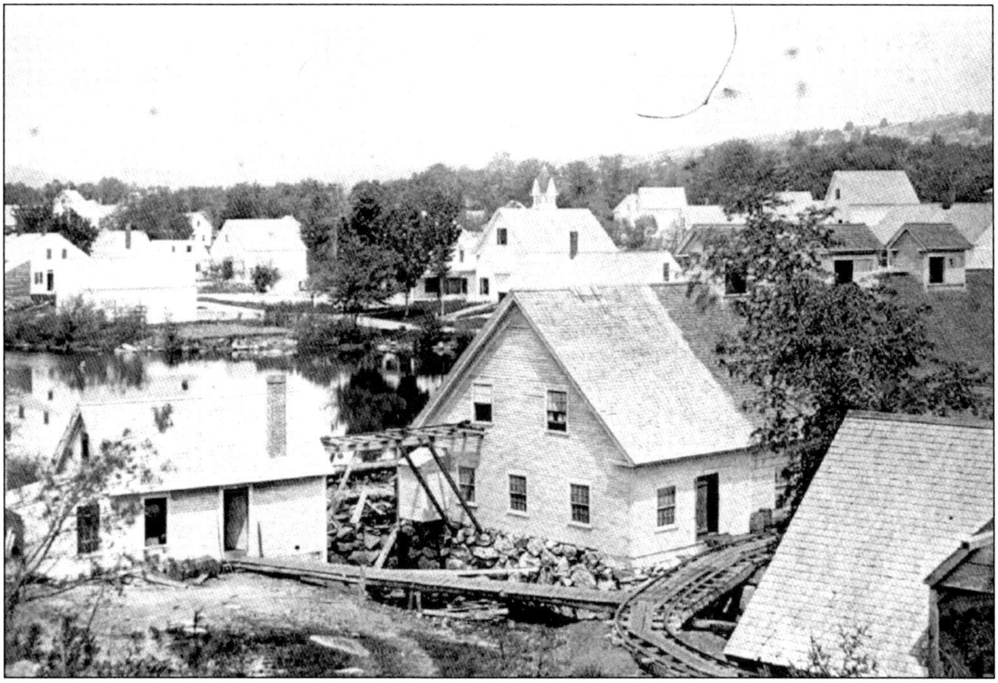

THE ELKINS FORGE SHOP. Most of the buildings in this photograph belong to the New London Scythe Company. To the left across the pond is the company's carriage shed and office and paint shop. The paint shop was later used as the Scytheville post office.

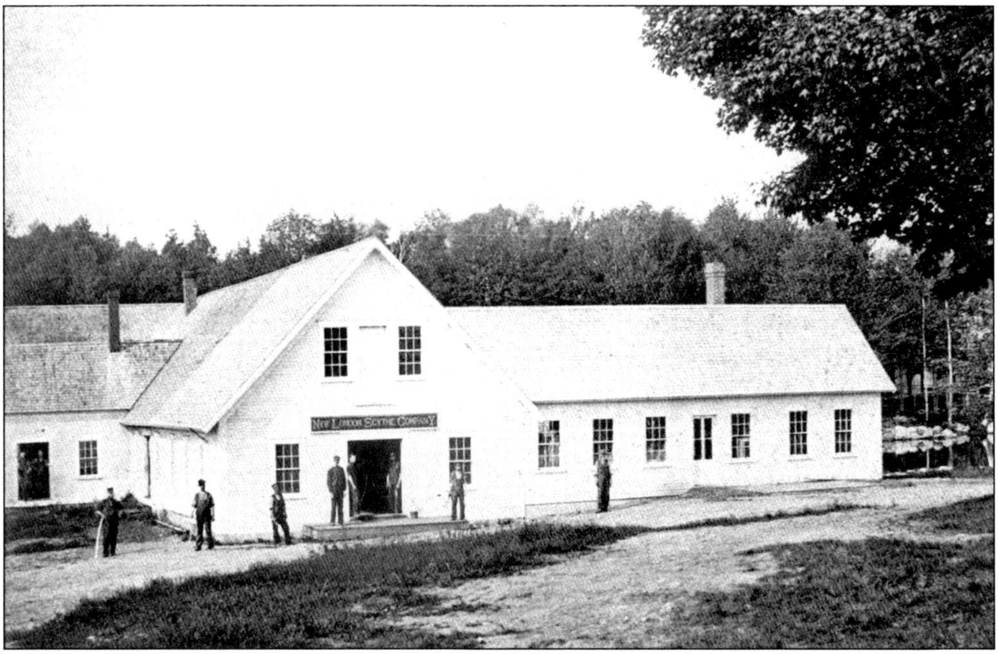

THE NEW LONDON SCYTHE COMPANY, 1871. The New London Scythe Company was established in 1837 and was in operation until 1888. At the height of its production, it turned out 120,000 scythes, 12,000 hay knives, and 60,000 axes in a year. This building was used for polishing, painting, packing, and shipping articles, as well as the company office.

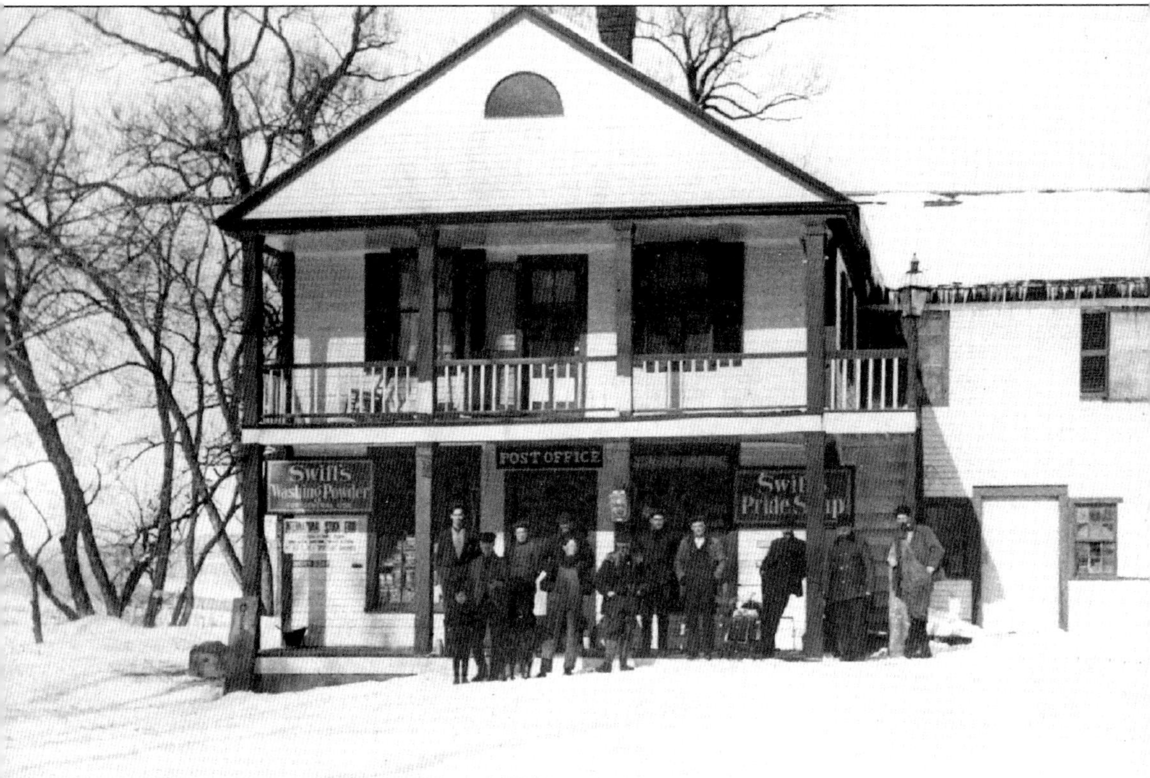

THE ELKINS STORE, PLEASANT LAKE. This general store provided goods and also housed a post office for residents of Elkins Village.

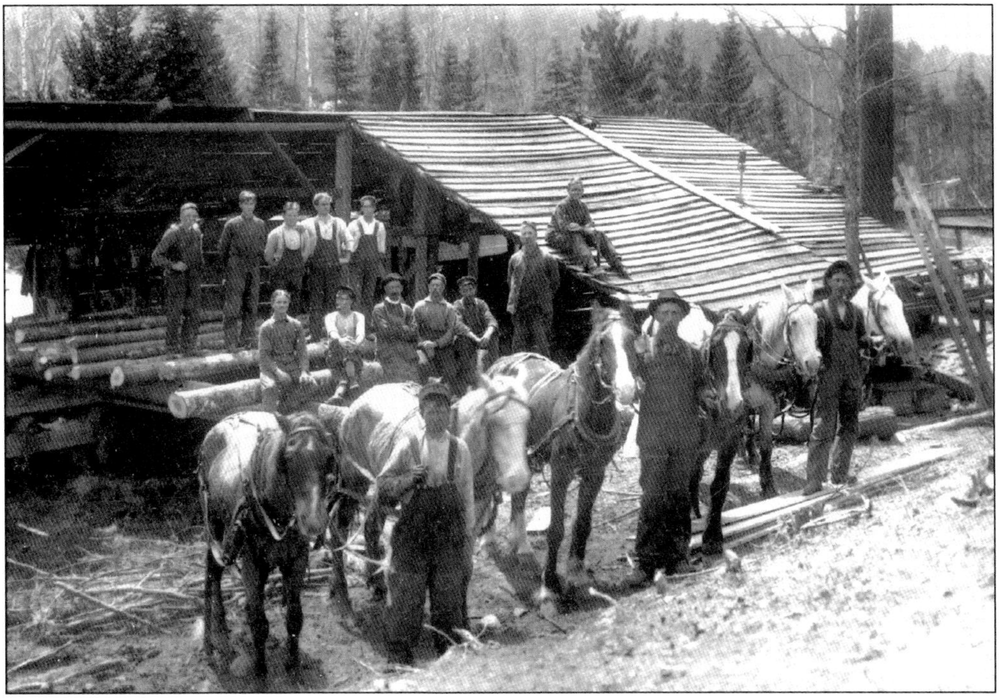

Sawmill Workers. New London had three main industrial areas: Elkins Village, at the southern end of Pleasant Lake; an area called Otterville, located northwest of Little Lake Sunapee; and Hominy Pot, in the southern part of town near Clark Pond.

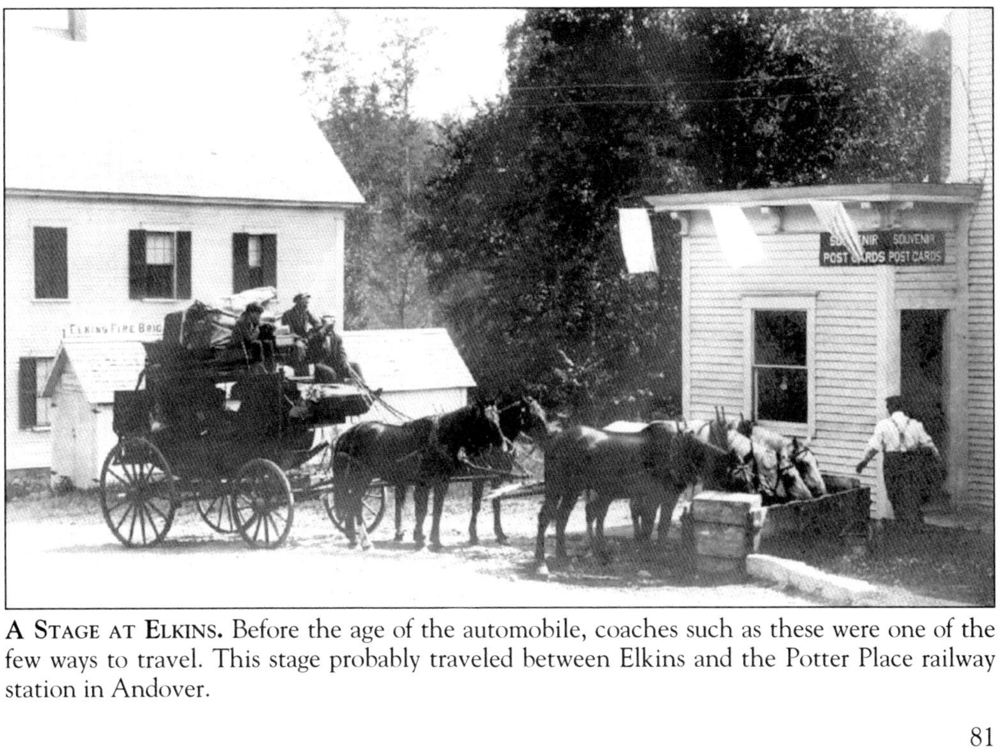

A Stage at Elkins. Before the age of the automobile, coaches such as these were one of the few ways to travel. This stage probably traveled between Elkins and the Potter Place railway station in Andover.

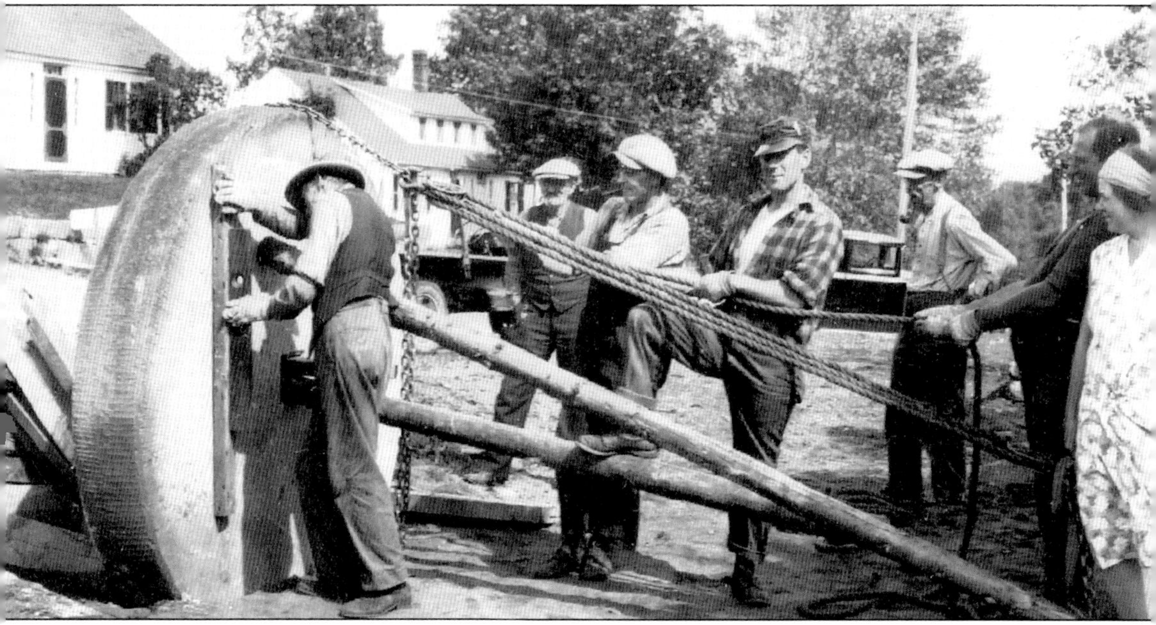

SETTING THE GRINDSTONE AT SCYTHEVILLE PARK, 1929. Erected on the site of Herbert Swett's tin shop, the Grindstone and surrounding park stand as a tribute to Elkins's industrial past.

Four

INSTITUTIONS

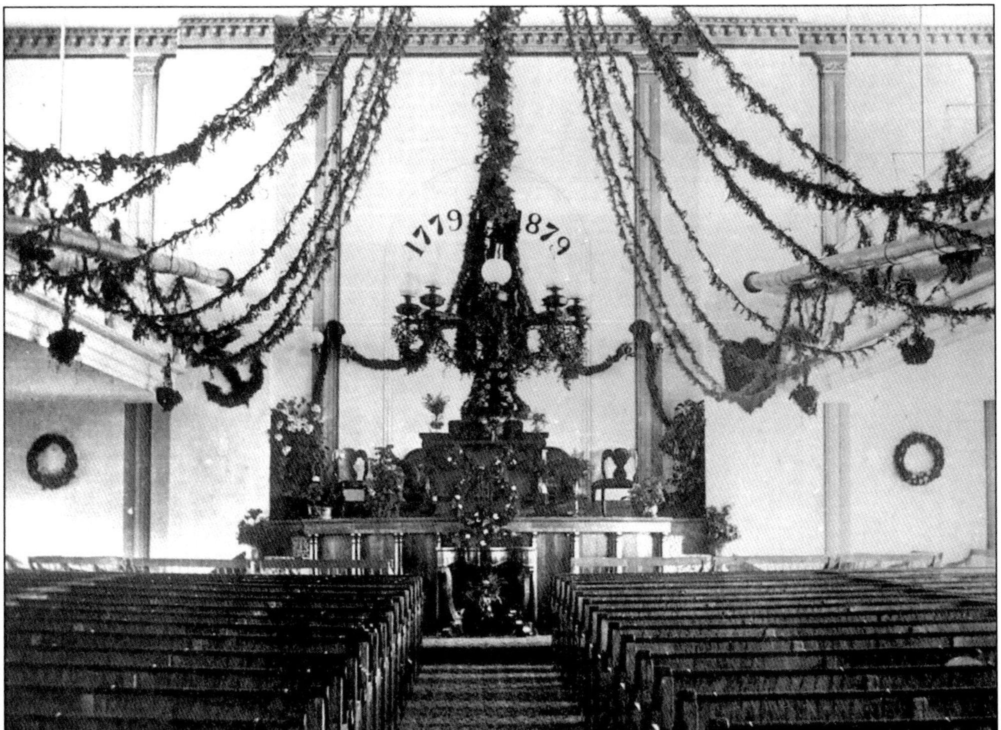

THE NEW LONDON CENTENNIAL, 1879. The interior of the Baptist church on Main Street is decorated for centennial celebrations.

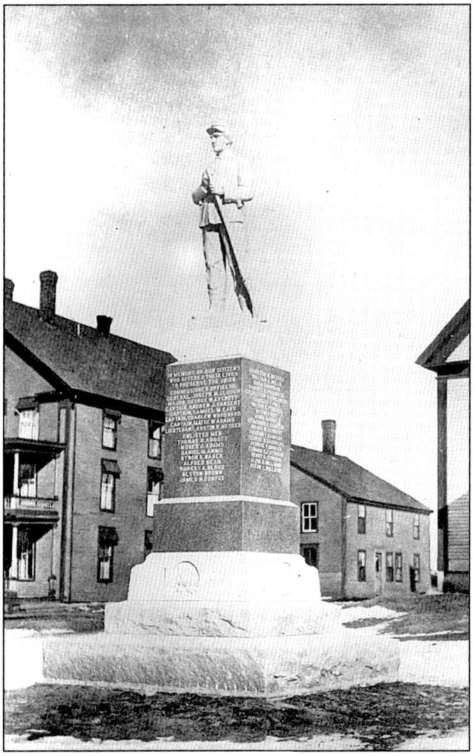

The War Memorial. Located in front of the town hall, this monument was erected at a cost of $800 in 1914 to pay tribute to the town's Revolutionary War and Civil War veterans. In 1919, names of veterans from the world war were added. A monument commemorating World War II veterans now stands next to this memorial. (Courtesy of Colby-Sawyer College Archives.)

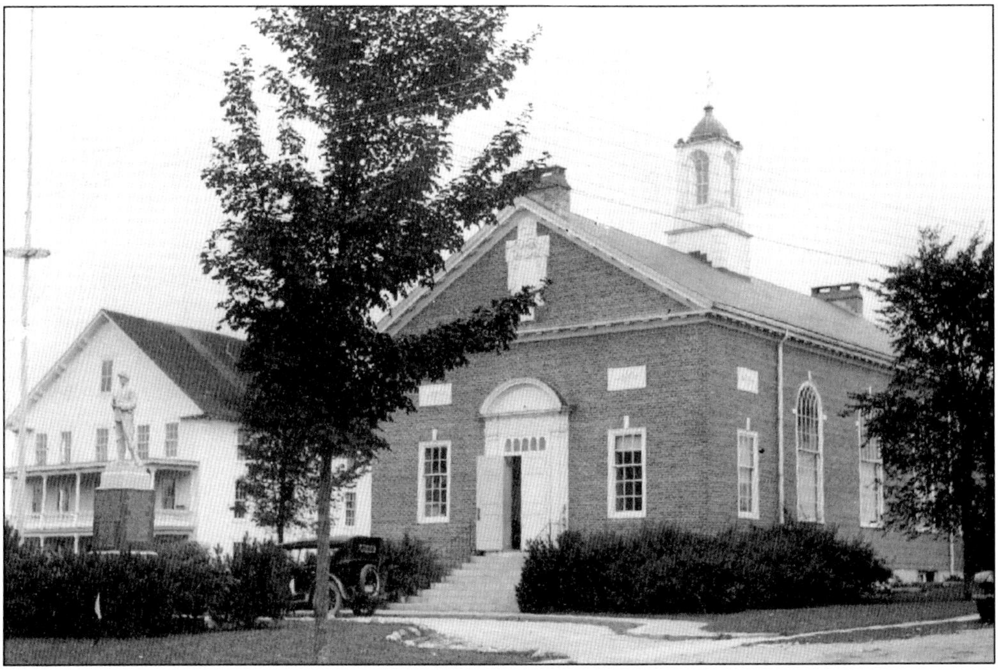

Whipple Memorial Town Hall. Built on land given to the town by a bequest from Amos H. Whipple, the town hall was constructed in 1918 at a cost of $9,000. The former town hall was built in 1853 and was starting to look its age. It was torn down and sold to William M. Kidder and Joseph Cutting, who used the beams for an extension to Kidder Garage.

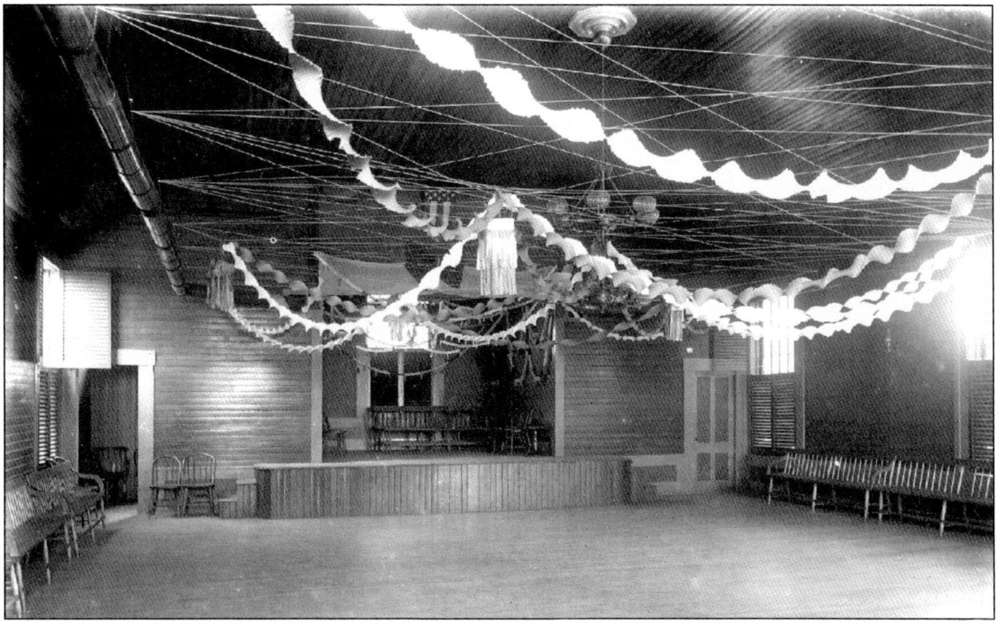

WHIPPLE MEMORIAL TOWN HALL, AN INTERIOR VIEW. In addition to its official business, the town hall was the site of the first motion picture showings in town and, until 1942, was also the site of basketball games.

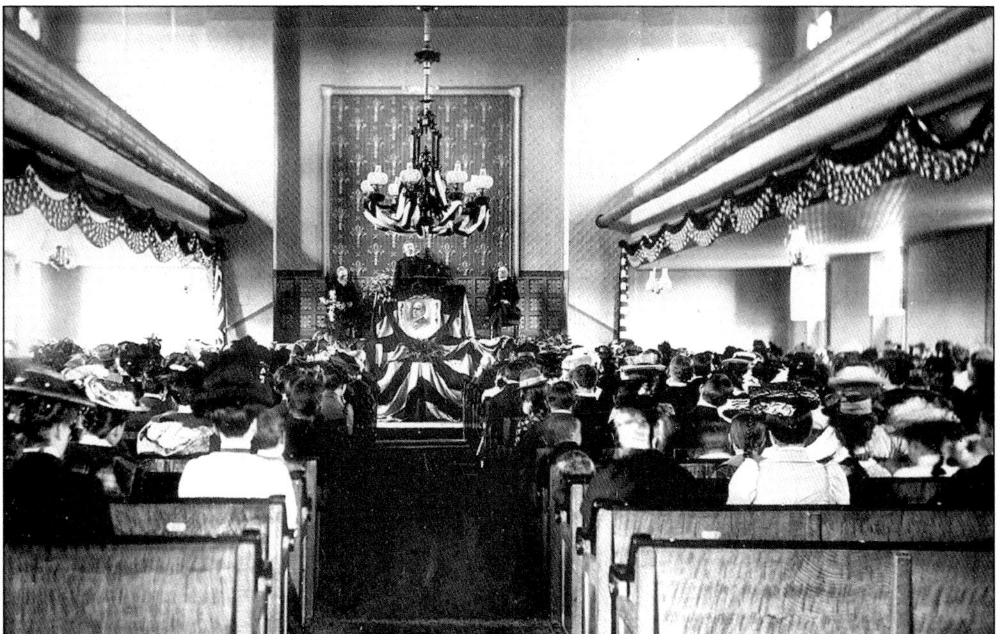

PRESIDENT MCKINLEY'S MEMORIAL SERVICE, 1901. The assassination of President McKinley in September 1901 was a terrible blow to people across the nation. This photograph depicts the service held at the Baptist church. (Courtesy of Colby-Sawyer College Archives.)

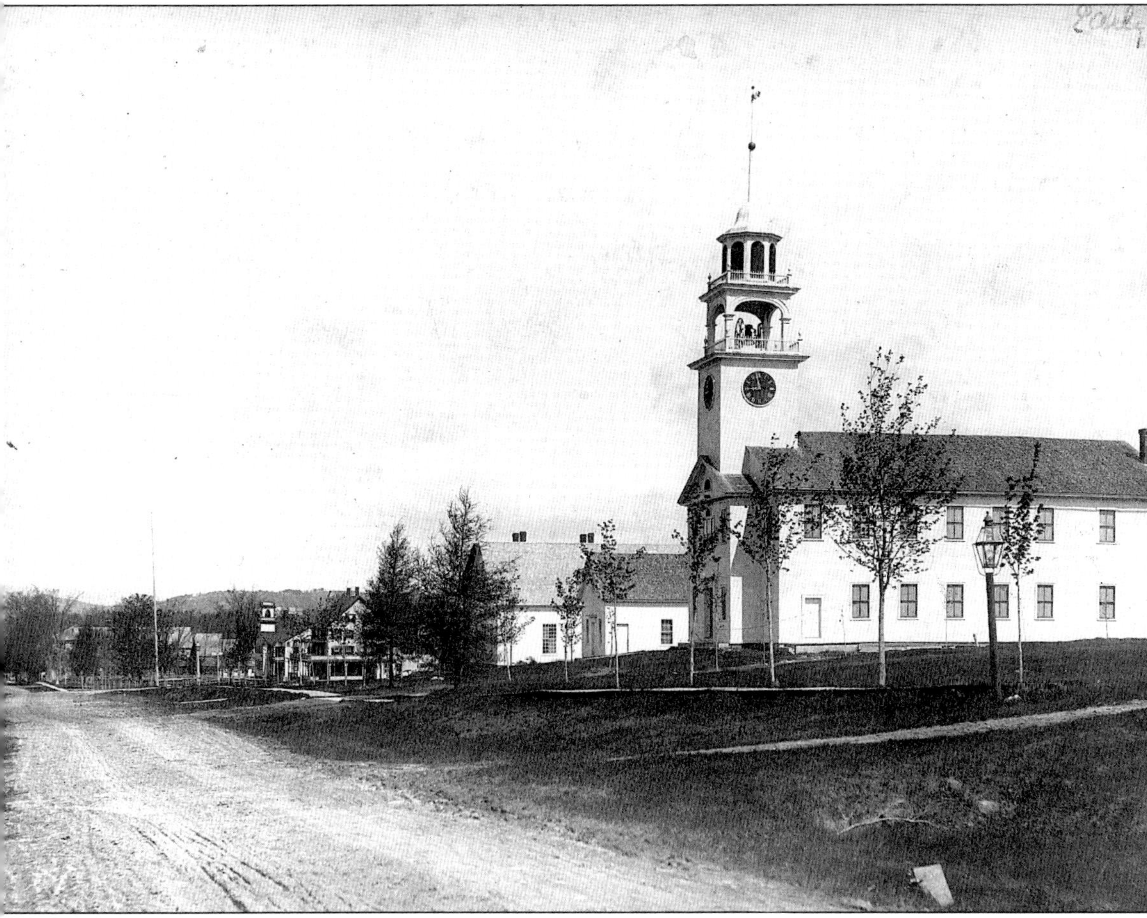

MAIN STREET. The Baptist church (right) was built in 1826. Its distinctive clock was added in 1884. (Courtesy of Colby-Sawyer College Archives.)

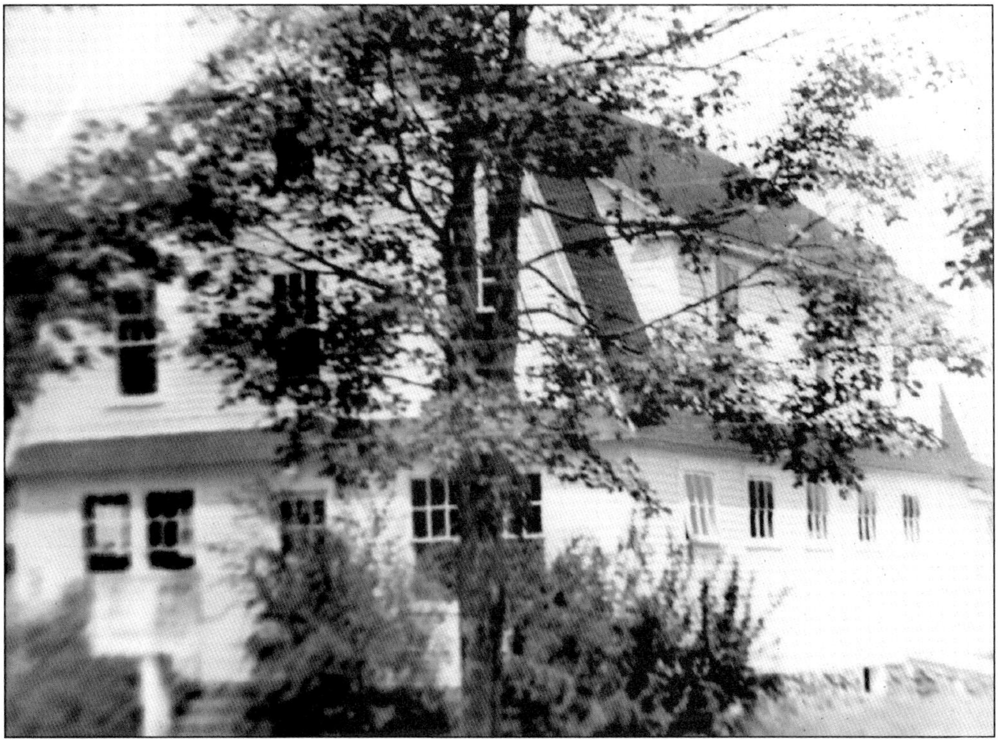

THE CATHOLIC CHURCH. Before the building of Our Lady of Fatima Church in 1960, Catholic services were held in the former Green Maples Restaurant building on Main Street. This building became the middle school annex.

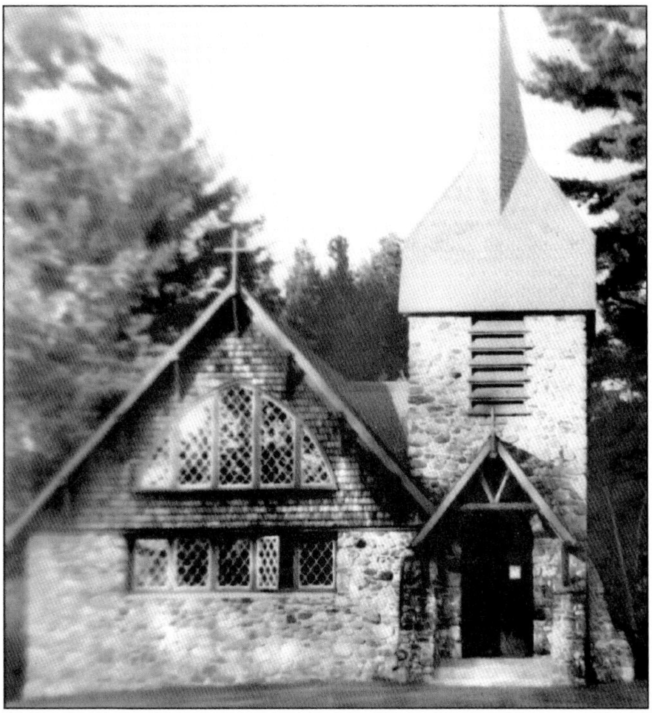

THE OLD ST. ANDREW'S EPISCOPAL CHURCH. Until this chapel was built on King Hill Road in 1906, Episcopal services were held at the West Part Schoolhouse. The new St. Andrew's, located on Gould Road, was consecrated in 1965.

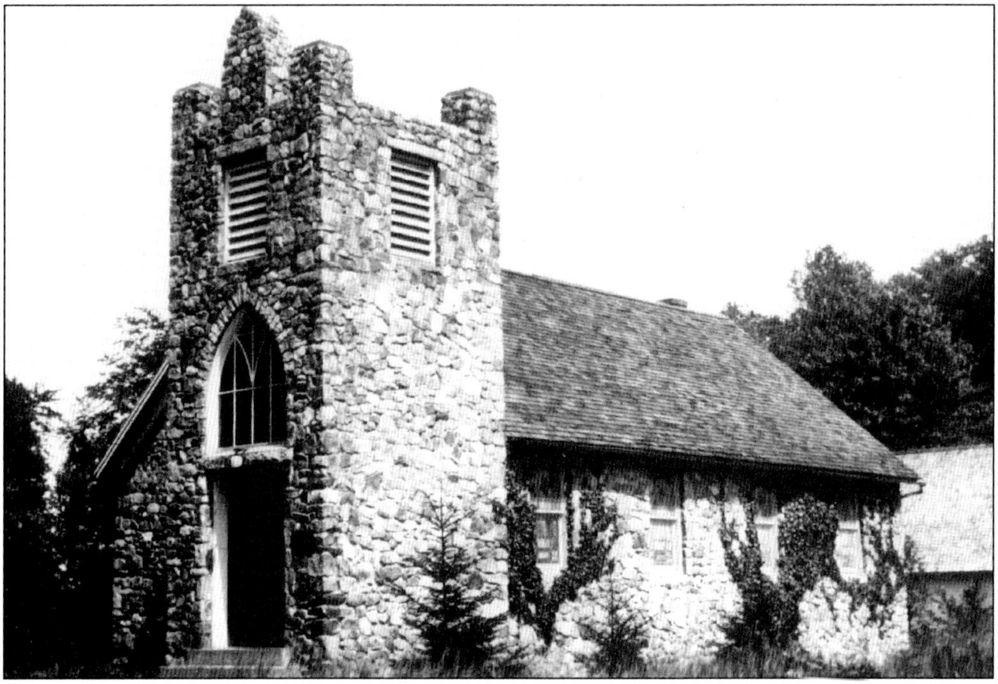

The Elkins Chapel. Stones from the Emery Burpee place were used to construct this building in 1916. Although the chapel is administered by the Elkins Church Society, the minister from the Baptist church performs the services here. This chapel bears a striking similarity to the Otterville chapel (below).

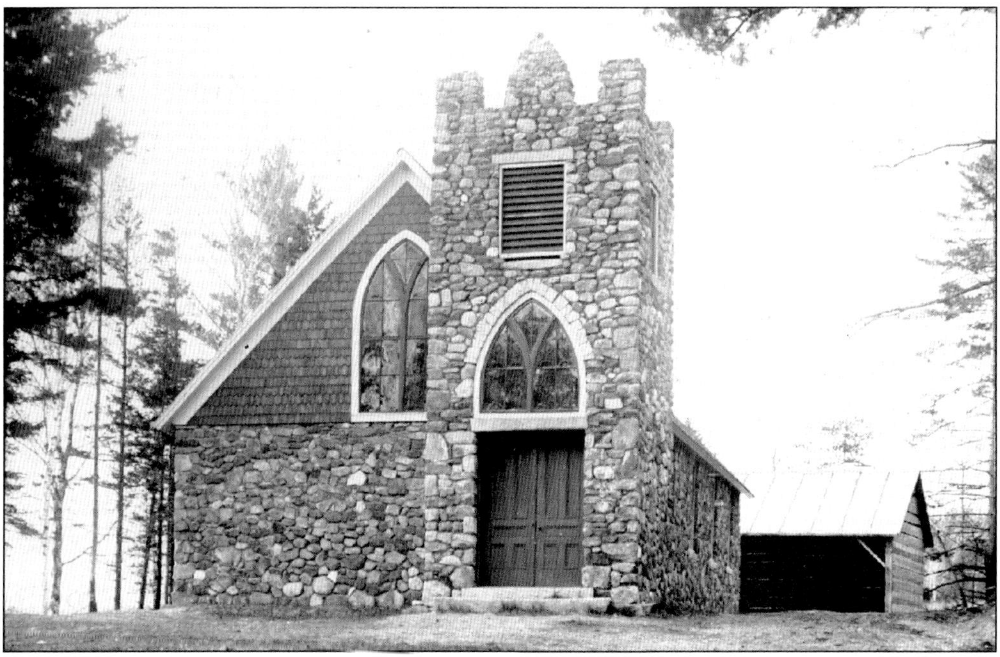

The Wayside Chapel in Otterville. This chapel was built by the First Union Religious Society in 1902 in the northwest area of town, known as Otterville. The last service here was in 1926, and now the building is a private residence.

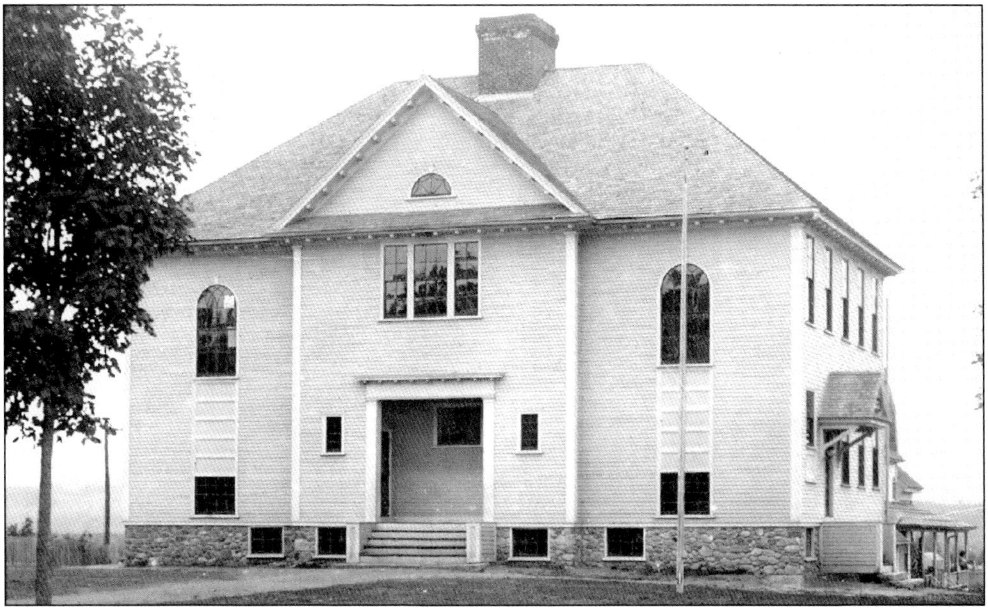

The Central School. Located at Four Corners (the intersection of Main and Pleasant Streets), this school was built in 1906 at a cost of $8,891. It replaced the Colby Hill School and Pleasant Street School and was torn down in 1949.

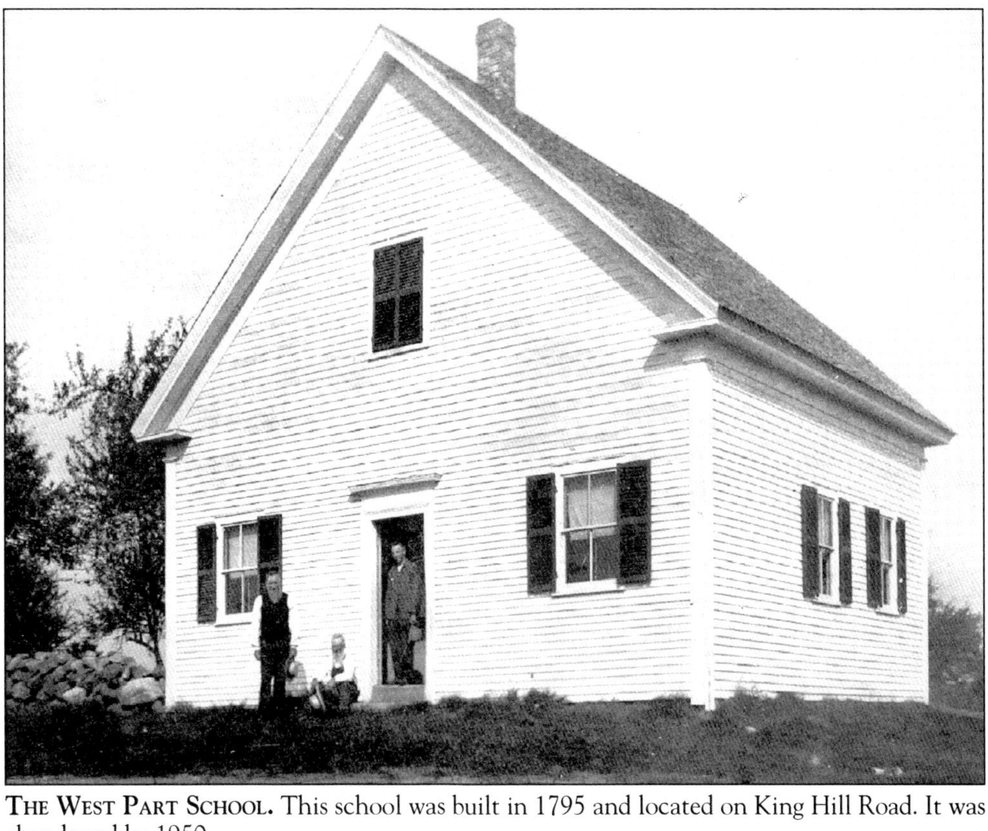

The West Part School. This school was built in 1795 and located on King Hill Road. It was abandoned by 1950.

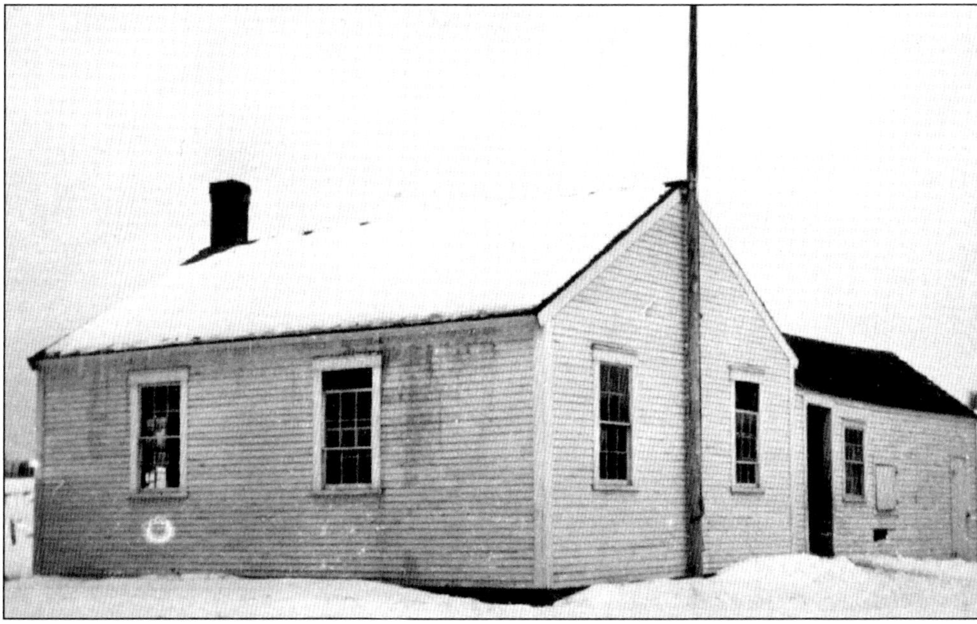

THE BURPEE HILL ROAD SCHOOLHOUSE. Built in the 1820s, this building was moved to the grounds of the historical society and is used for the society's country store exhibit. In 1900, this school served 10 students. It was closed in 1914.

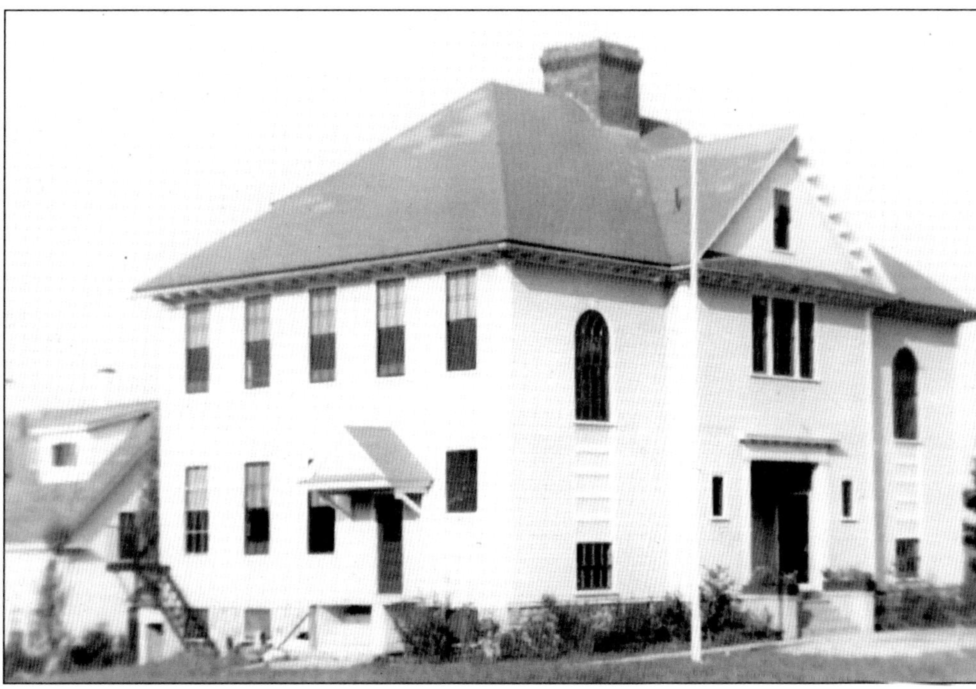

THE COLBY HILL SCHOOL. This school served 25 students in 1900. It was shut down in 1906, and its students were sent to the new Central School.

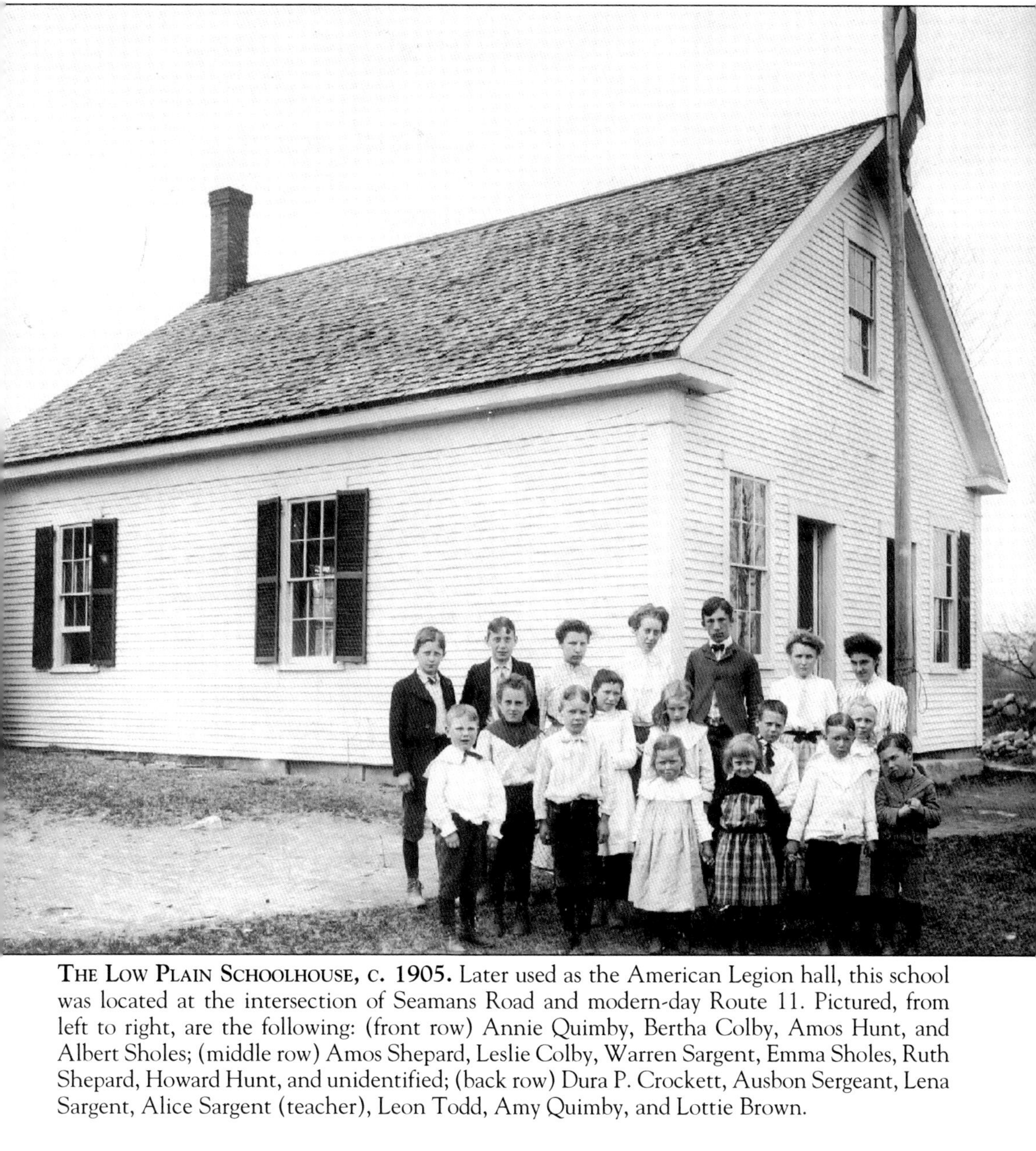

THE LOW PLAIN SCHOOLHOUSE, C. 1905. Later used as the American Legion hall, this school was located at the intersection of Seamans Road and modern-day Route 11. Pictured, from left to right, are the following: (front row) Annie Quimby, Bertha Colby, Amos Hunt, and Albert Sholes; (middle row) Amos Shepard, Leslie Colby, Warren Sargent, Emma Sholes, Ruth Shepard, Howard Hunt, and unidentified; (back row) Dura P. Crockett, Ausbon Sergeant, Lena Sargent, Alice Sargent (teacher), Leon Todd, Amy Quimby, and Lottie Brown.

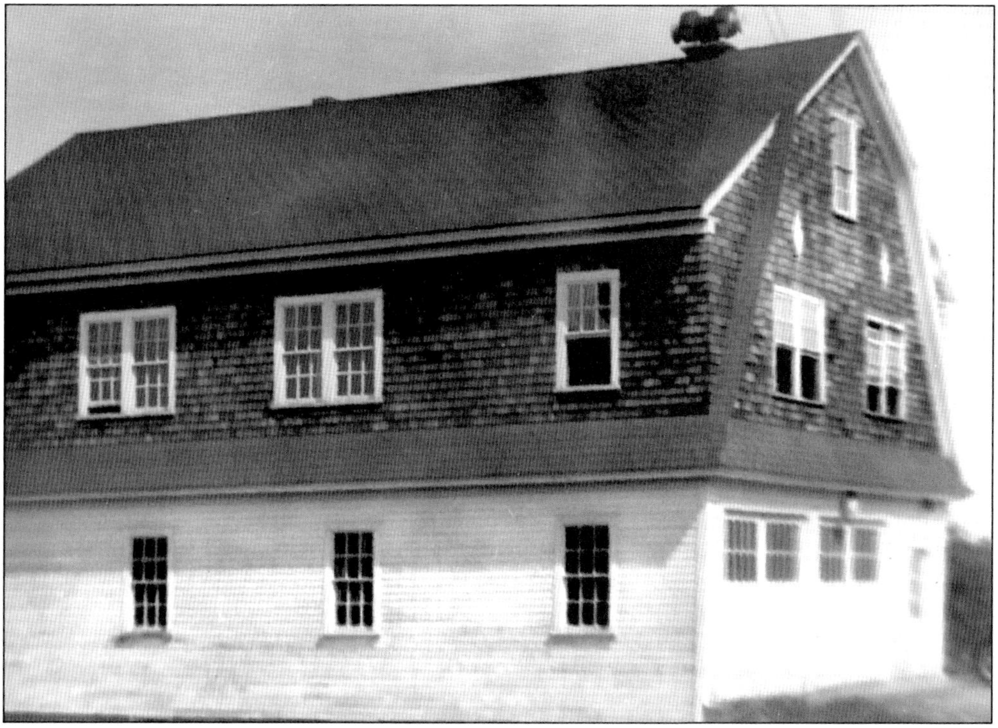

THE FIREHOUSE. Built in 1930 at a cost of $6,000, this firehouse is located on North Pleasant Street on land donated by Louisa Sargent. A cupola was added to the building during World War II for airplane spotting.

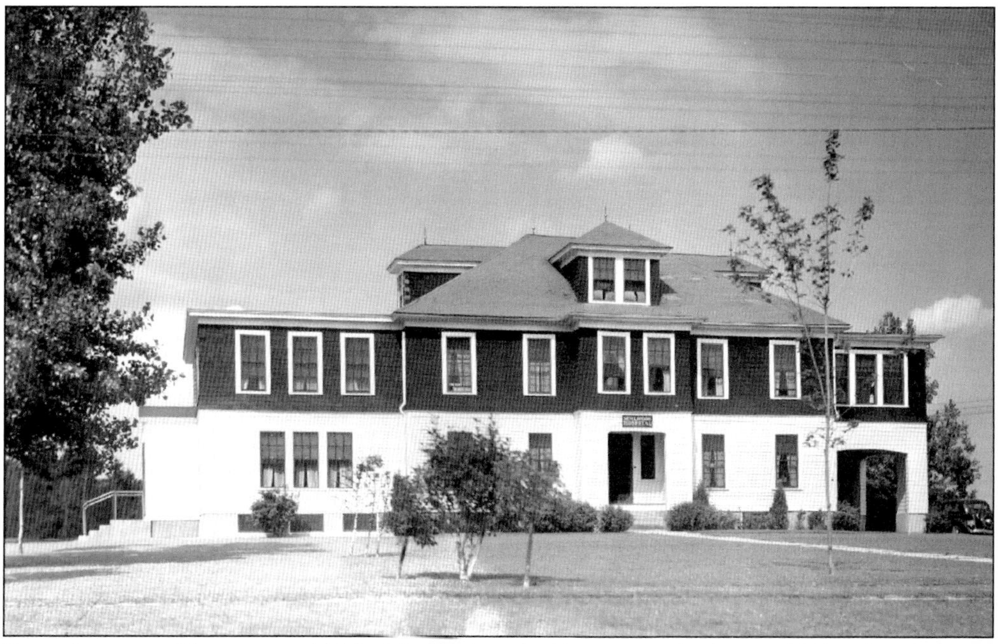

NEW LONDON HOSPITAL, 1936. Until this building was built in 1923, the hospital was located in the building now known as the Tracy Memorial Library. (Photograph by Herbert D. Swift.)

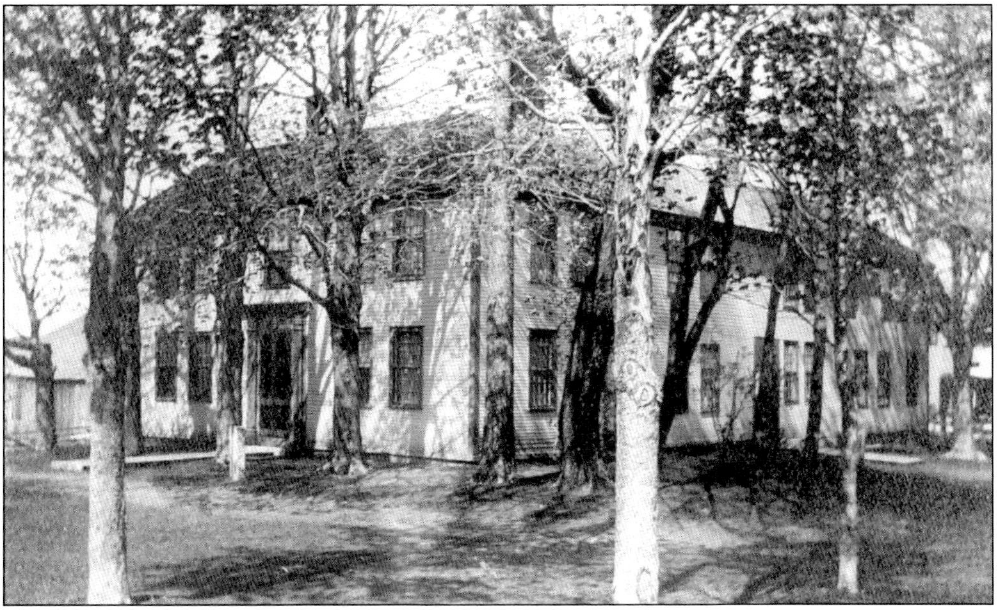

The Everett Homestead. Located at Four Corners, this building was the site of New London Hospital from 1918 until 1923. In 1926, Jane A. Tracy bought and renovated the building as a library for the town. She also paid $125,000 as a gift-in-trust for its maintenance. (Courtesy of Colby-Sawyer College Archives.)

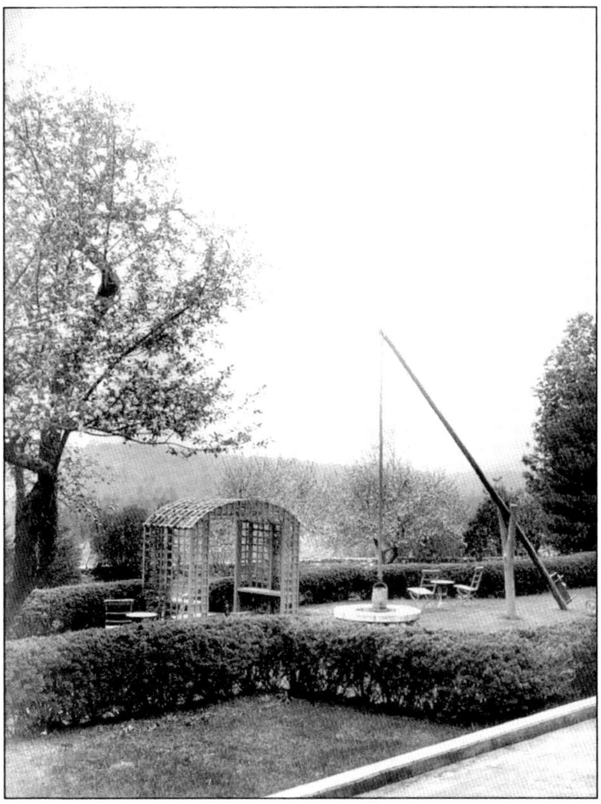

The Everett Homestead Garden. Although it is hard to determine when this photograph was taken, it is likely that it was before the homestead was converted into the hospital in 1918. (Courtesy of Colby-Sawyer College Archives.)

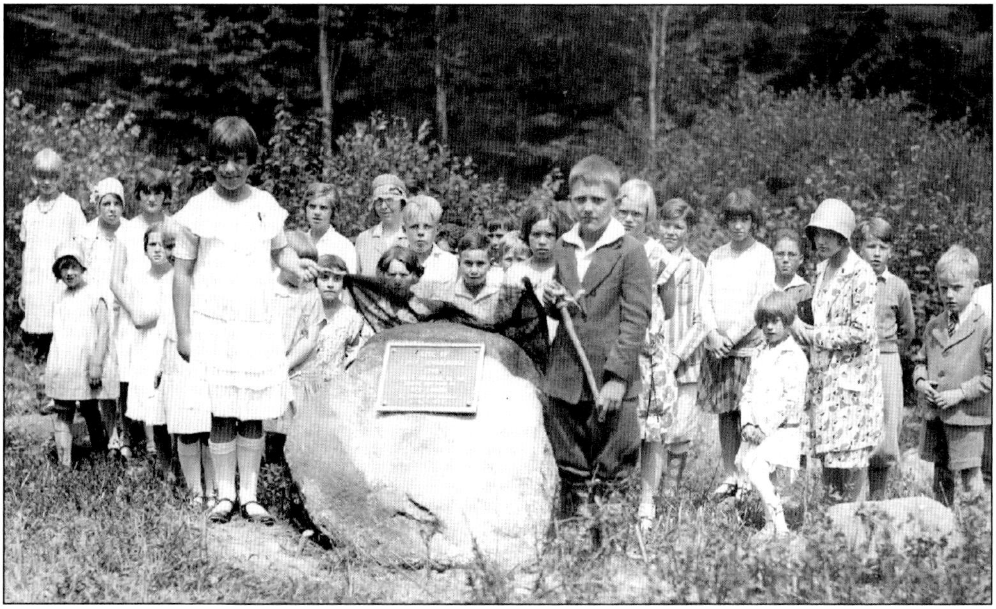

The Hominy Pot Schoolhouse Marker, 1929. During the 1929 sesquicentennial of the founding of New London, most of the historical markers still apparent today were installed. Here, Mary and David Crockett pose with others at the installation of the marker commemorating the town's first schoolhouse.

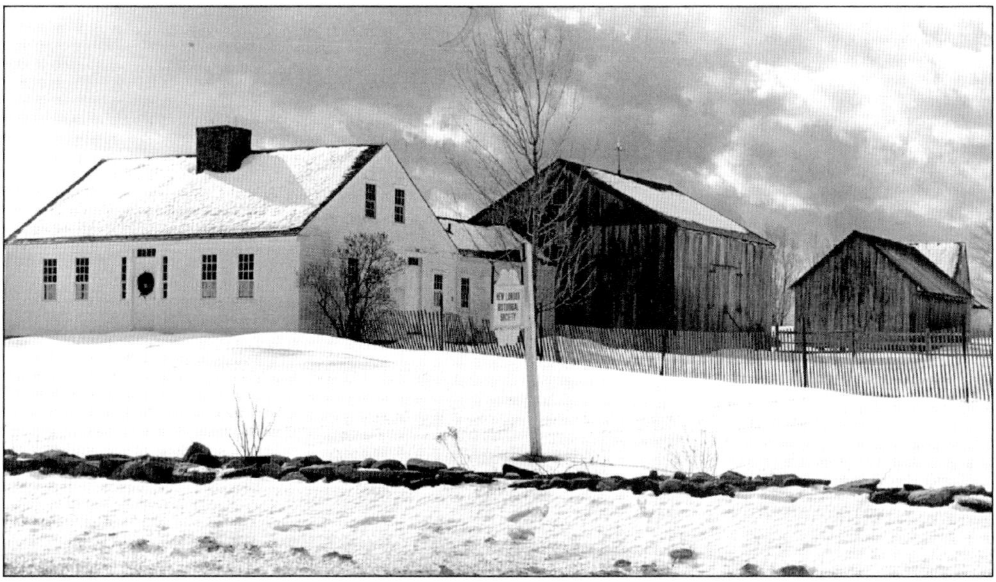

The New London Historical Society. Founded in 1954, the historical society is concerned with preserving the history of the New London area. Located on Little Sunapee Road, the society is a complex of historic buildings and modern buildings based on historic designs. The organization holds many activities throughout the year, including an open house for the holidays and a summer art show.

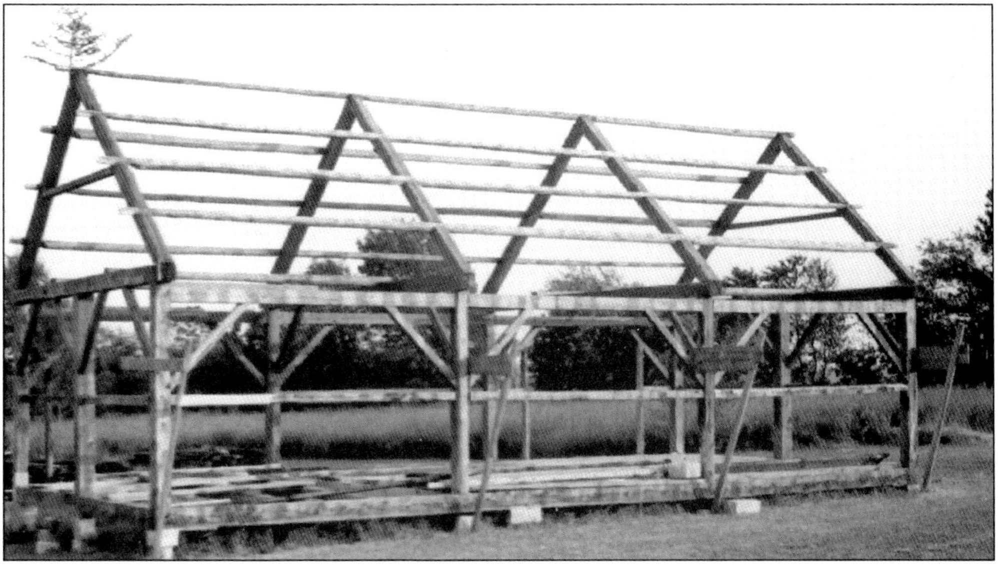

THE CARRIAGE SHED FROM THE MORGAN FARM, 1970. This shed, originally built in 1860, was dismantled and moved to the historical society site.

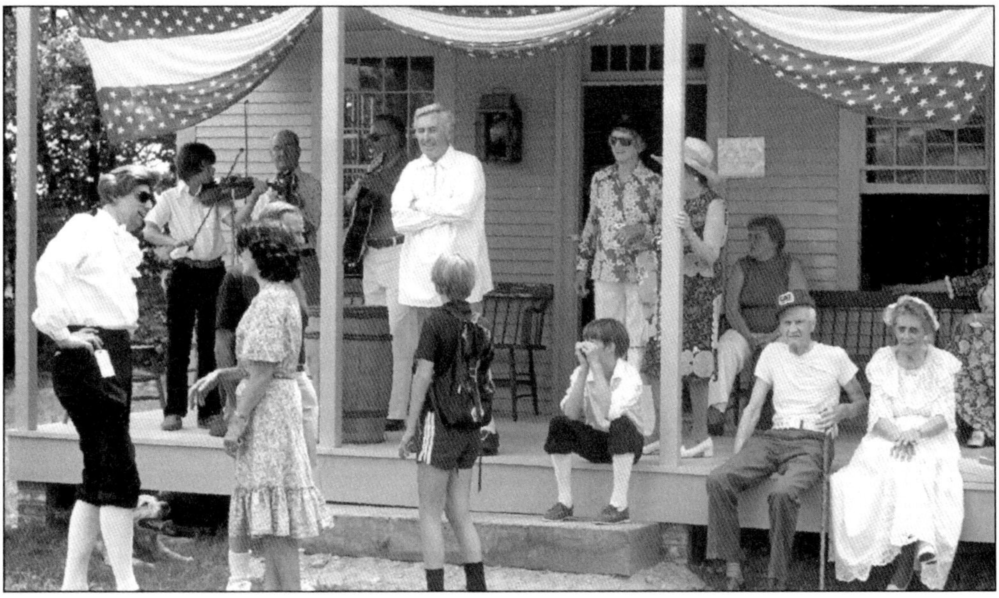

NATIONAL BICENTENNIAL CELEBRATIONS, 1976. History fever swept the nation as its 200th anniversary of the signing of the Declaration of Independence approached. Many institutions across the country held special events to celebrate, and the New London Historical Society was not left behind.

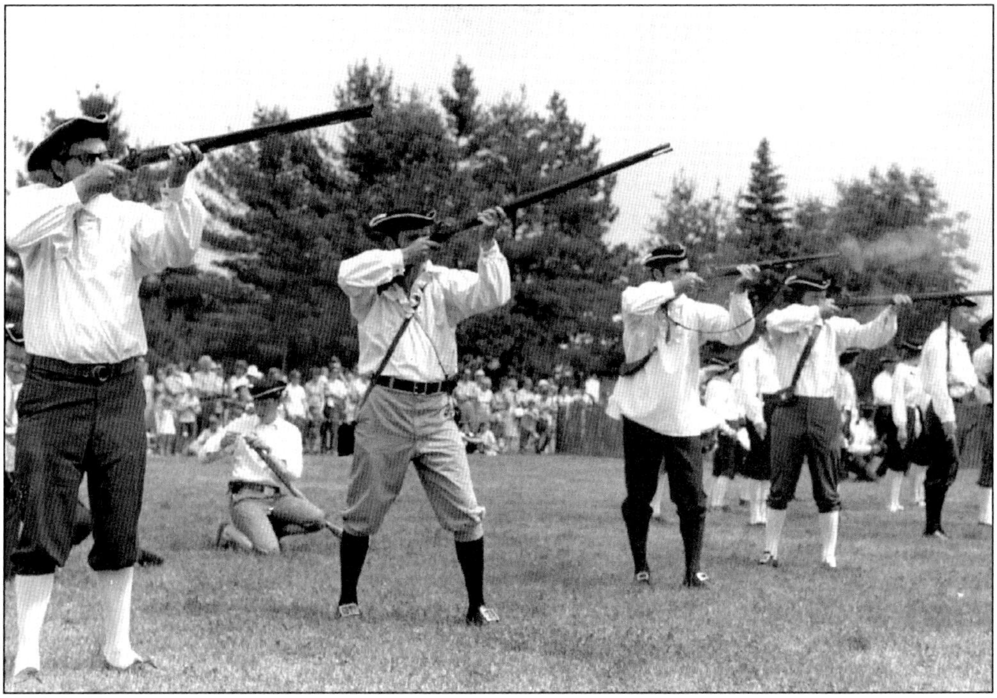

MUSTER DAY, THE 1970S. Battle reenactments and other events, such as this Muster Day at the historical society, were very popular across the country around the time of the bicentennial.

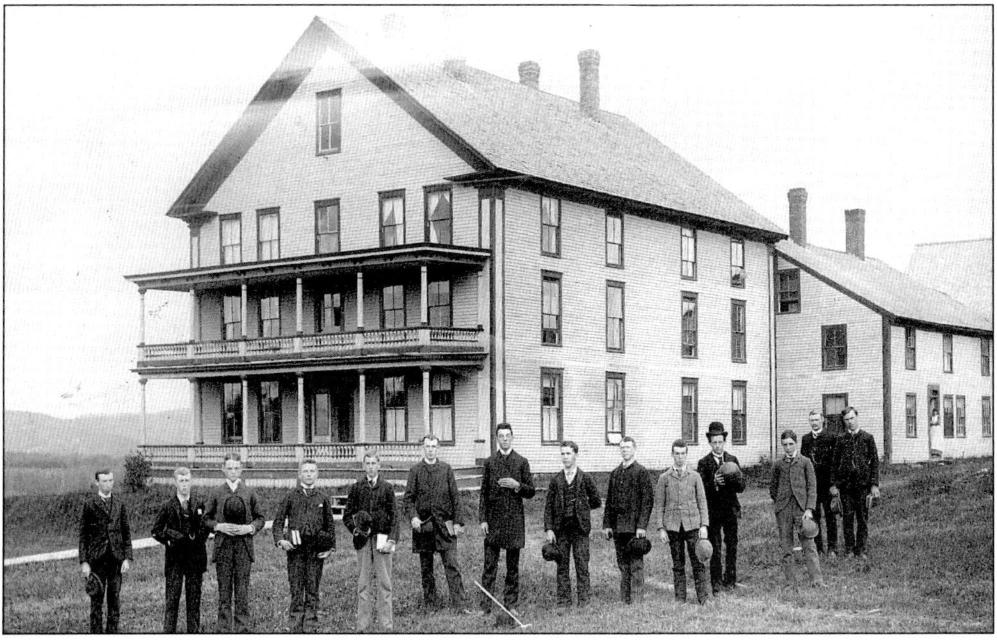

OLD COLBY HALL. Constructed with beams from the original town meetinghouse in 1854, Colby Hall was used as a boys' dormitory for Colby Academy. It was dismantled, and the beams were used again for the Colbytown Camp lodge on Colby Point on Little Lake Sunapee. In the 1990s, the beams were used one more time to build the Lodge, a student center on the Colby-Sawyer College campus. (Courtesy of Colby-Sawyer College Archives.)

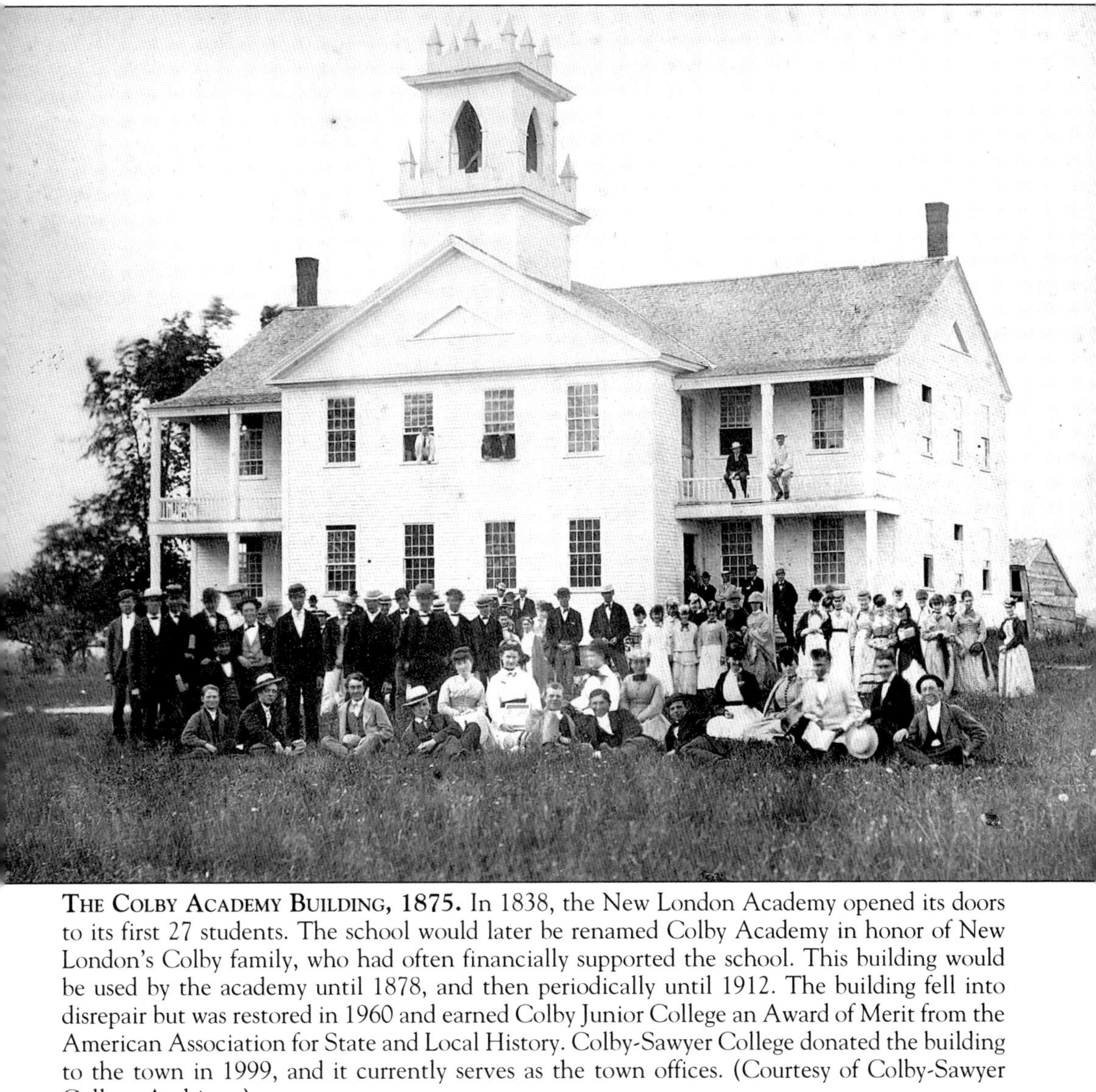

The Colby Academy Building, 1875. In 1838, the New London Academy opened its doors to its first 27 students. The school would later be renamed Colby Academy in honor of New London's Colby family, who had often financially supported the school. This building would be used by the academy until 1878, and then periodically until 1912. The building fell into disrepair but was restored in 1960 and earned Colby Junior College an Award of Merit from the American Association for State and Local History. Colby-Sawyer College donated the building to the town in 1999, and it currently serves as the town offices. (Courtesy of Colby-Sawyer College Archives.)

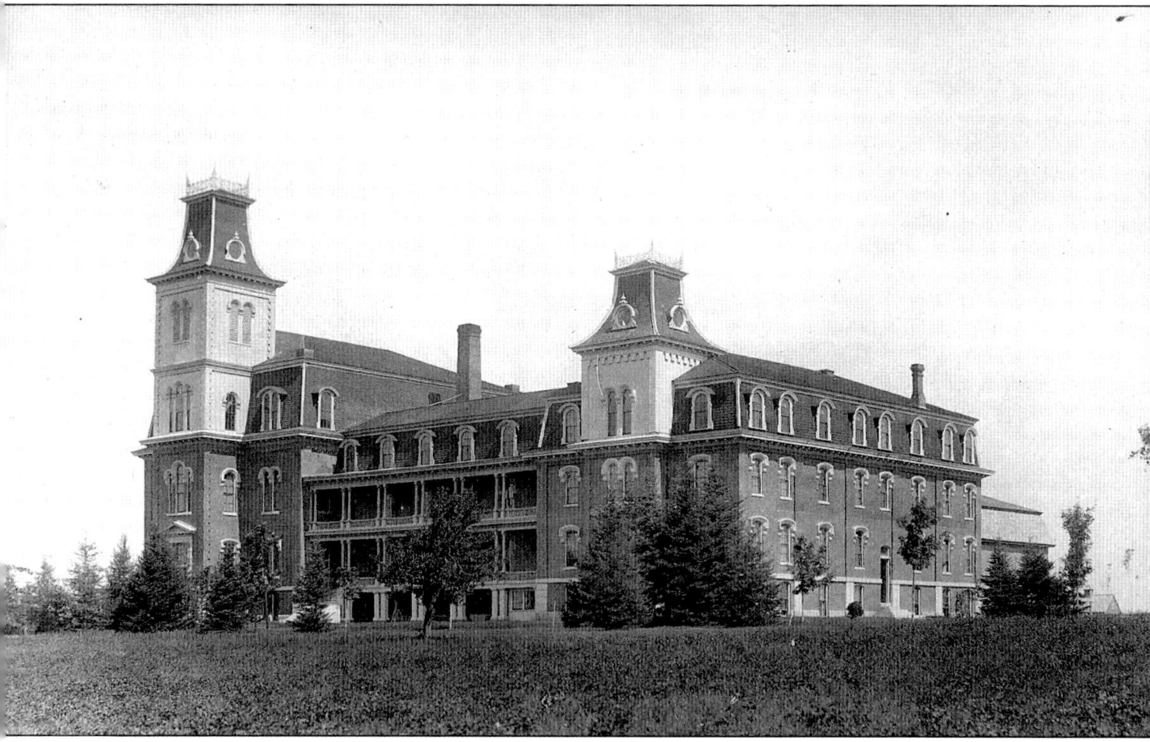

The Brick Colby Academy Building, c. 1890. Built in the 1860s, the impressive building boasted a 111-foot-high belfry tower and included a library, classrooms, two chapels, and dormitory space for 100 students. (Photograph by J.B. Warren, courtesy of Colby-Sawyer College Archives.)

The Academy Building Fire, 1892. On the afternoon of April 25, while most of the student body was away on a field trip to Mount Kearsarge, a fire broke out in one of the towers (most likely in the photographic laboratory) and quickly spread to the rest of the building. Most of the furniture and library books on the lower floors were saved, but the building was a total loss. Students boarded with families in town, and classes resumed the very next morning in buildings around town. (Courtesy of Colby-Sawyer College Archives.)

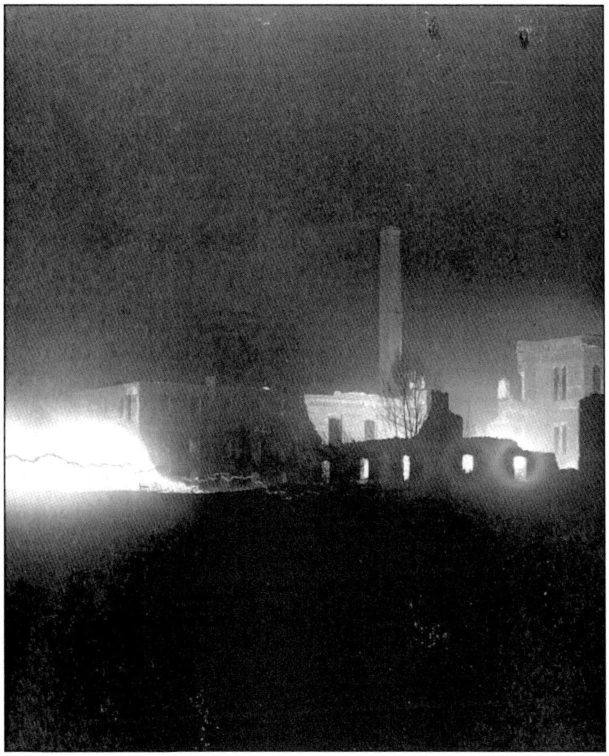

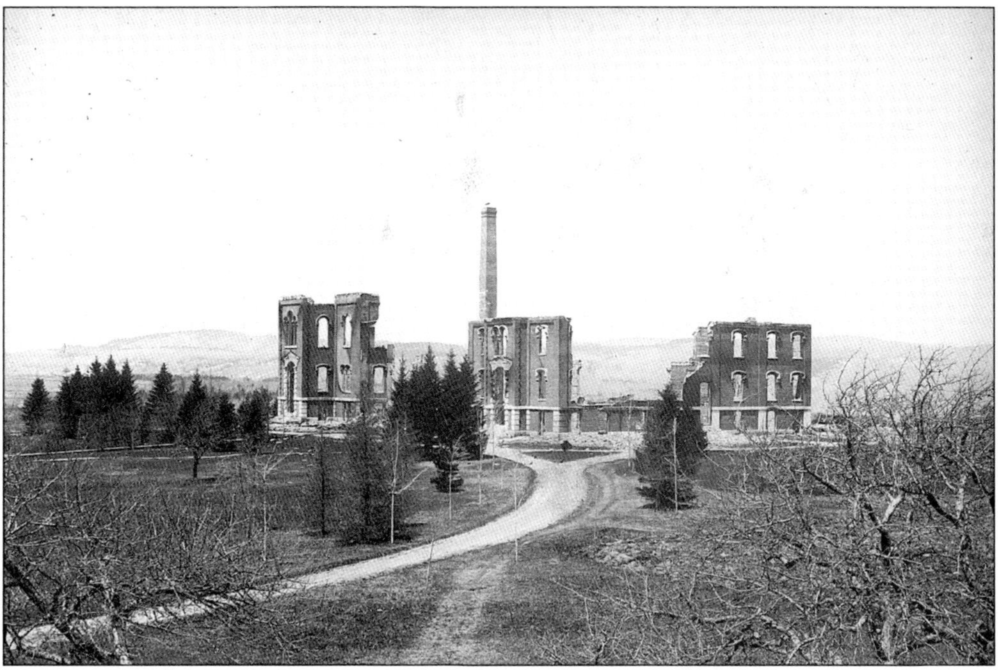

The Ruins. Fundraising to replace the building was started immediately. However, despite the best efforts of school administrators, it took almost 20 years to secure the funds and agree on a design for the replacement building. Ruins from the fire were still apparent on campus as late as 1904. (Courtesy of Colby-Sawyer College Archives.)

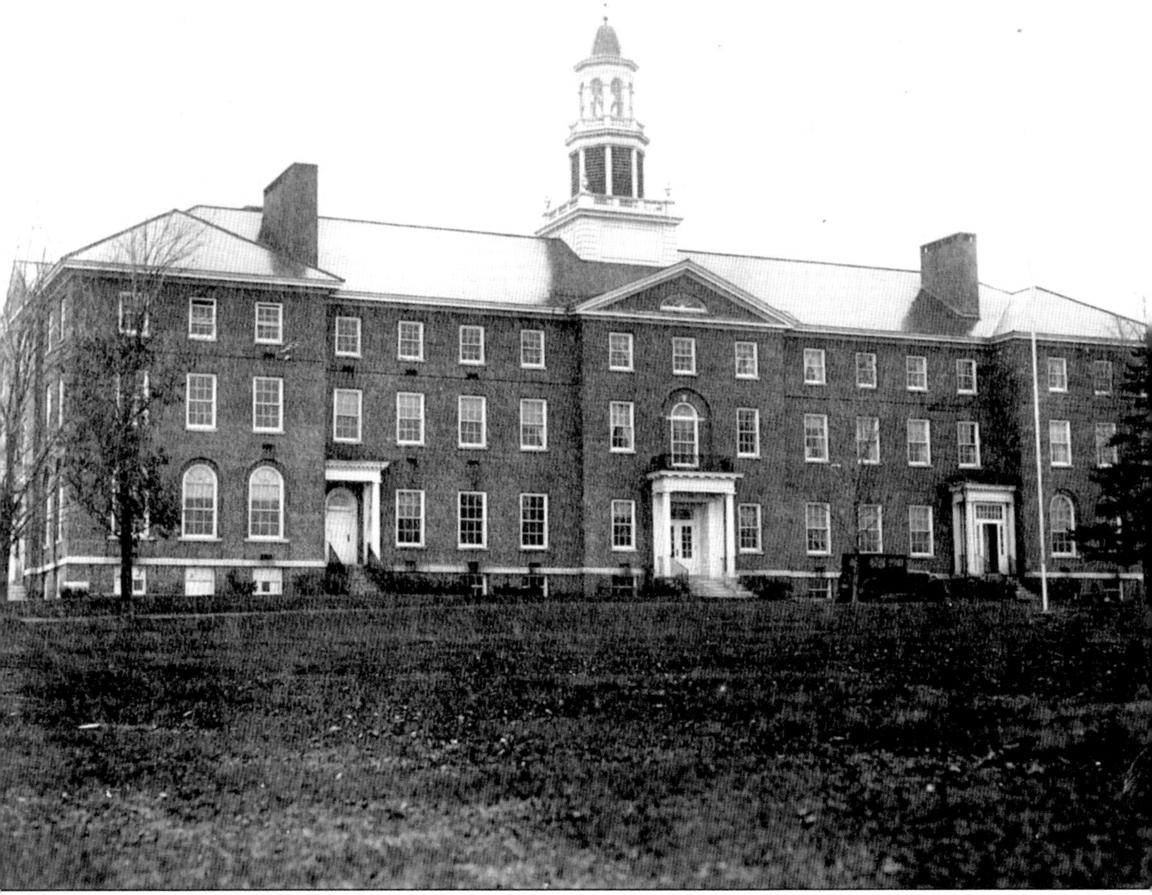

COLGATE HALL, C. 1920. Built in 1911 on the site of the building that was destroyed by fire, Colgate Hall was named for the Colgate family, who helped finance the building and the school for many years. This building has been renovated and enlarged many times in its history and serves as the main administration and classroom building for the college. (Courtesy of Colby-Sawyer College Archives.)

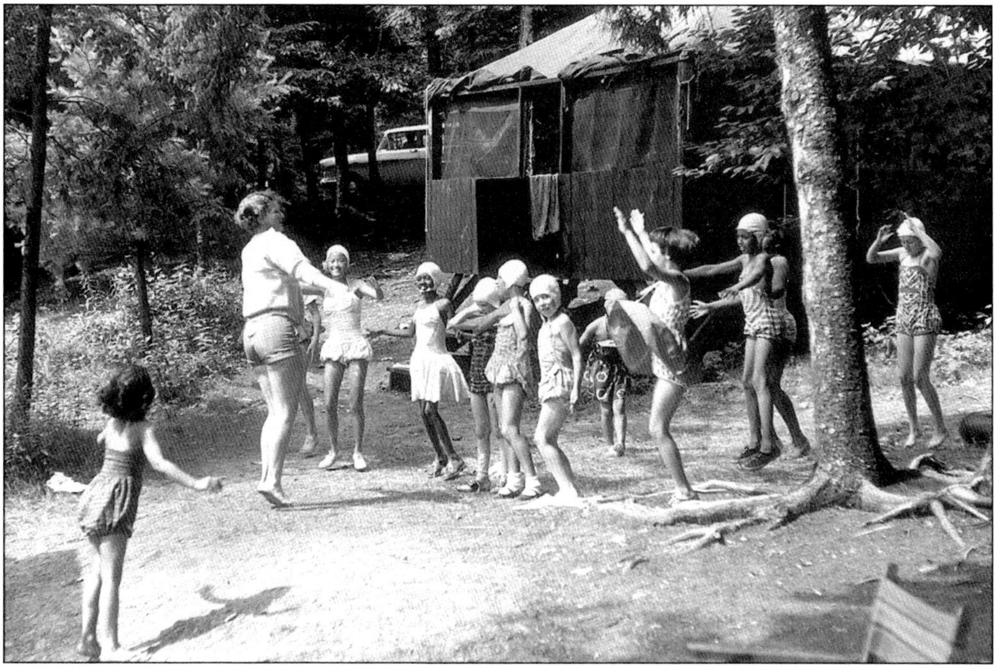

COLBYTOWN CAMP. Instituted in 1941 on the shores of Little Lake Sunapee, Colbytown Camp was a one-month summer camp program for European refugee children during the war. Later, the camp's mission was changed to include underprivileged American children as well. Colby Junior College administered the camp, and the counselors were students at the college. (Above photograph by Adrienne Fussiner, both courtesy of Colby-Sawyer College Archives.)

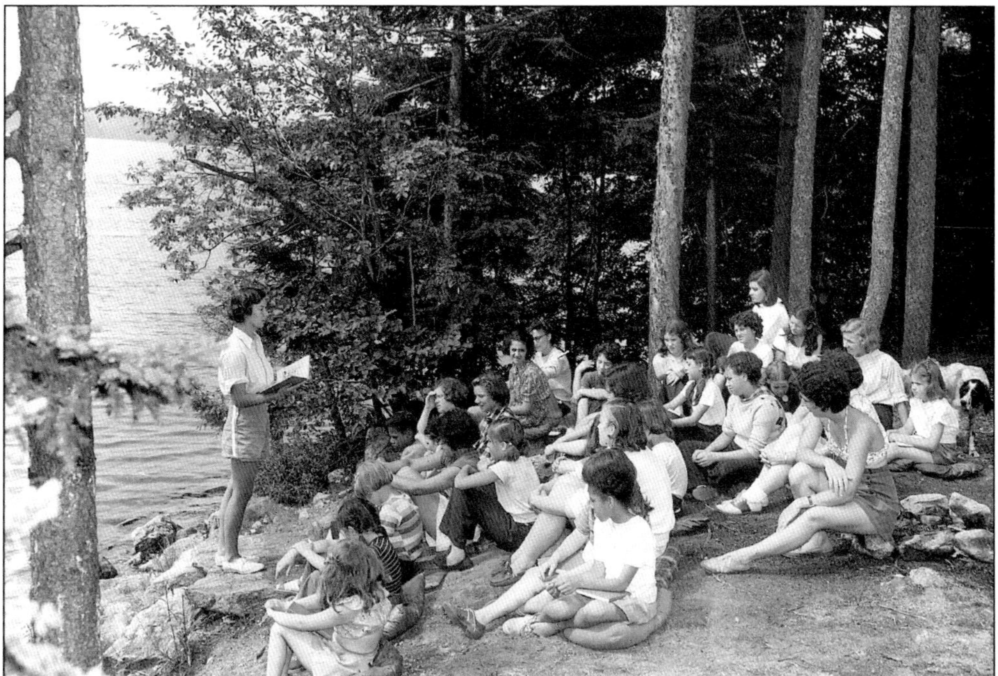

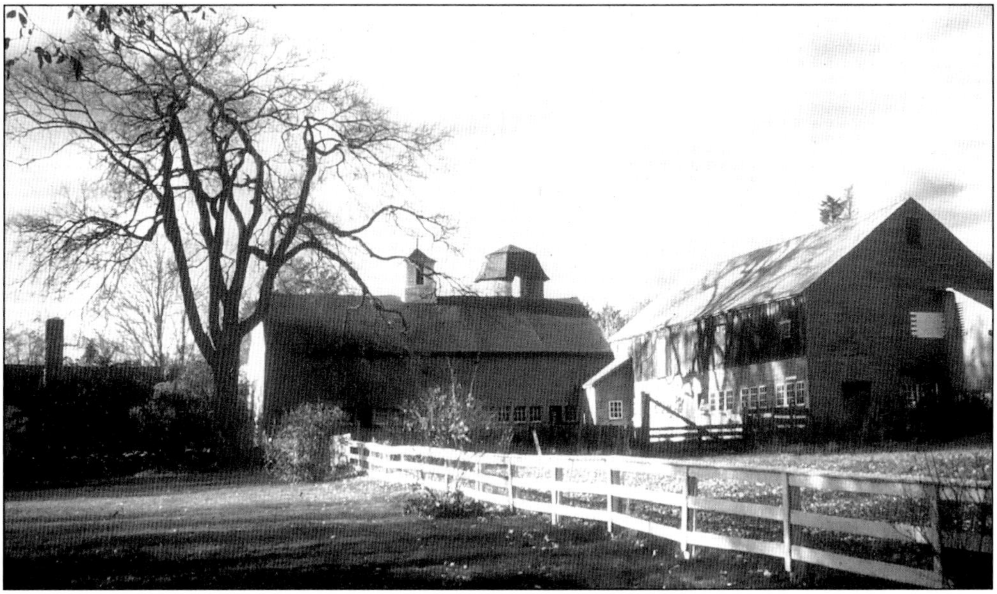

The Barns of the Colby Homestead, the Early 1980s. Colby Junior College purchased the Colby Homestead in the early 1970s, and when the school expanded its programs as a four-year institution, the homestead seemed a logical place to expand. With the support (financial and otherwise) of townspeople, the Colby barns, which were built before the Civil War, were renovated and used for Colby-Sawyer's library and learning center, named for Susan Colgate Cleveland, a longtime trustee and former resident of the homestead. (Courtesy of Colby-Sawyer College Archives.)

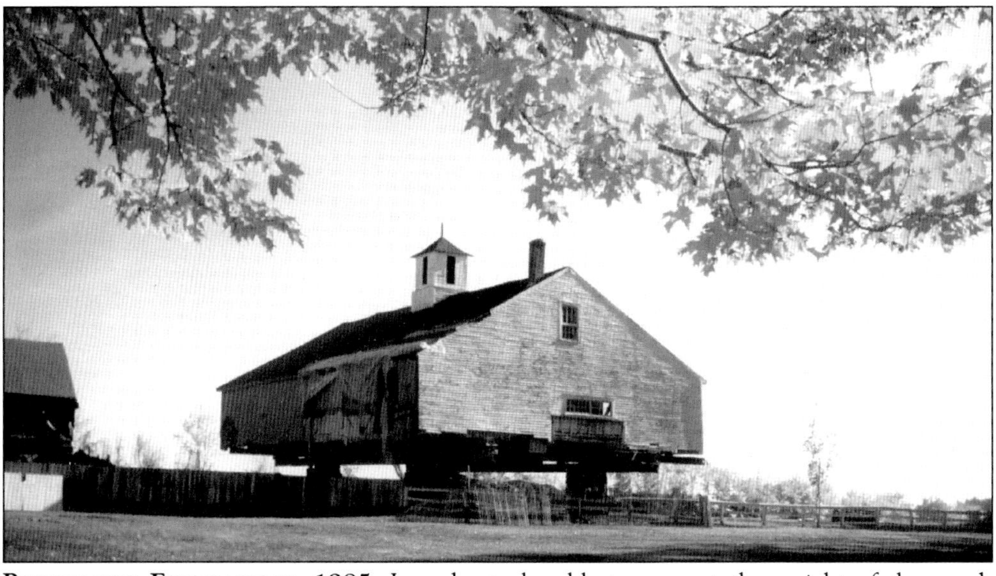

Reinforcing Foundations, 1985. In order to be able to support the weight of thousands of books, the foundations and floors of the Colby Homestead barns needed to be reinforced with concrete. The buildings were moved for this process and then replaced. The library won numerous awards for its unique preservation of these historic structures. In addition to the college's constituents, residents of New London and surrounding towns may use the library's resources. (Courtesy of Colby-Sawyer College Archives.)

Five

Recreation and Tourism

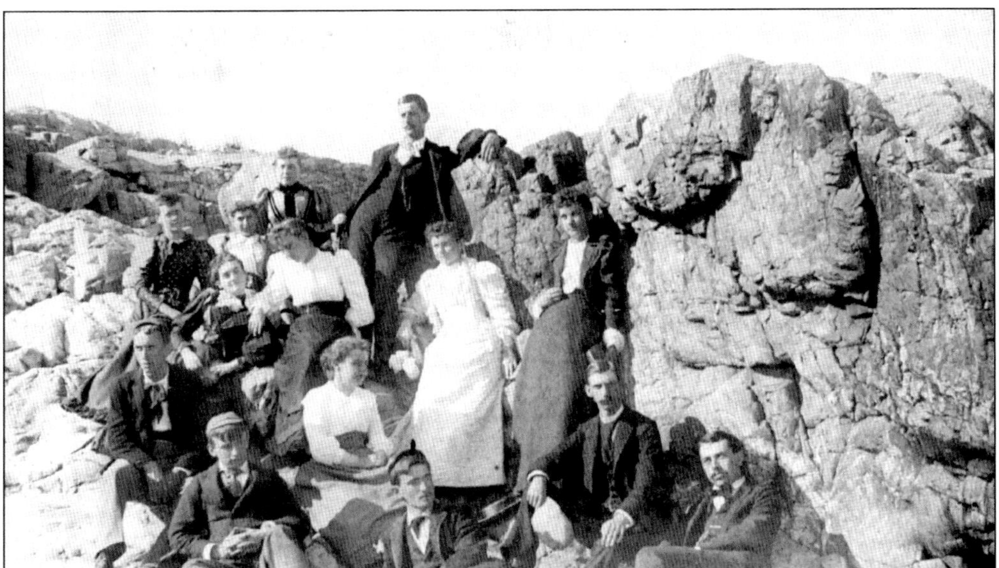

The Kearsarge Summit, c. 1890. The fantastic views from the summit of Mount Kearsarge have always made it a popular tourist destination. Although not apparent in this photograph, many visitors have inscribed names and dates on the rocky summit. A 21st-century visitor to the summit can see inscriptions made as early as 1832.

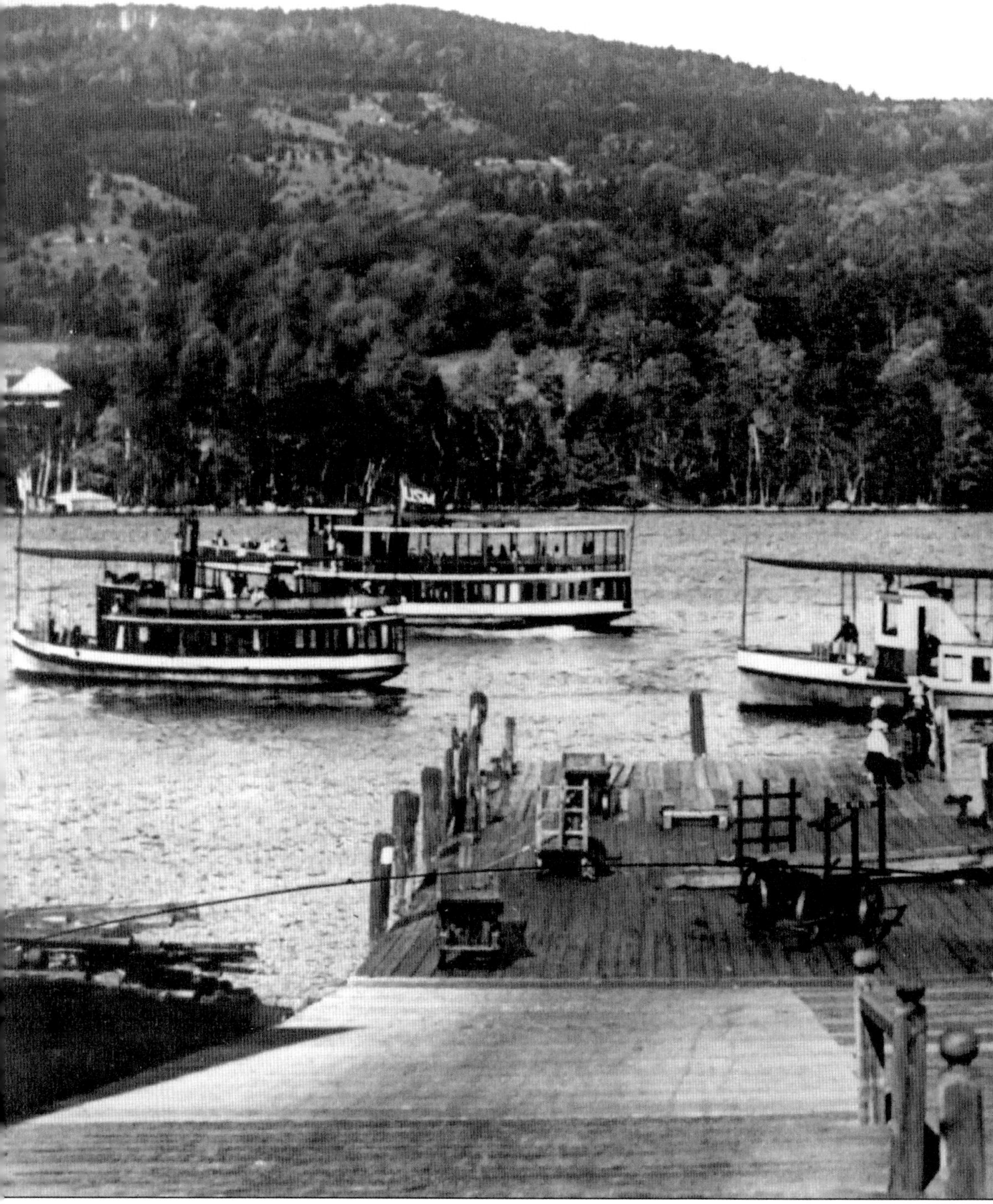

Lake Sunapee Steamboats, c. 1910–1920. Pictured, from left to right, are the *Ascutney*, *Kearsarge*, *Weetamo*, and *Armenia White*. Steamboats were a popular way to get from place to place until the emergence of the automobile, and the Great Depression made them no longer profitable to run. The *Ascutney*, built in 1907 for 150–200 passengers, stopped running in 1932 and was sold for scrap. The *Kearsarge*, built in 1897, was the last to succumb to change. It was

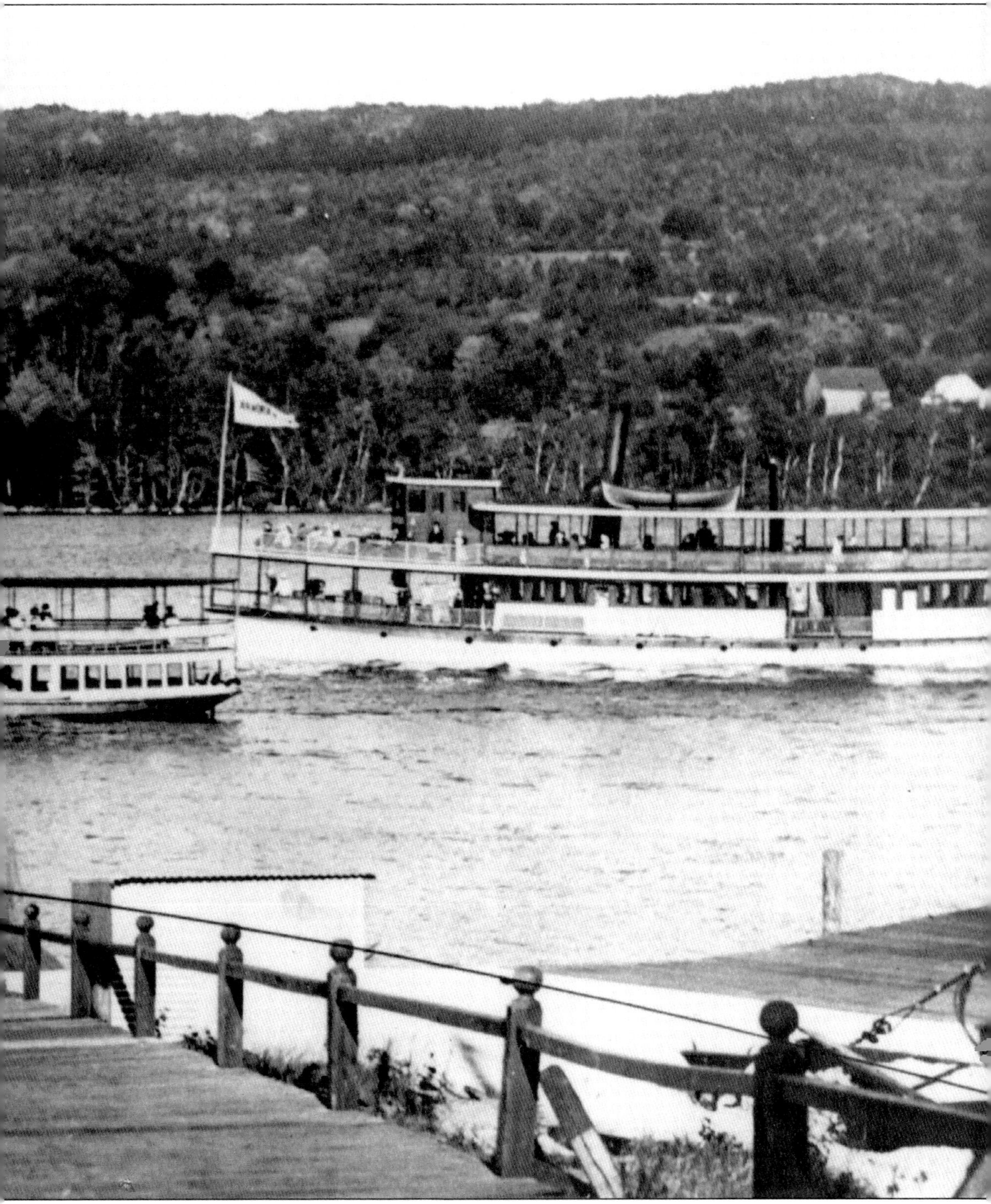

tied up for good in 1933 and lingered rusting away at Lake Sunapee Station for years until it too was sold for scrap. The *Weetamo*, built in 1902, was stripped for parts, and the hull was sunk near Pinecliff Landing in 1925. The *Armenia White* was in use from 1887 until 1917, when it was tied up at Georges' Mills and sold for scrap years later.

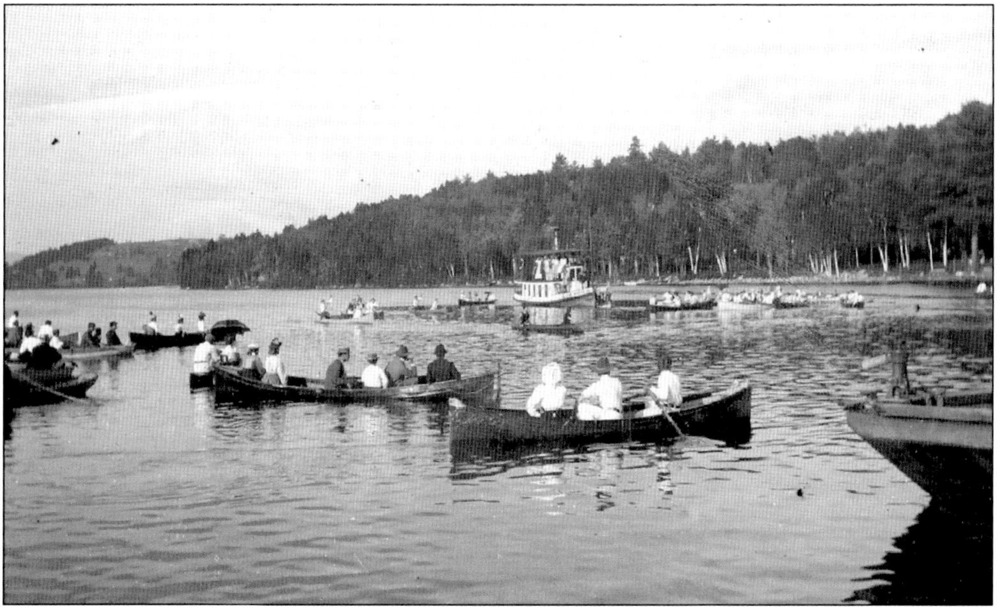

THE STEAMBOAT *LADY WOODSUM*. Another popular Lake Sunapee steamboat, the *Lady Woodsum* was built in 1876 and could hold 75 passengers. Fire destroyed it in 1910 near Lake Sunapee Station.

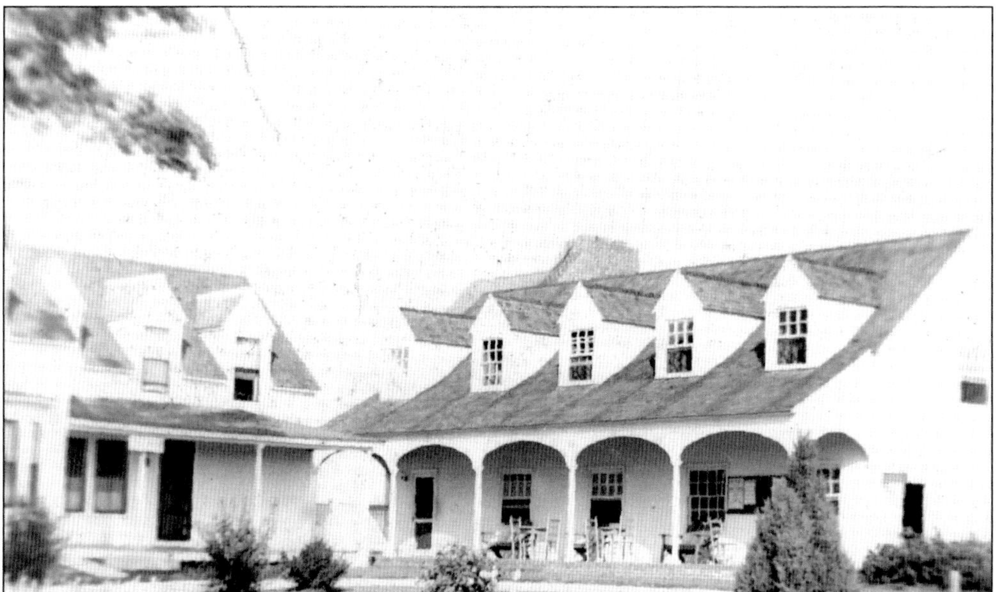

THE LAKE SUNAPEE COUNTRY CLUB. Located to the east of Crockett's Corner, the country club was formerly J.E. Shepard's farm, Sheepfold. The club's first nine holes were completed in 1928, and nine more holes followed a year later.

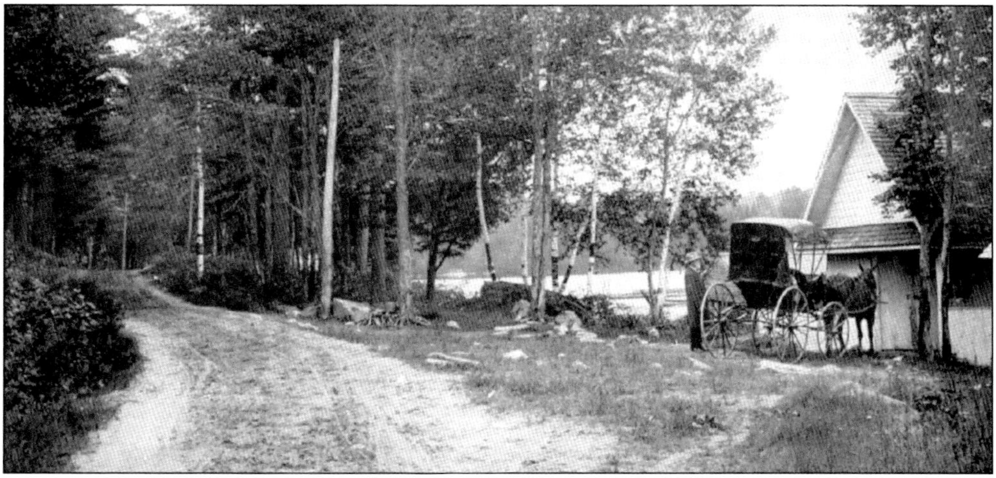

LAKESIDE LANDING, 1906. Lakeside Landing, located in Herrick's Cove on Lake Sunapee, was the principal landing point for New London.

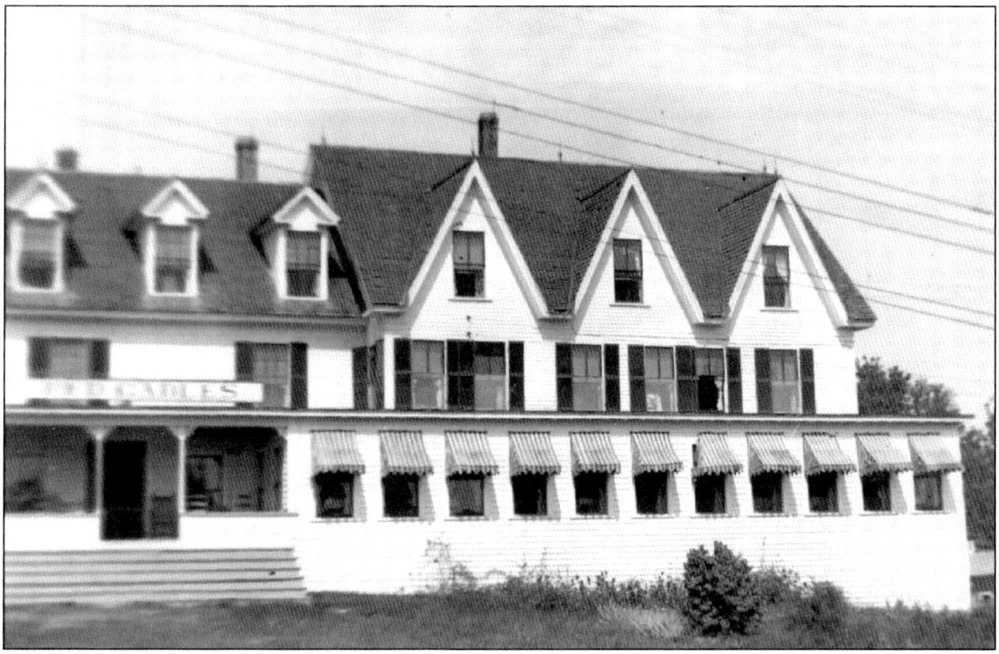

RED GABLES. This hotel is still in operation today as the Inn at Pleasant Lake.

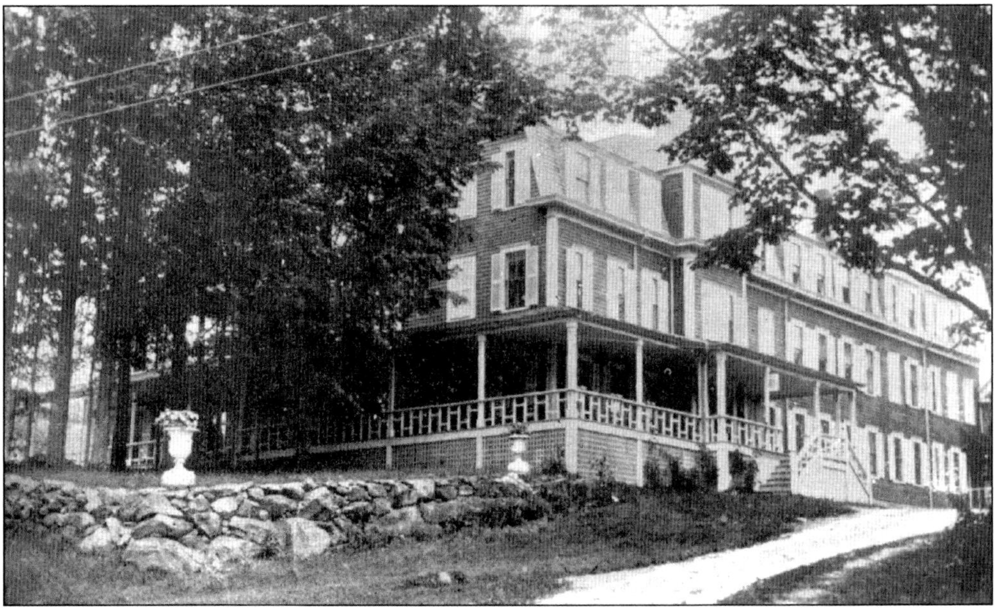

Lakeside Lodge. This hotel on Lake Sunapee was established in the 1890s by George Prescott.

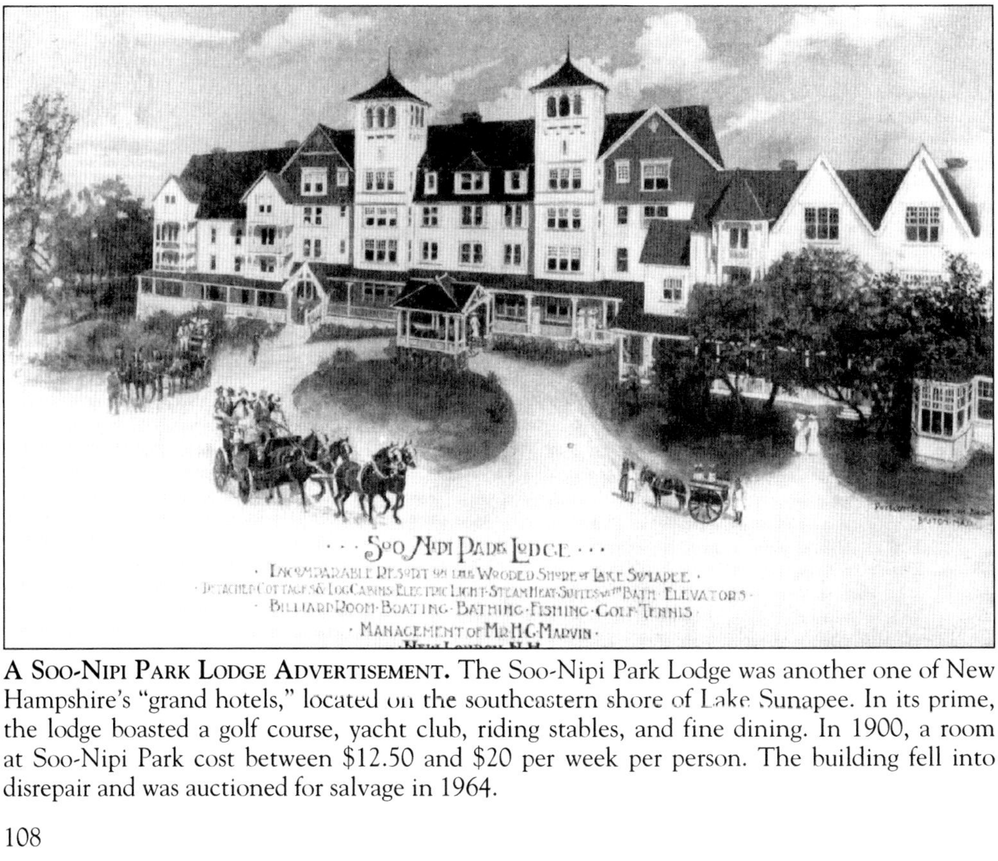

A Soo-Nipi Park Lodge Advertisement. The Soo-Nipi Park Lodge was another one of New Hampshire's "grand hotels," located on the southeastern shore of Lake Sunapee. In its prime, the lodge boasted a golf course, yacht club, riding stables, and fine dining. In 1900, a room at Soo-Nipi Park cost between $12.50 and $20 per week per person. The building fell into disrepair and was auctioned for salvage in 1964.

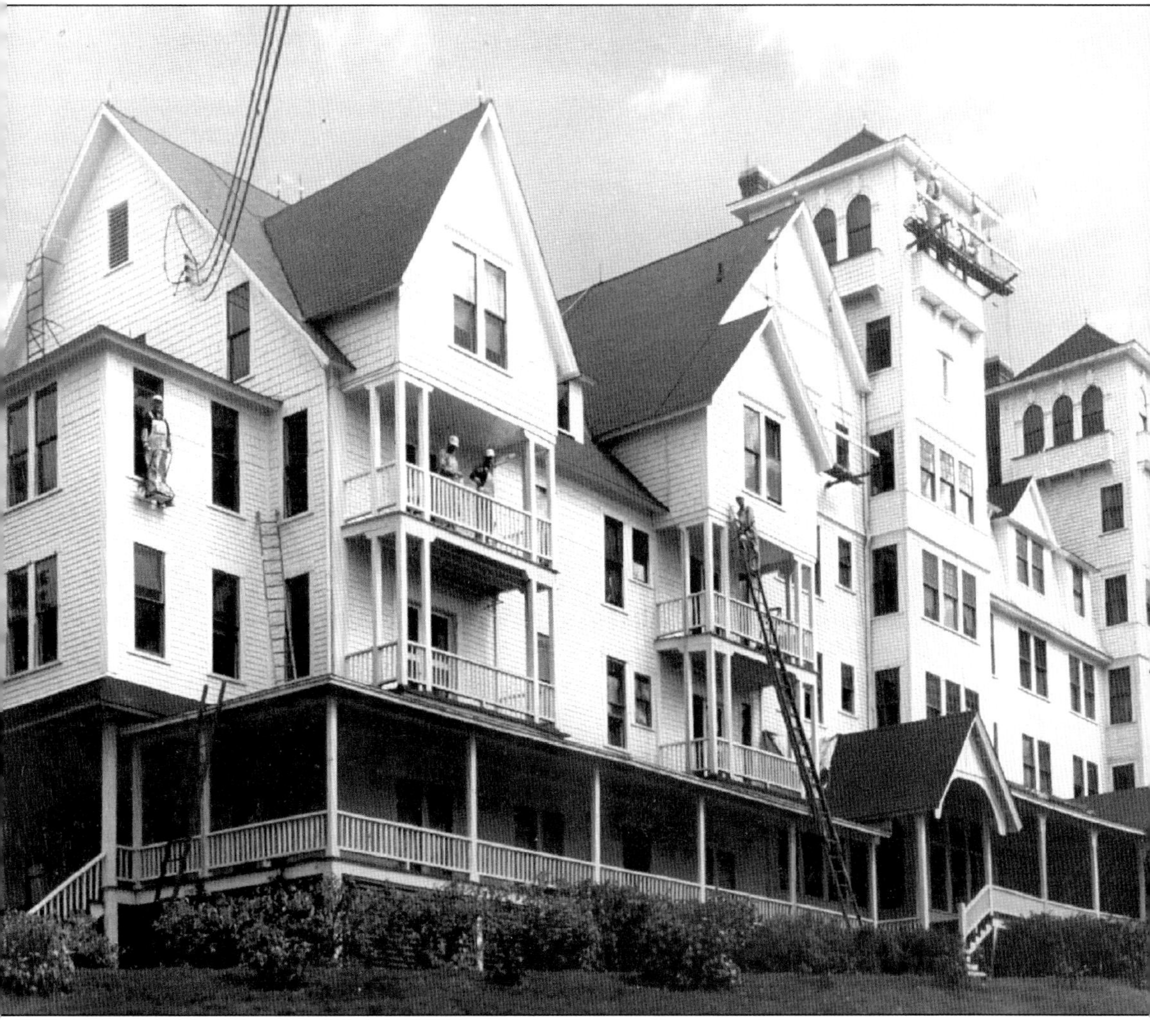

REPAINTING THE SOO-NIPI PARK LODGE, C. 1960. Pictured, from left to right, are Raymond Gay, Herb Hayes, Bob MacMichael, Leon Stowell, Warren Sargent, and Berk Hunter.

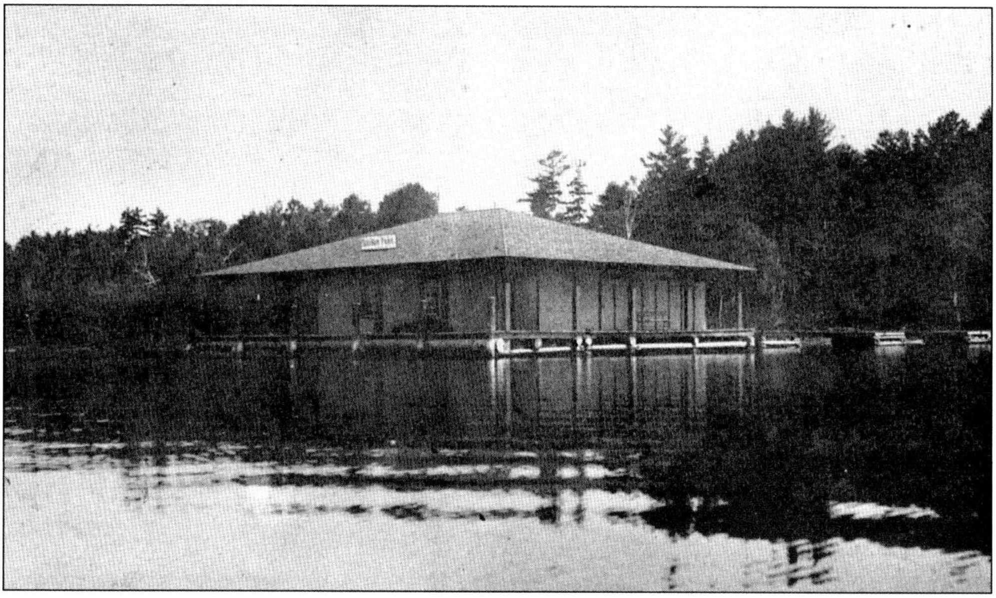

The Pier at Soo-Nipi Park. Visitors of Soo-Nipi Park could swim and take boats out from this pier in Lake Sunapee.

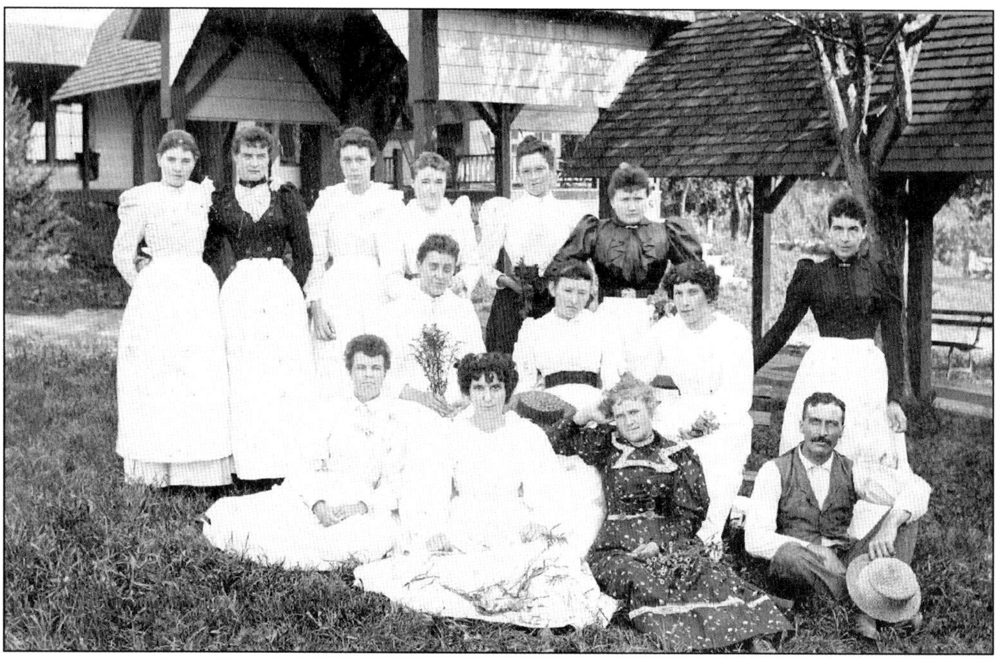

Employees at Soo-Nipi Park, c. 1900. Large resorts required lots of summer help to keep visitors fed and entertained.

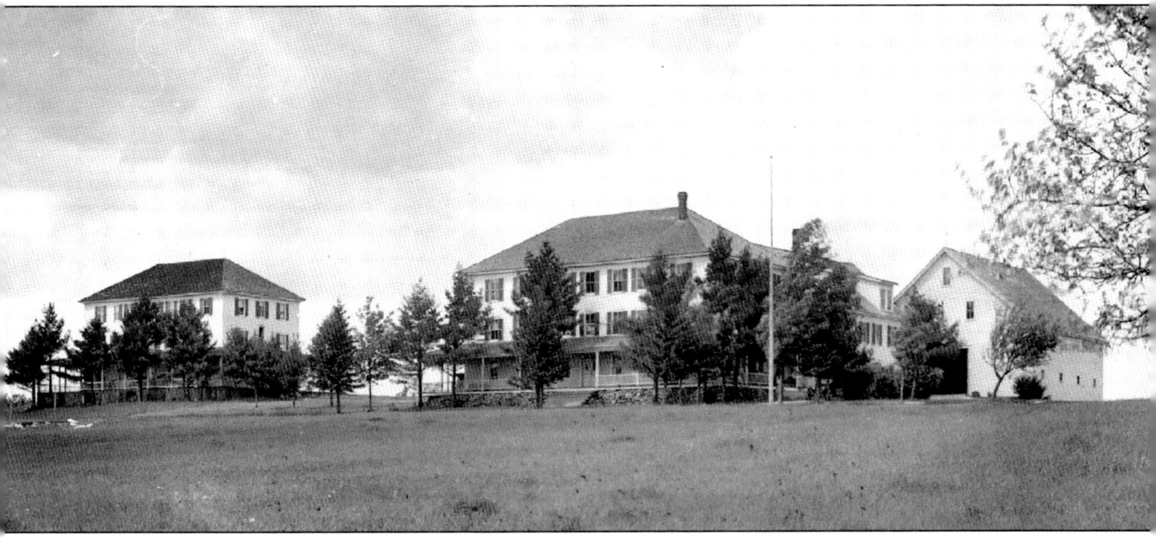

BROCKLEBANK. Another of New London's hotels, the Brocklebank was started by Fred B. Gay in the late 1890s and was enlarged in 1901 during the height of the area's tourism industry. In the 1970s, this property was developed into the condominium complex Hilltop Place.

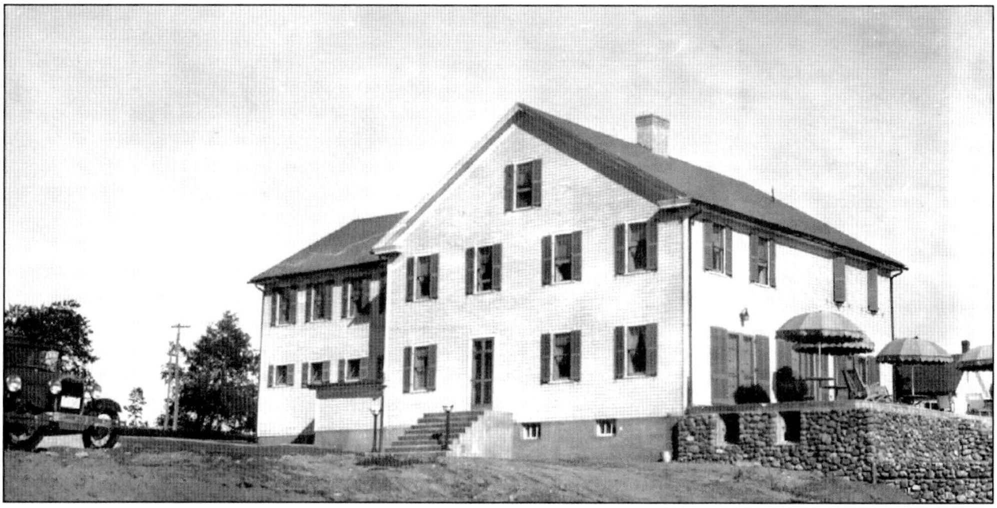

The College Inn, the 1920s. Located on Main Street, the College Inn opened to visitors in the autumn of 1946. The inn had been the former summer home of Jane A. Tracy.

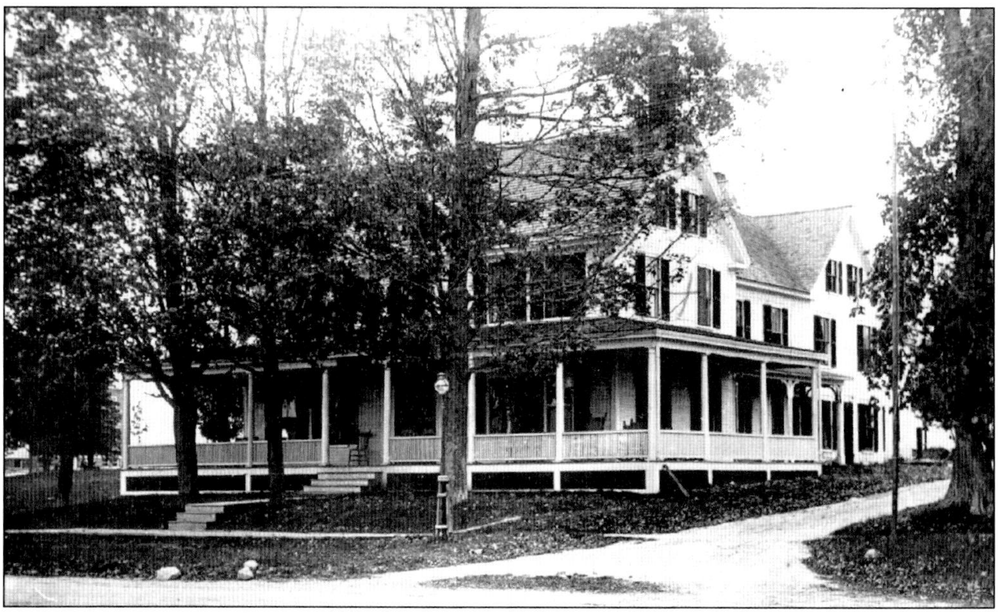

Cranehurst. Originally built by Manning Seamans in 1810, this building was a private residence before becoming an inn. The property changed hands several times before being purchased by Colby-Sawyer College (with financial assistance from residents in town) in 1976. The building is now used as the college's alumni relations office.

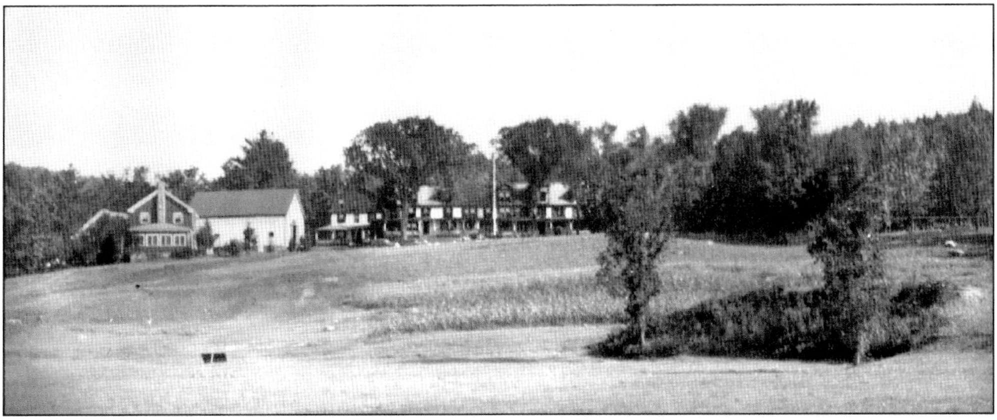

TWIN LAKE VILLA. Located on the eastern shore of Little Lake Sunapee, Twin Lake Villa is still in operation and boasts a golf course, as well as boating and swimming.

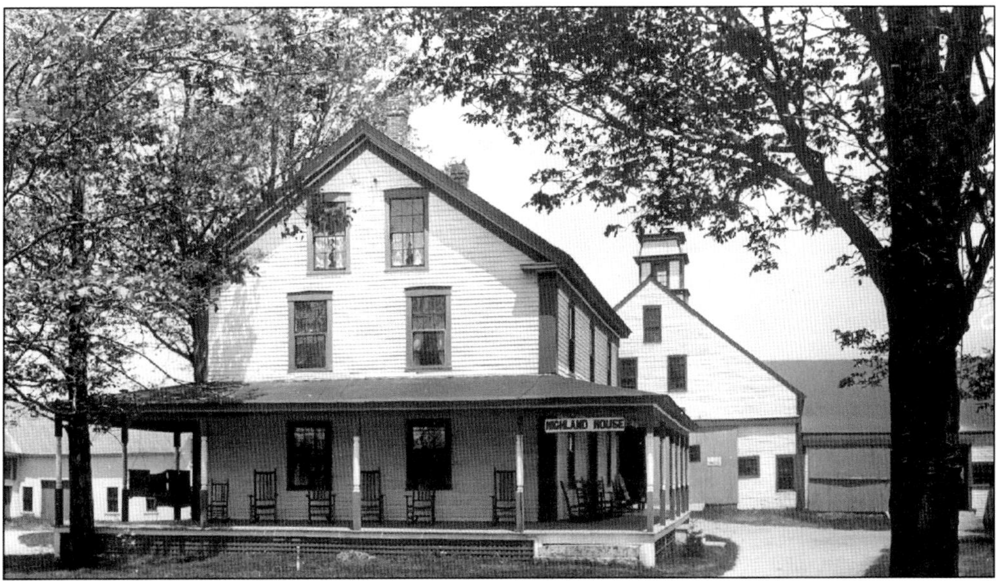

HIGHLAND HOUSE. Located on County Road, this boardinghouse was started in 1903 by Herman Messer.

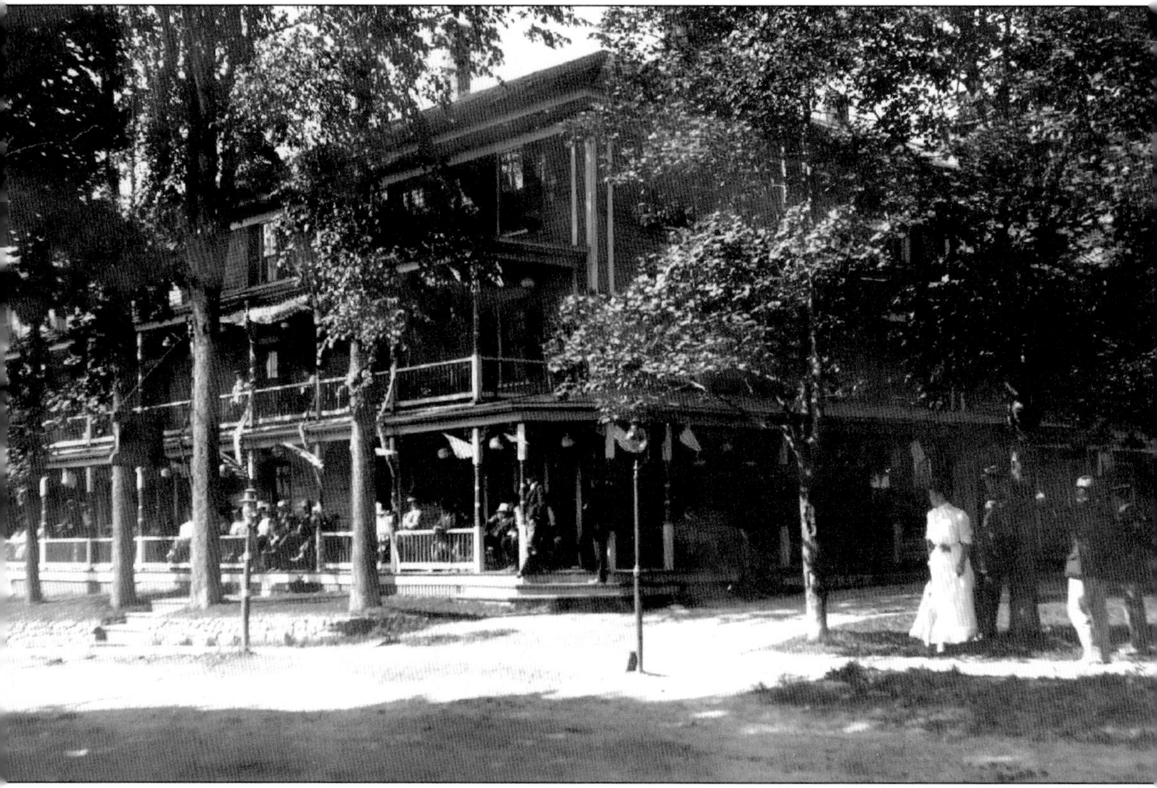

THE ELMS HOTEL, THE LATE 1890S. Located on Main Street just south of Four Corners, the Elms has changed hands and names many times in its history. At one point, it was called the Hotel Sargent and, in 1903, was renamed the New London Inn. The inn was used briefly by Colby Academy as dormitory space.

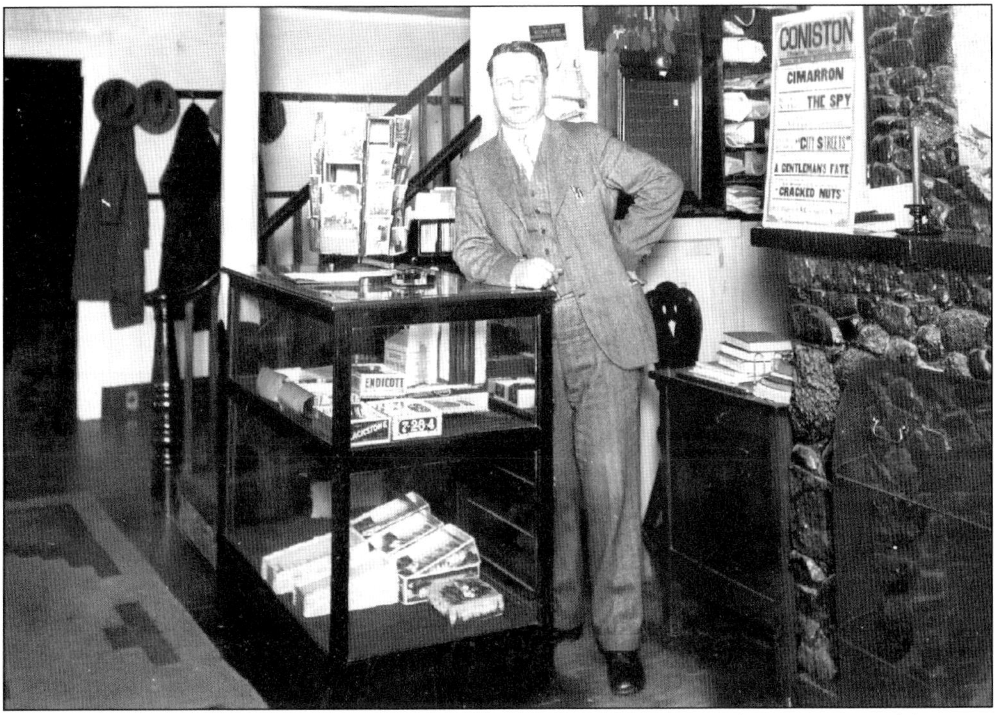

THE NEW LONDON INN, C. 1938. Wendell Hobbs, pictured here, was the proprietor of the New London Inn for 38 years. He first leased the property from Colby Junior College, which used the building for extra dormitory space, before purchasing it in 1938. Hobbs also managed the Soo-Nipi Park Lodge for a time.

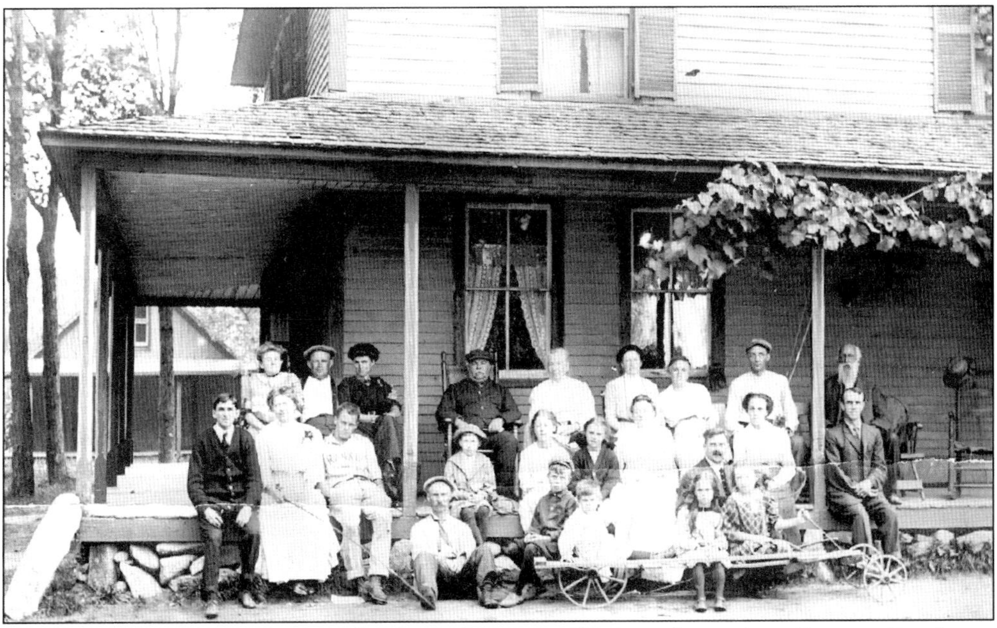

VISITORS AT GLENGAE. The boardinghouse known as Glengae, located on Newport Road, was one of the area's first inns. The site is now the location of the Gallery, a group of retail shops.

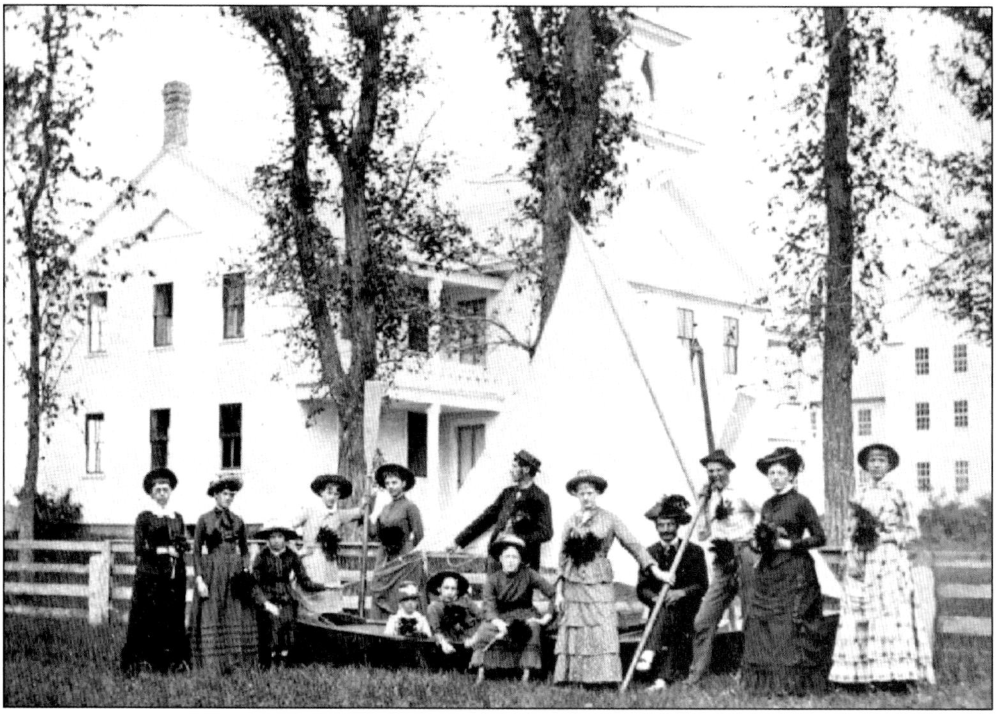

A Boat out of Water. This photograph presents a bit of a mystery and was so unusual it had to be included in this book. In the background is the Colby Academy building, but the reason for this boat to be about two miles away from the shore of any lake in New London (and photographed there) remains a mystery.

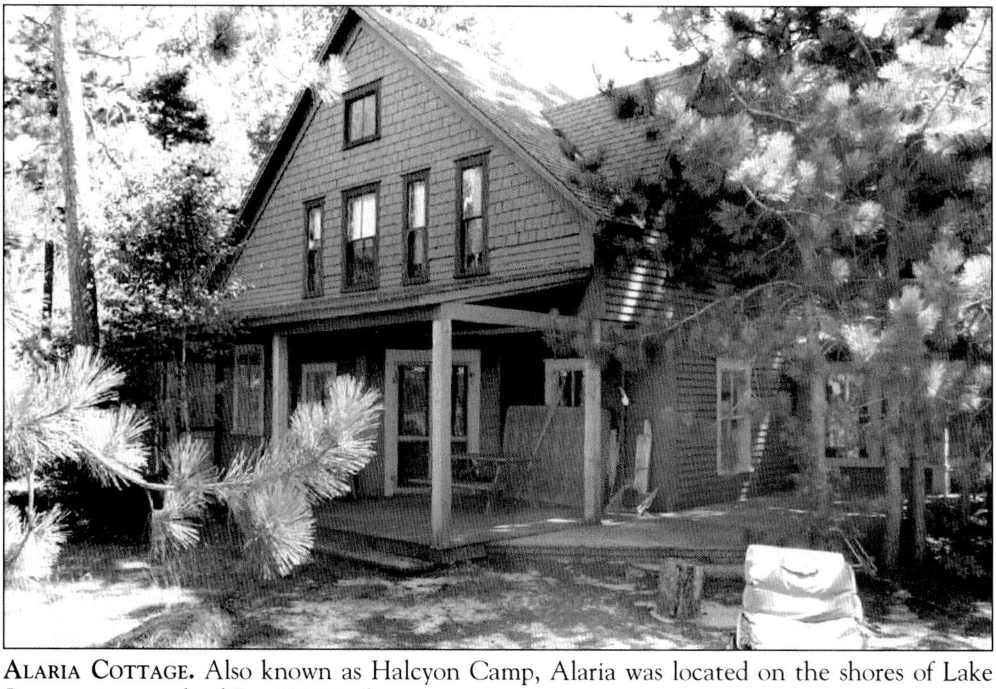

Alaria Cottage. Also known as Halcyon Camp, Alaria was located on the shores of Lake Sunapee just south of Soo-Nipi Park.

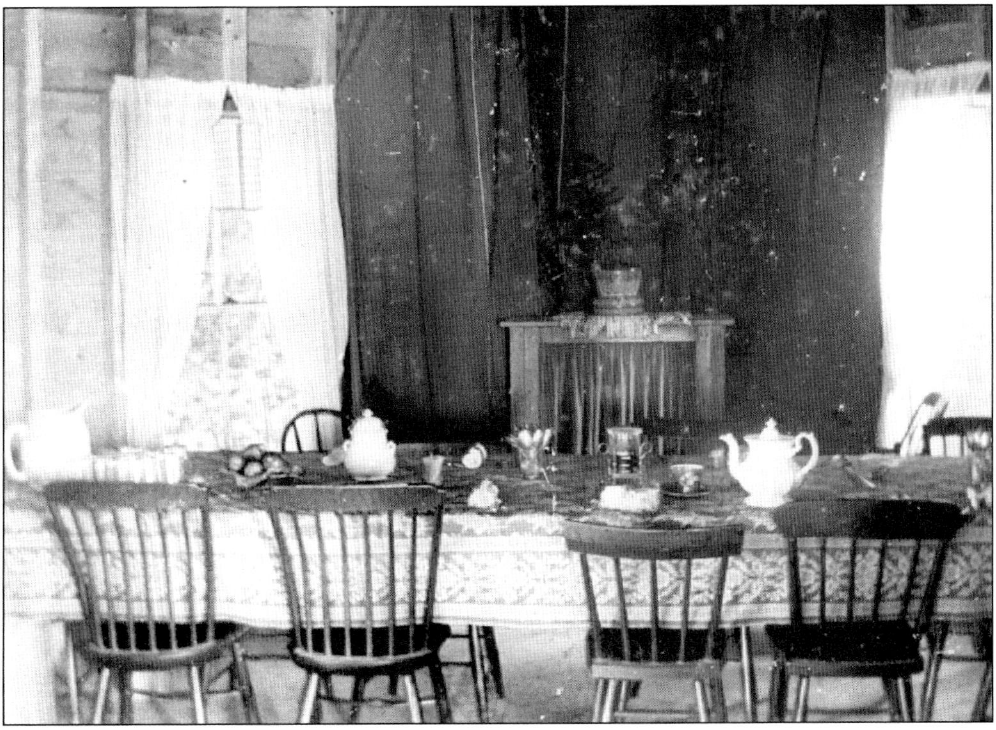

ALARIA COTTAGE, INTERIOR VIEWS. These interior photographs were taken in 1893.

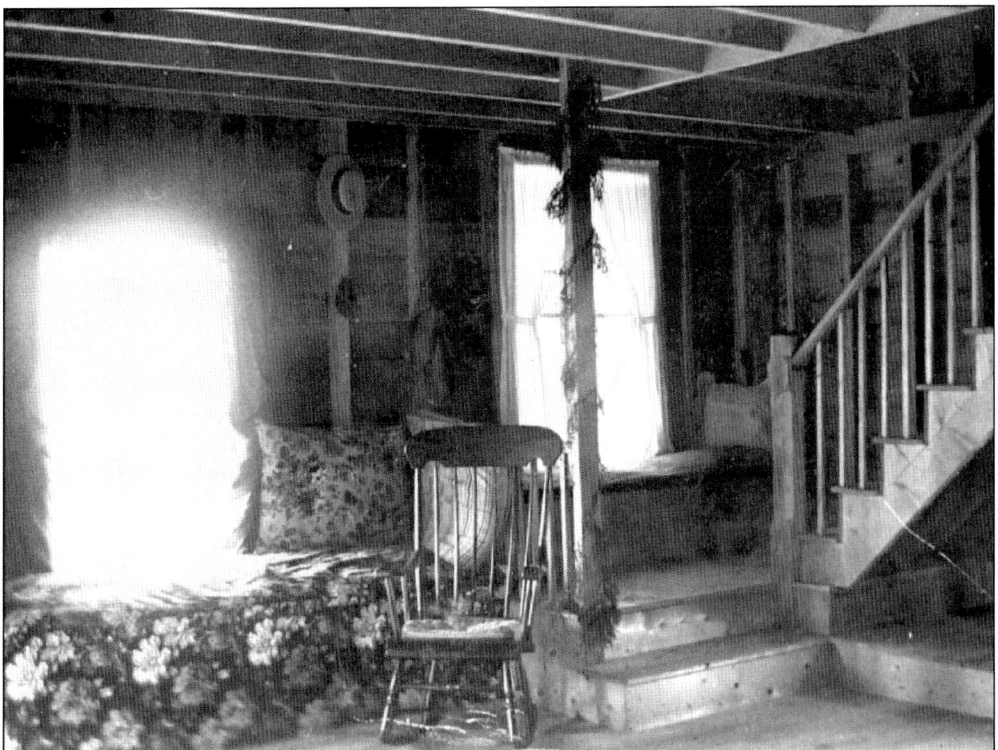

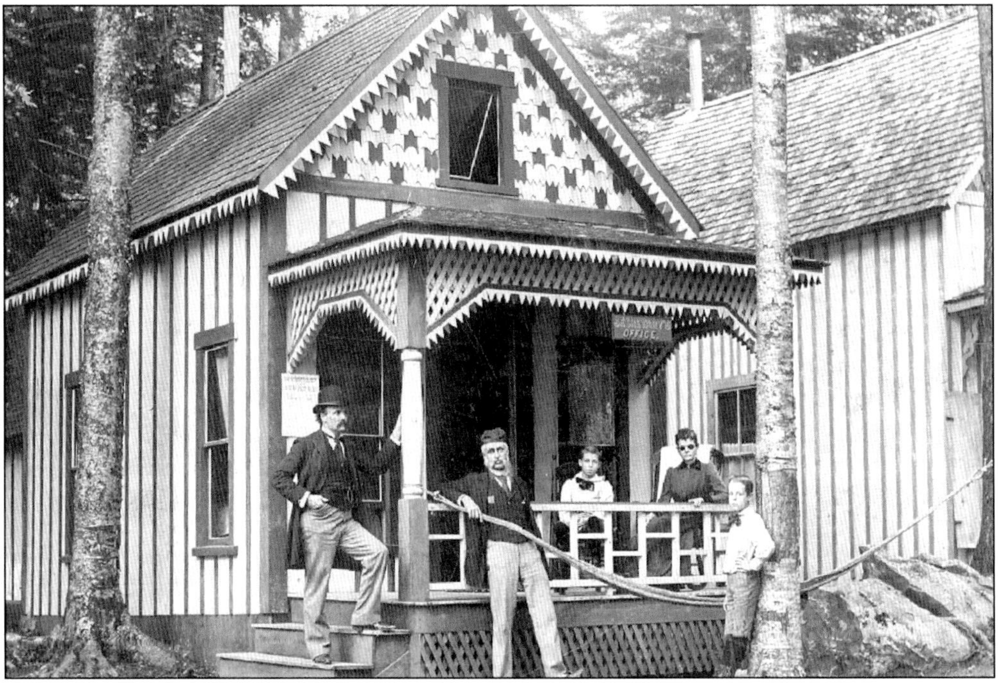

Blodgett's Landing. Located on the shores of Lake Sunapee, Blodgett's Landing was a summer camp. The writer Thornton Wilder worked at this camp for a few summers in the 1920s while teaching at a school in New Jersey. It has been argued that his experiences in New London inspired his famous play *Our Town*.

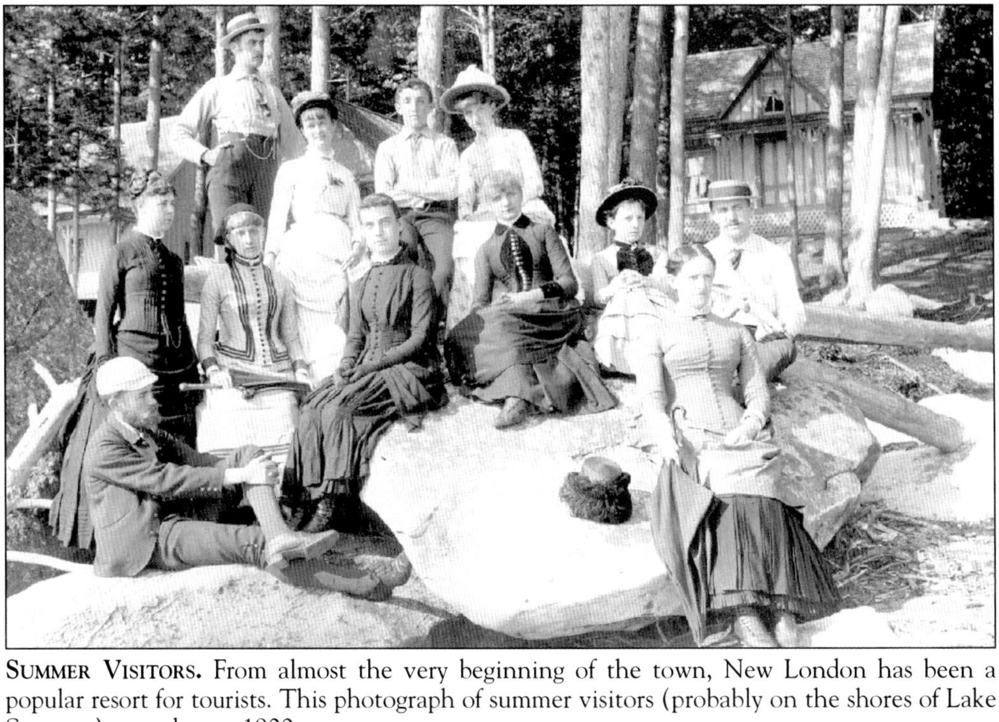

Summer Visitors. From almost the very beginning of the town, New London has been a popular resort for tourists. This photograph of summer visitors (probably on the shores of Lake Sunapee) was taken *c.* 1900.

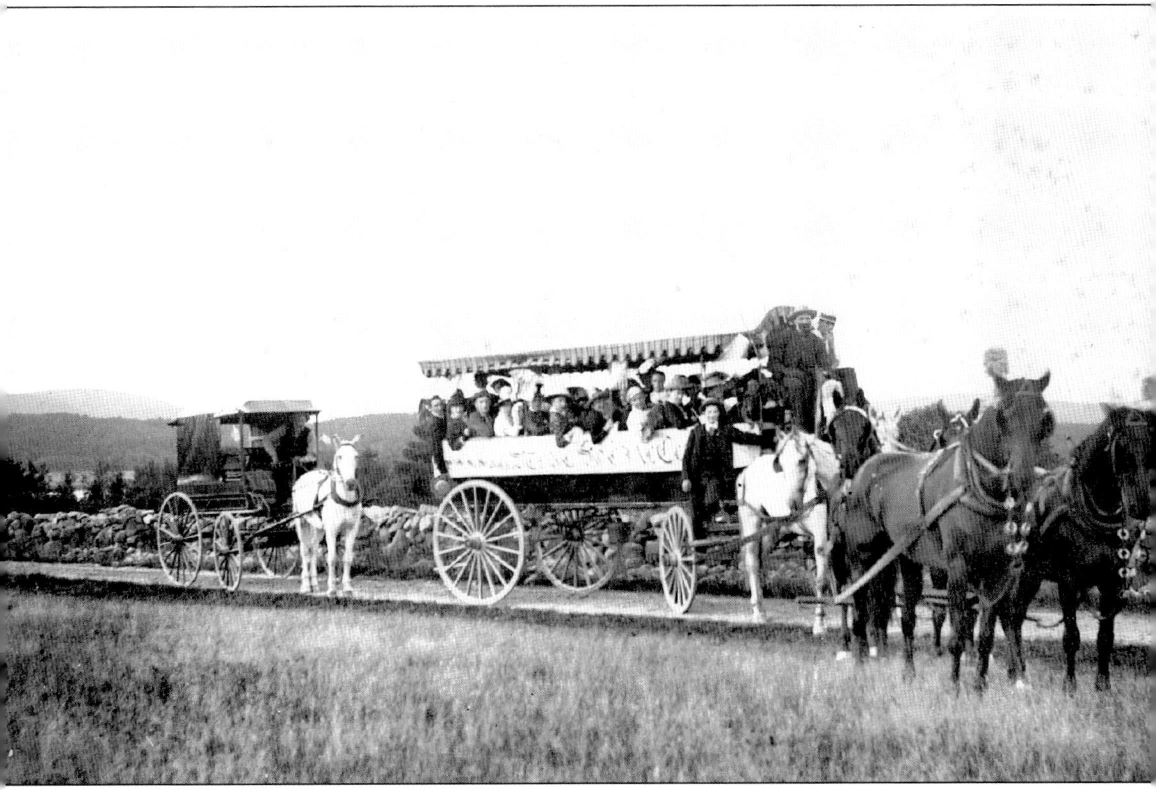

THE STONE SOCIAL CLUB PARADE ENTRY, THE 1890S. Parades of all kinds of decorated horse-drawn vehicles were popular amusements during the summer, and most of the guesthouses and social groups in town would have their own entries. This entry is from the Stone Social Club.

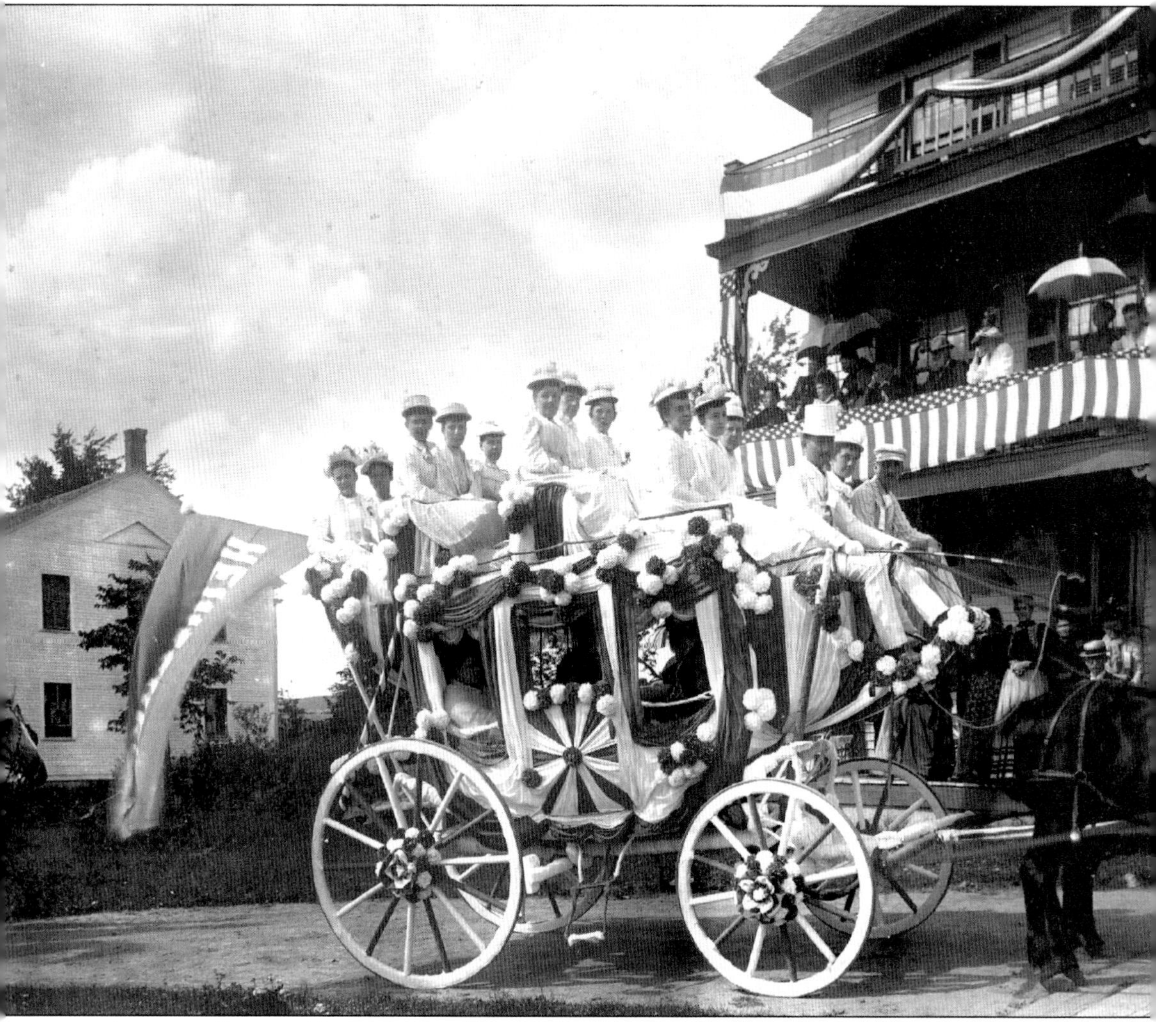

ANOTHER PARADE ENTRY, THE 1890S. Like most guesthouses, the Heidelberg competed in the summer coaching parades, partially for bragging rights and partially to advertise their establishment. These parades were annual events, but as time wore on, the automobile made elaborate coaches obsolete. The last parade of this kind was held in August 1906. (Photograph by J.B. Warren.)

PRIZEWINNING FISH. P.H. Killelea of Leominster, Massachusetts, proudly displays his 18.5-pound catch from Pleasant Lake. This was the largest landlocked salmon caught in New England for the 1914 season. (Courtesy of Colby-Sawyer College Archives.)

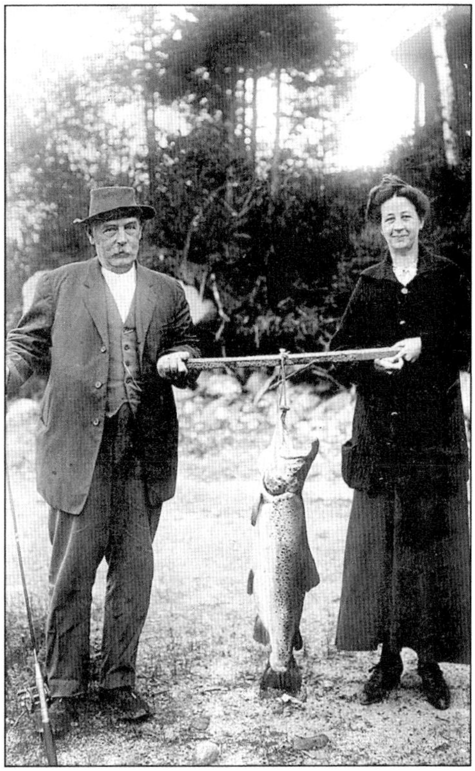

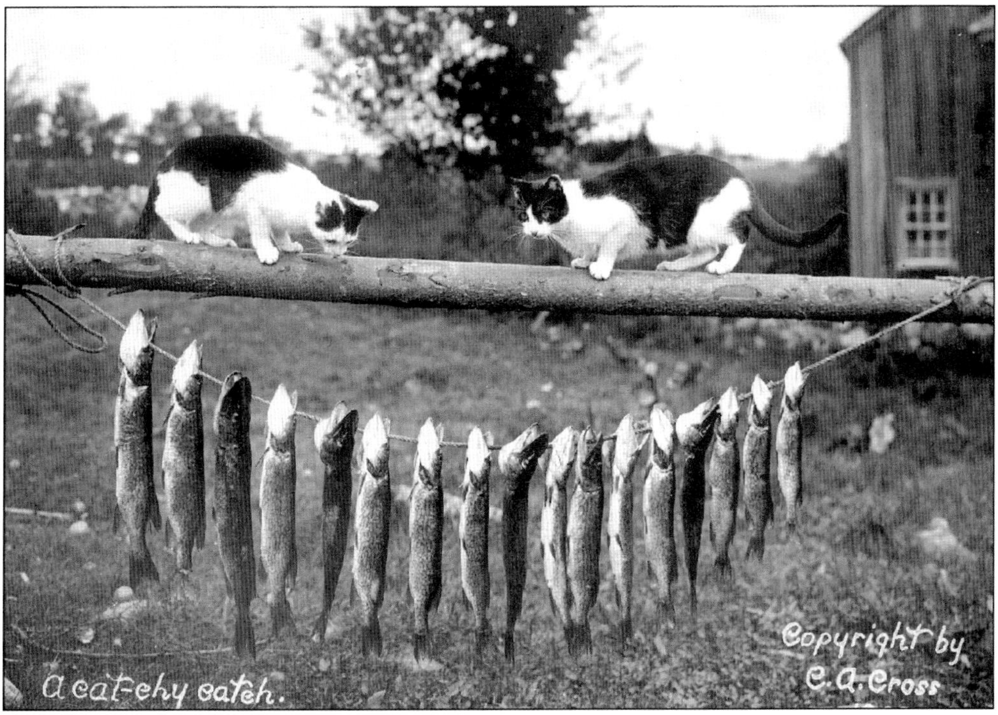

A CATCH OF FISH, 1902. These chain pickerel were caught in Pleasant Lake. (Photograph by C.A. Cross.)

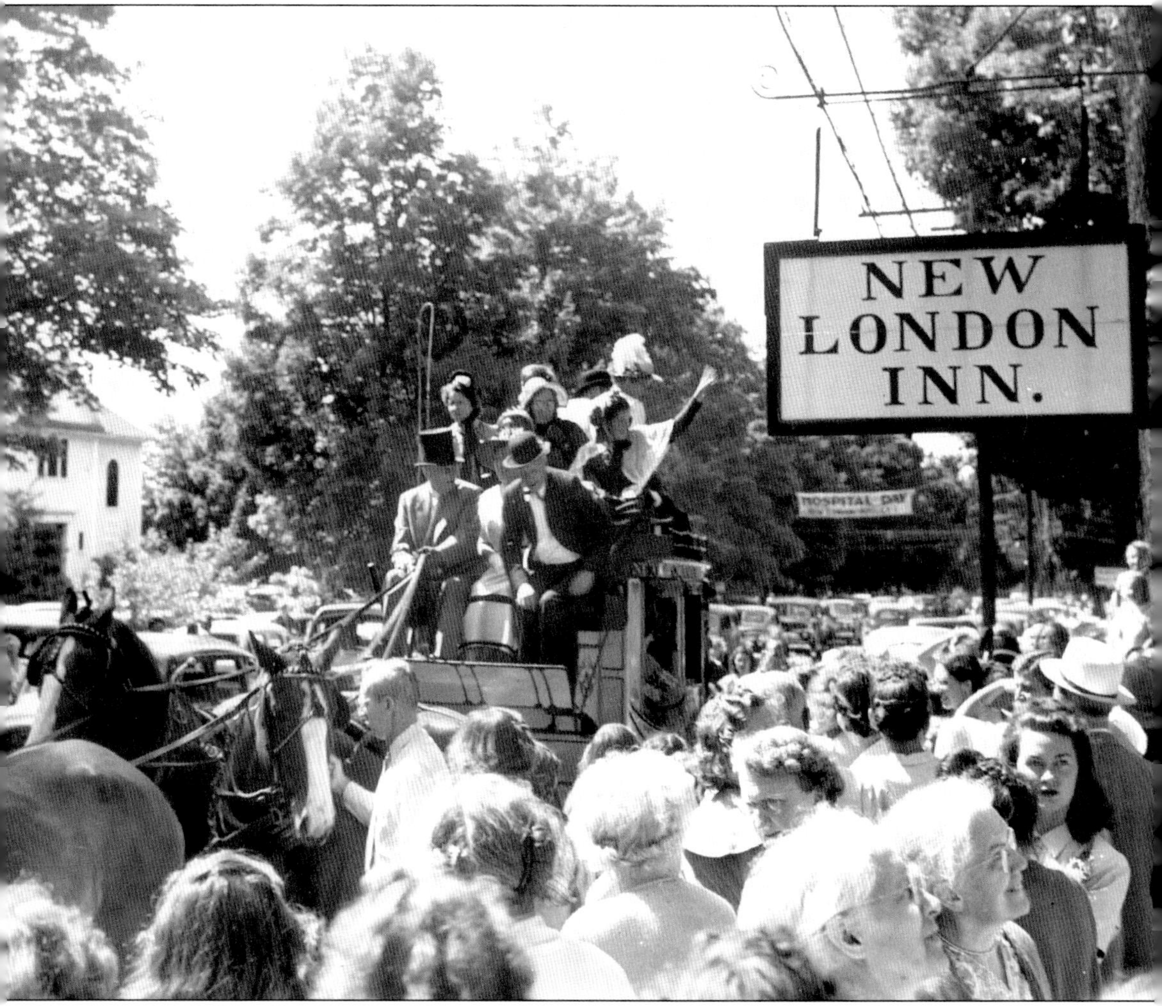

The Hospital Day Parade, August 1948. Started in 1924 as "Tag Day" as a way to raise funds for New London Hospital, Hospital Day has always been a popular summer tradition. Festivities include concerts, a flea market, and of course, a parade. In this photograph, a Concord coach passes by the New London Inn on Main Street.

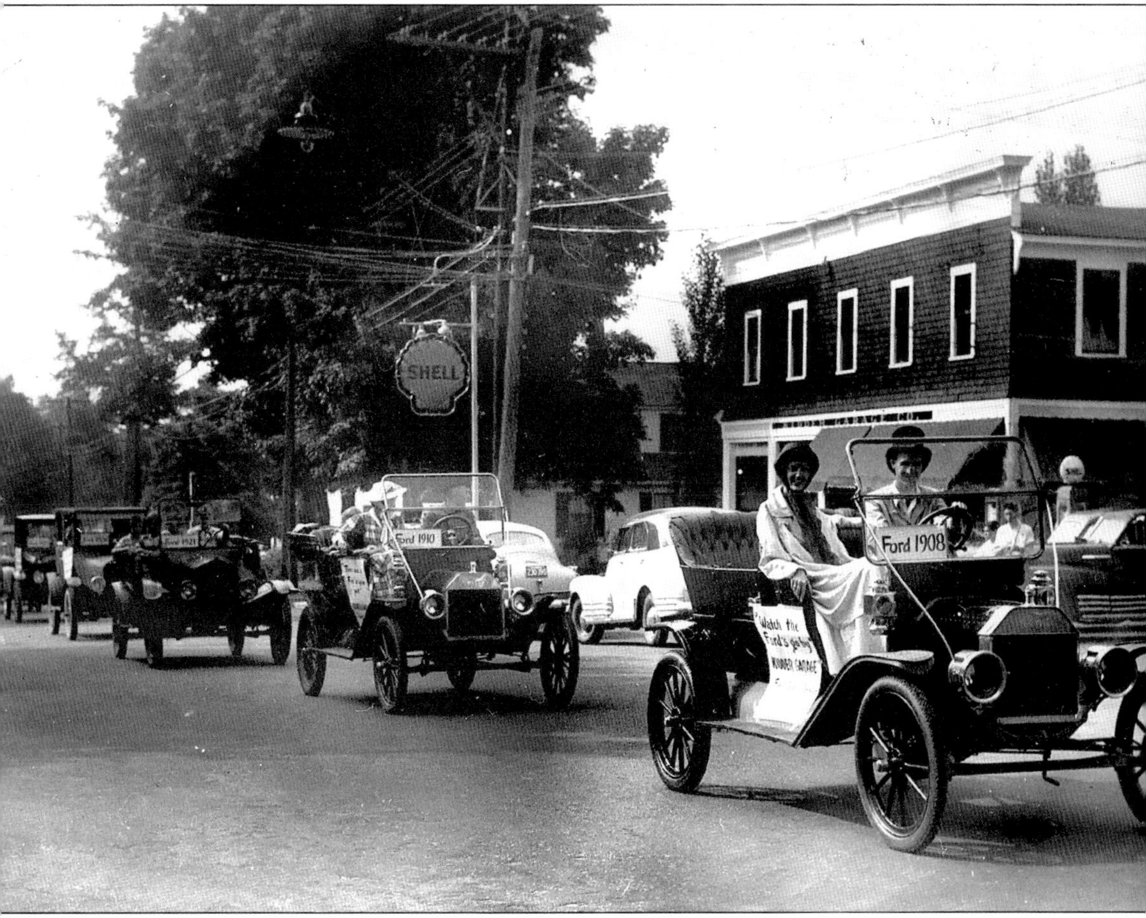

The Hospital Day Parade, the 1940s. Antique Fords advertise Kidder Garage in the parade. (Courtesy of Colby-Sawyer College Archives.)

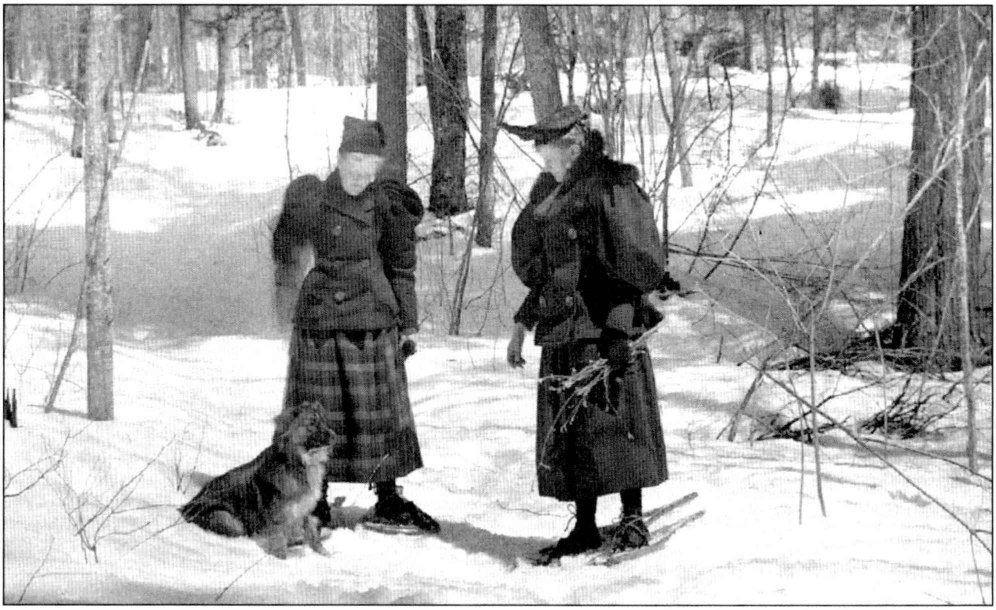

SNOWSHOEING, 1896. Eliza Burpee (left) and A. Macomber get some exercise and enjoy the New London scenery on April 10, 1896.

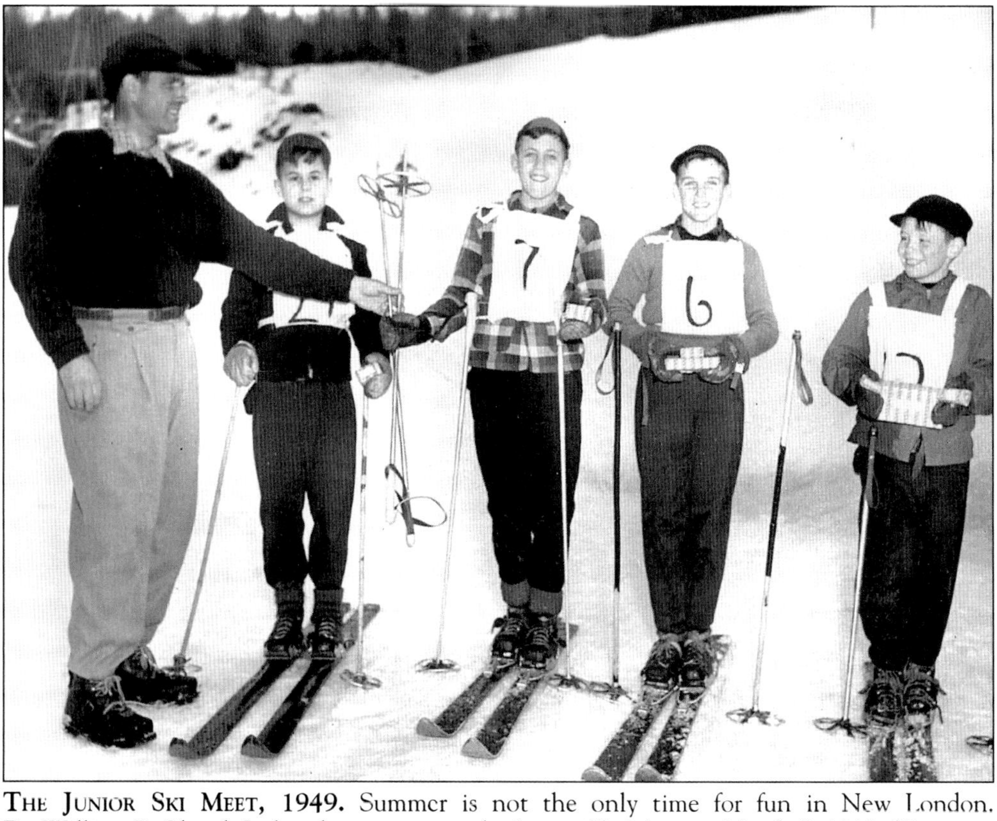

THE JUNIOR SKI MEET, 1949. Summer is not the only time for fun in New London. Dr. William P. Clough Jr. hands out prizes at the Junior Ski Meet on March 5, 1949. (Courtesy of Colby-Sawyer College Archives.)

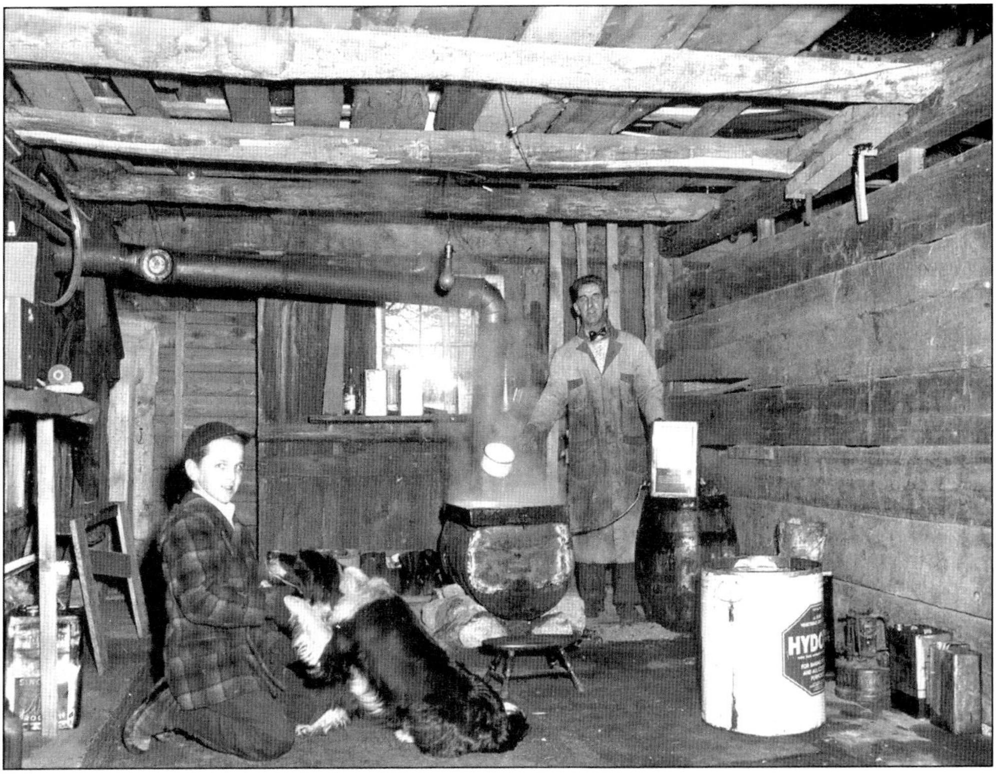

MAPLE SUGARING, THE 1950S. Springtime in New England often means spending time boiling sap to make maple syrup, and New Londoners are up to the challenge.

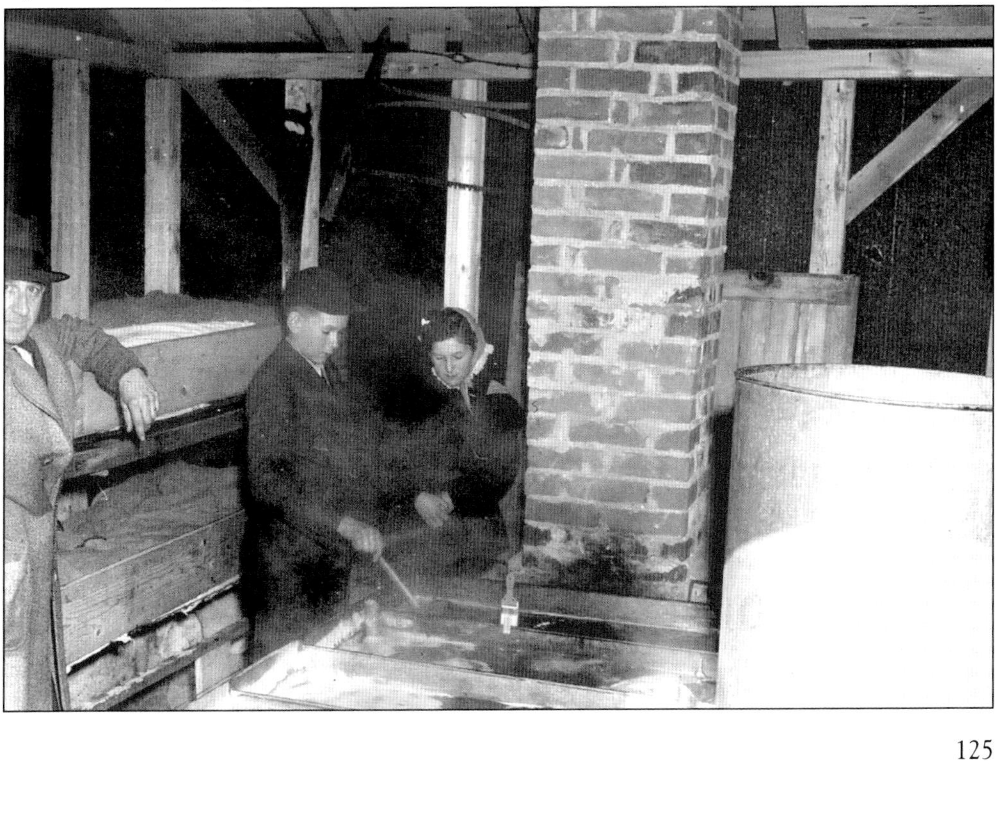

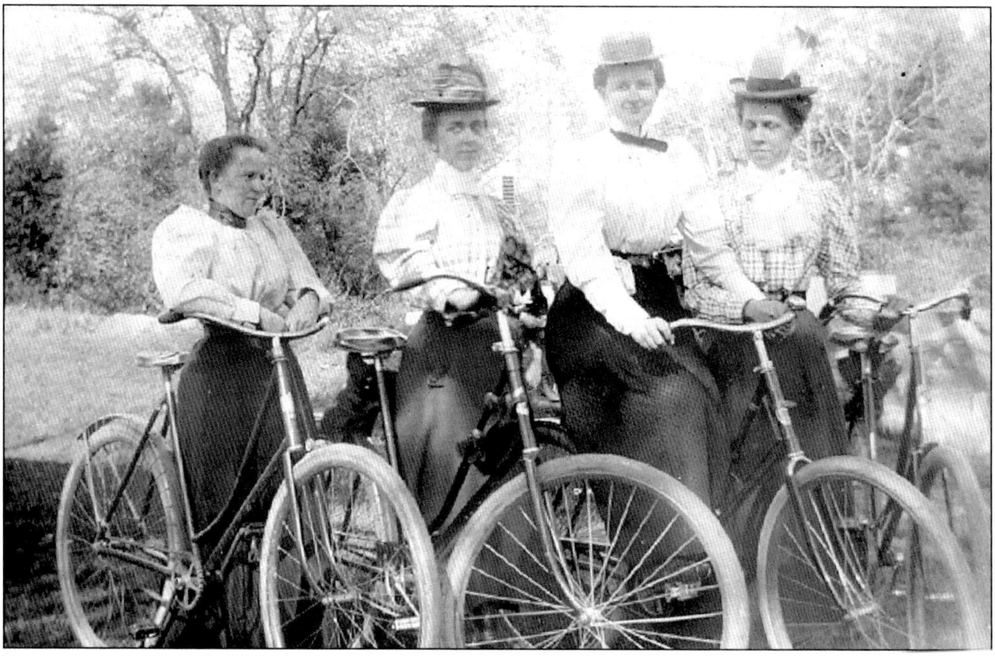

BICYCLISTS, C. 1895. These young women are most likely students from Colby Academy.

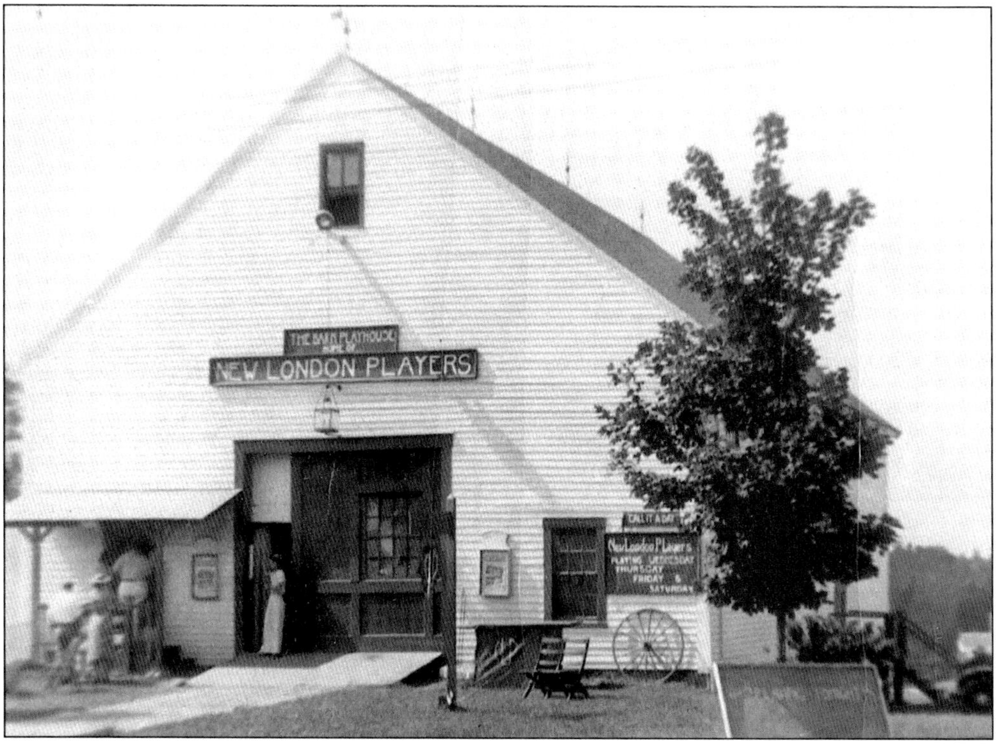

THE BARN PLAYHOUSE. The barn on the Robert Knight property, on Main Street, was bought by Josephine Etter Holmes and remodeled as a summer theater in 1934. The Barn Playhouse had eight plays that season and is still in operation, entertaining residents and visitors alike. (Courtesy of Colby-Sawyer College Archives.)

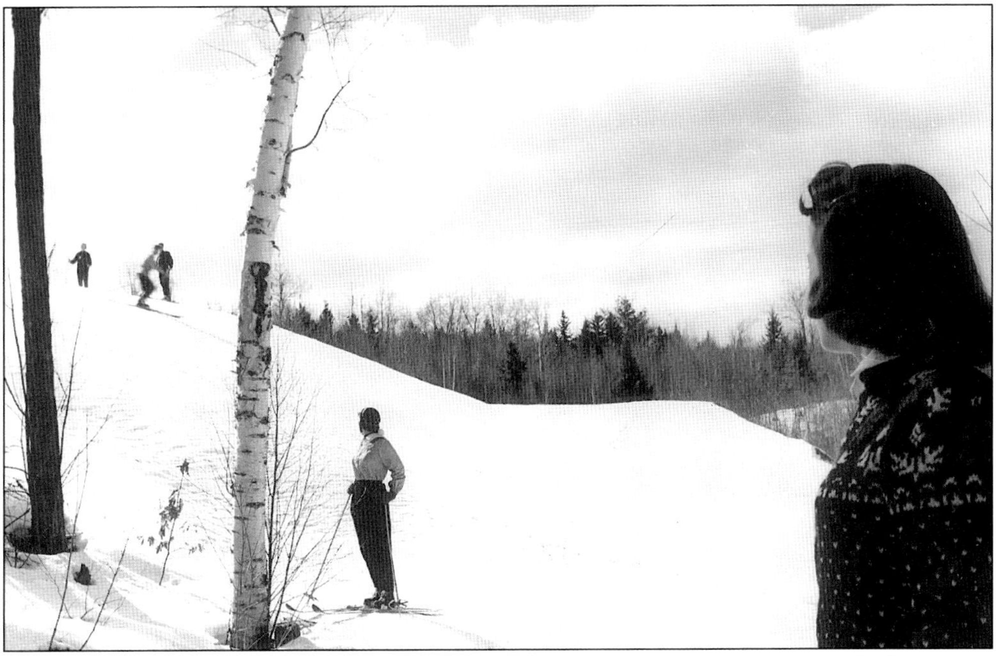

The New London Ski Tow, c. 1953. Located on a slope behind Seaman's Road, the ski tow was opened in the winter of 1939–1940 by Harold W. Buker Jr., Richard Messer, and Maurice Shepard. This slope operated for only two years, but another 800-foot tow rope on the west side of Pleasant Lake was started in January 1948. Townspeople and college students alike used both of these areas. (Photographs by Don Sieburg and William Rittase, courtesy of Colby-Sawyer College Archives.)

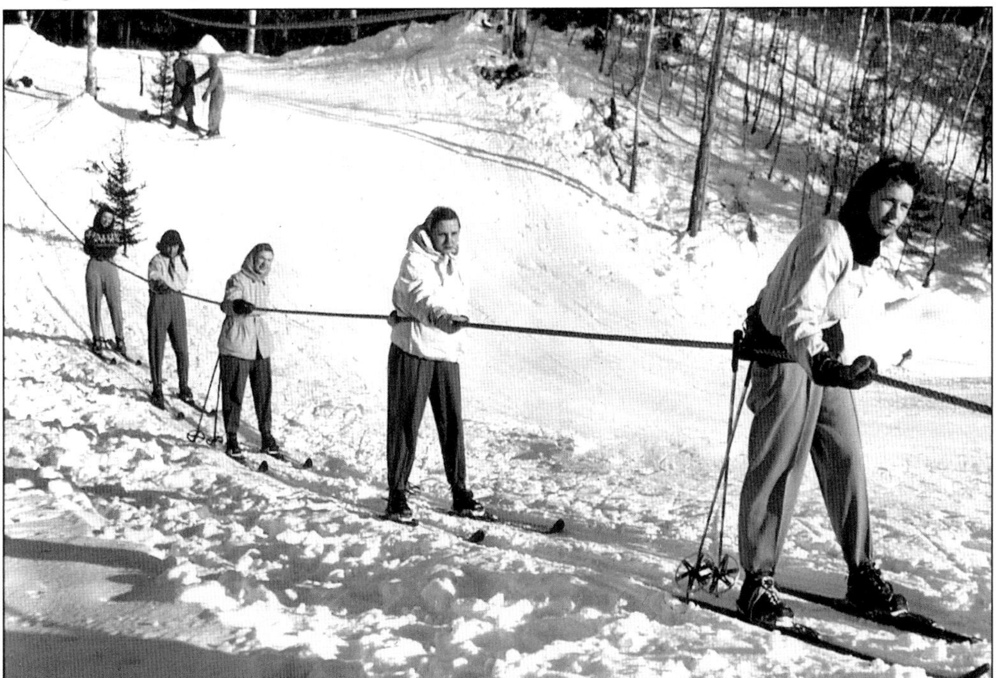

BIBLIOGRAPHY

Atlas of New Hampshire. Boston: D.H. Hurd and Company, 1892.

Charlton, Edwin A. *New Hampshire As It Is*. Claremont: Tracy and Sanford, 1855.

History and Archives Committee of New London. *Historical Sketches from New London, New Hampshire: Selections from "The Mountaineer."* New London: Country Press, 1977.

Lord, Myra A. *A History of the Town of New London, Merrimack County, New Hampshire*. Concord: Rumford Press, 1899.

Squires, James Duane. *Mirror to America: A History of New London, New Hampshire, 1900–1950*. Concord: Evans Printing Company, 1952.

Stecker, Ann Page. *Our Voices, Our Town: A History of New London, New Hampshire, 1950–2000*. Portsmouth: Peter E. Randall, 2000.